access to his

Rebellion and Disorder Under the Tudors 1485–1603

Geoff Woodward

HODDER
EDUCATION
AN HACHETTE UK COMPANY

The Publishers would like to thank the following for permission to reproduce copyright material: Woburn Abbey, Bedfordshire, UK/The Bridgeman Art Library, page 105.

Hachette Livre UK's policy is to use papers that are natural, renewable and recyclable products and made from wood grown in sustainable forests. The logging and manufacturing processes are expected to conform to the environmental regulations of the country of origin.

Orders: please contact Bookpoint Ltd, 130 Milton Park, Abingdon, Oxon OX14 4SB. Telephone: (44) 01235 827720. Fax: (44) 01235 400454. Lines are open 9.00–5.00, Monday to Saturday, with a 24-hour message answering service. Visit our website at www.hoddereducation.co.uk

© Geoff Woodward 2008
First published in 2008 by
Hodder Education,
an Hachette UK Company,
338 Euston Road
London NW1 3BH

Impression number   5 4 3 2
Year   2012 2011 2010 2009

Cover photo: Pontefract Castle, c.1620–40, Keirincx, Alexander (1600–c.1652)/ © Wakefield Museums and Galleries, West Yorkshire, UK/The Bridgeman Art Library
Typeset in 10/12pt Baskerville and produced by Gray Publishing, Tunbridge Wells
Printed in Malta

A catalogue record for this title is available from the British Library.

ISBN: 978 0340 983713

Contents

Chronology of Key Events

Introduction

Apart from scholars and A-level students, few people have heard of the Tudor rebellions, or indeed are aware of the main protagonists, or that at least 19 occurred in England and Ireland during this period. Lambert Simnel and Perkin Warbeck may ring a bell, Henry VIII and his wives may be well known, and most are familiar with the main events of Elizabeth I's reign, but it is generally not known that each of the Tudors faced at least one rebellion that threatened to destabilise their throne. In early modern England, the term 'rebellion' was an imprecise concept. Contemporaries understood that it was an armed uprising and that, unlike a riot, it could last for several weeks, involve thousands of people and be much more than a local disturbance. Yet, if the objectives of a rebellion were to right a perceived wrong, whether political, religious, social or economic, not all rebellions sought violence and many, like the Pilgrimage of Grace, were genuinely passive. All protests, however, were seen as a challenge to the established order; it therefore suited the government to label the protesters as 'rebels', and so apply the full force of the law against them.

Of course, rebellion was not unique to the Tudor age. The second half of the fifteenth century saw Jack Cade's uprising, the Wars of the Roses and Henry VI's 'readeption', Buckingham's rebellion and Henry Tudor's victory at Bosworth Field that led to the overthrow of Richard III. The early seventeenth century also witnessed several large rebellions that included the Midland peasant uprising, major revolts in Scotland and Ireland, and, of course, the Great Rebellion from 1642 to 1649. Tudor rebellions, however, were different in their causes, variety, frequency, size and nature, and, for the first time, religious issues became a prominent influence. How and why revolts occurred has long puzzled historians but equally intriguing is how Tudor authorities dealt with each disturbance. The value of a synoptic study that analyses and synthesises the key developments of Tudor rebellions is that it clearly demonstrates the concepts of continuity and change in an important historical period.

The purpose of this book is to provide an analysis and synthesis of the main rebellions that occurred in Tudor England and Ireland. It does not seek to narrate the events or tell the story of Tudor rebellions but attempts to draw together common features and to focus on elements of continuity and change during this period. Narrative is, of course, an important aspect of informing and explaining events, as well as exciting students about historical developments. Moreover, a narrative account provides students with a clear sense of chronological progression, which is essential to any understanding of continuity and change. To this end, a brief outline of each rebellion discussed in this book appears on pages vii–x: it is not intended to replace a detailed narrative but to provide the reader with an appropriate context and point of reference.

Chapter 1 aims to analyse the causes of Tudor rebellions, to discern similar and dissimilar themes and to separate the more important causes from subsidiary factors. Chapter 2 focuses on the nature of rebellion. It seeks to explain the changing nature of rebellions, analyses their strengths and limitations, and examines why some disturbances were more threatening than others. Chapter 3 looks at how Tudor governments dealt with individual rebellions and considers their impact on government and society. Finally, Chapter 4 explores how governments tried to maintain stability and so prevent the outbreak of disorder. Did Tudor society become more communally responsible?

Synoptic understanding

While forming a chronological framework is essential, so too is understanding how events may be connected both in the short and long term. To achieve this, it is important at the end of studying a particular era or rebellion to consider what has changed and what remains the same, and to practise cross-referencing thematic developments. Sometimes these links highlight points of similarity and continuity; sometimes they emphasise differences and change. When a key event has been analysed and tied to another event to show change and continuity, then ideas and concepts will have been synthesised. In this way, the skills of synthesis may be used to achieve a synoptic understanding of the period and theme. Of course, any synthesis requires specific examples to support and evaluate an assertion, so in building up a body of knowledge, students should ask themselves how this evidence might be useful when constructing an argument. Being able to use knowledge flexibly is a key skill and one that students should regularly practise.

Note making

Before you begin to make any notes, read through the introductory section of each chapter to get an overview of the main themes and familiarise yourself with any notes you already have on a particular topic. You will not need to make notes on every part of each section since some of the material will be well known to you. Use the headings and sub-headings as starting points for the principal arguments in each section. Decide how many examples are needed to back them up and use the ideas and examples to complement existing notes and knowledge. Be selective, but have at least two examples in reasonable detail so that you can explain their historical significance. Use the summary diagrams in a similar way to help synthesise your thoughts and organise your notes.

Essays

A-level questions have been set at the end of each chapter, together with two contrasting answers of a very good and average standard. Each essay has been evaluated and a mark and grade awarded according to official mark schemes. The commentary in the margins of the sample essays is a descriptive analysis of each paragraph and is used by the examiner to make the summative comments at the end of the essay on which the level and mark assessment is based. The intention of each essay is to indicate to students how they might improve their own standard of work with the ultimate objective of achieving the top grade. Students approach A-level essays in different ways and there is no correct approach or 'right' answer. Nevertheless, some techniques clearly work better than others and, by comparing essay plans, approaches, styles, and how students use their knowledge synoptically, it should be possible to see why one answer has merited a higher mark. If you compare a Grade C with a Grade A answer, ask yourself which features in a C-grade essay prevented it from gaining a higher mark. And how much of a Grade A essay do you need to read before you feel it has the making of a top-class answer? A point worth remembering is that the best students are not always the most knowledgeable but they do know how to make best use of their knowledge.

If, as a result of reading this book and incorporating some of the ideas and skills contained within it, students deepen their knowledge and develop a synoptic understanding of the topic, then it will have fulfilled its purpose.

Main rebellions
Henry VII (1485–1509)

Lovel 1486
Having survived the battle of Bosworth, Francis Lovel, a councillor to Richard III, sought to overthrow Henry VII. Lovel took sanctuary in Colchester and then escaped before raising troops at Middleham (Yorkshire) in a bid to overthrow Henry VII. He failed and fled to Flanders.

Stafford 1486
Humphrey and Thomas Stafford had eluded capture after the battle of Bosworth and taken sanctuary in Colchester abbey. They then fled to Worcester, escaped again and were finally captured at Culham church (Oxfordshire). Humphrey was executed.

Simnel 1486–7
Lambert Simnel claimed to be Edward, Earl of Warwick, and therefore had a better claim to the English throne than Henry VII. He won the support of several English and Irish nobles, including Lincoln and Kildare, as well as foreign troops, but was captured on the battlefield of East Stoke. The king made him a servant in the royal household.

Yorkshire 1489

Unwilling to pay taxes to fund a war against France, protesters in Yorkshire led by Sir John Egremont killed the Earl of Northumberland before royal troops dispersed them. Some rebels were executed but Egremont escaped to France.

Cornish 1497

Unwilling to pay taxes to fund a war against Scotland, Cornish protesters marched towards London. They were slaughtered at Blackheath, the ringleaders – Audley, Flamank and Joseph – were executed, and the county received a heavy fine.

Warbeck 1497

Perkin Warbeck claimed to be Richard Duke of York, the younger of the two princes in the Tower, who disappeared in 1483. He won support from a few English nobles, notably Sir William Stanley, the Lord Chamberlain, from Cornish peasants still smarting from their treatment at Blackheath, and at varying times, from foreign states. He was captured, imprisoned in the Tower and eventually executed in 1499.

Henry VIII (1509–47)

Amicable Grant 1525

Unwilling and, allegedly, unable to pay taxes to fund a war against France, protesters in several counties, but mainly in Suffolk, forced the government to back down. No rebels were punished.

Silken Thomas 1534–7

'Silken' Thomas O'Neill began a rebellion in Dublin upon hearing of the arrest and imprisonment of his father, the Earl of Kildare, in the Tower of London. Thomas and his five uncles attacked Henry's administration before submitting to an Anglo-Irish army. The leaders were brought to London and executed.

Pilgrimage of Grace 1536–7

Three separate risings in Lincolnshire (led by Dymoke), Yorkshire and other northern counties (led by Aske), and a later brief disturbance in Yorkshire and Cumberland (led by Bigod) challenged Henry's religious reforms. They also had economic, social and political grievances. The pilgrimage was the largest and longest rebellion in Tudor England and resulted in over 200 executions in 1537.

Edward VI (1547–53)

Western 1549

Cornish and Devon protesters besieged Exeter and demanded an end to Protestant reforms and recent taxes on sheep and wool. Their rebellion lasted for five weeks and was ended at the battles of Clyst St Mary and Sampford Courtenay in Devon.

Kett 1549

Robert Kett led a rebellion in Norfolk against illegal enclosures and agrarian practices adopted by the county gentry. Rebel camps were set up in several market towns in East Anglia and the principal one at Mousehold Heath was only dispersed after the battle of Dussindale. Kett and other ringleaders were hanged in Norfolk.

Mary I (1553–8)

Northumberland 1553

The Duke of Northumberland attempted to prevent Mary from gaining the throne by asserting the claim of Lady Jane Grey, his daughter-in-law. He and his supporters submitted without a fight at Cambridge. He was taken back to London and executed.

Wyatt 1554

Sir Thomas Wyatt raised troops in Kent in protest at Mary's proposed marriage to Philip of Spain. Planned uprisings in several English counties failed to materialise and Wyatt was captured at Ludgate (London) and subsequently executed.

Elizabeth I (1558–1603)

Shane O'Neill 1558–67

He resented losing the earldom of Tyrone in Ulster to his brother, murdered him and turned on English settlers and the administration in Dublin. The uprising only ended when he was killed in a brawl with rival clans.

Northern Earls 1569–70

The earls of Westmorland and Northumberland planned to release Mary Stuart from captivity, marry her to the Duke of Norfolk and force Elizabeth to recognise Mary as her successor. The Catholic earls wanted greater power for themselves in the north and called for the dismissal of William Cecil, the queen's secretary. Few supported the rebellion outside Yorkshire and Durham and when a royal army approached, the earls fled. Northumberland was later executed but Westmorland was never caught.

Munster 1569–73

James Fitzmaurice Fitzgerald rose up against English plantations in Munster and his colleague Edmund Butler attacked settlements in Leix-Offaly. Over 800 rebels were executed but Fitzgerald escaped to France.

Geraldine 1579–83

Fitzgerald returned from abroad and raised Irish rebels in protest at Elizabeth's religious and political policies. Fitzgerald was killed but the Earl of Desmond assumed command and received aid from Italian and Spanish troops at Smerwick. The rebels were rounded up by an English army and Desmond was executed.

Tyrone 1595–1603

Hugh O'Neill, the Earl of Tyrone, raised support from every Irish province against English rule. Elizabeth underestimated the scale of his revolt, made several unwise appointments and deployed insufficient resources until her military commander, Lord Mountjoy, persuaded Tyrone to submit.

Oxfordshire 1596

In spite of severe economic problems, the only armed uprising in England in the 1590s occurred near Oxford and involved a handful of protesters. The government declared it was a rebellion and meted out harsh punishments to the leaders.

Essex 1601

The Earl of Essex attempted to raise London in a show of popular support for him against Robert Cecil and the queen's councillors. Despite having the nominal support of many nobles, none was willing to risk his life or threaten the queen and the rebellion collapsed within a few hours. Essex was executed along with a handful of his household servants.

Summary diagram: The Tudors

1485	1509	1547	1553	1558	1603
Henry VII	Henry VIII	Edward VI	Mary I	Elizabeth I	

1

The Causes of Tudor Rebellions

> **OVERVIEW**
>
> This chapter analyses the causes of Tudor rebellions under the following headings:
>
> - Political causes: dynastic issues and the succession, 'evil councillors' and factions, reaction to government policies
> - Religious causes: reaction to the Reformation from Catholics and Protestants
> - Economic and social causes: taxation, enclosures, famine, inflation, landlord–tenant relations
> - Conclusion: why did rebellions occur?
> - An assessment of two A2 essays: Grades A and D

> **Note making**
>
> This chapter aims to analyse the causes of Tudor rebellions, to identify similar and dissimilar developments between historical periods and to distinguish the more important causes from subsidiary factors. Each section examines the main causes according to political, religious, economic and social factors, and seeks to assess their relative importance. Read a section to get an overview of the main themes before you begin to make any notes. Then decide what are the principal arguments and which examples are needed to back them up. Be selective but where possible have examples of several rebellions so that your points are fully illustrated.

1 | Political causes

Political factors were probably the most important and recurring theme as a cause of Tudor rebellions. They could be inspired by a wide range of issues: a desire to overthrow the dynasty or change the line of succession borne out of personal vengeance, ambition or principle; a wish to remove 'evil advisers' nominally in the interest of the country but often out of factional and self-advancement; a reaction to government centralisation which threatened to destroy traditional ways of life. Political causes were many and varied. Although they changed in the course of the period, other causes and personal motives were frequently interwoven.

Dynastic issues and the succession

Henry VII

Henry VII may have won the battle of Bosworth and established the Tudor dynasty, but his tenure on the throne was far from secure. To his enemies – and he had many – he was a usurper and, if he could overthrow a king, so could they. His very presence on the throne therefore sparked off three dynastic rebellions:

- Francis Viscount Lovel, a former lord chamberlain, and his Yorkist associates Humphrey and Thomas Stafford, raised troops in 1486 to kill the king as he progressed to the north of England.
- In 1487 Lambert Simnel 'pretended' to be the Earl of Warwick, a young prince with a strong claim to the throne whom Henry kept imprisoned in the Tower of London. Simnel's Yorkist supporters believed they would gain more from killing Henry than from serving him. The Earl of Lincoln was politically ambitious and dissatisfied with his court preferments and role that Henry had assigned him. Being a royal councillor and Lord Lieutenant of Ireland were not enough to satisfy this Yorkist claimant whom Richard III had named as his heir. Others like Lovel and Margaret of Burgundy, who funded the troops, were die-hard opponents of the king, while Gerald, Earl of Kildare and the 40 or so Irish nobles who backed Simnel, believed their end would be best served by overthrowing the regime.
- The third dynastic rebellion that Henry faced was led by Perkin Warbeck. He 'pretended' to be the Duke of York, the younger of two princes who had almost certainly been murdered by Richard III. In the early 1490s Warbeck was backed by France, Burgundy and Scotland, each intent on weakening if not actively wishing to remove Henry, but when this challenge came to a head in September 1497, all foreign support evaporated. A mixture of personal and political factors combined to bring about each of these revolts but they had a common link: they wished to remove the king.

Henry VIII

After this initial threat of opposition, Henry VIII faced no dynastic challenge until the 1530s when he was confronted with the greatest rebellion of the sixteenth century, the Pilgrimage of Grace. Henry's recent divorce from Catherine of Aragon and disinheritance of her daughter Mary had certainly alarmed some northern nobles. Among a wide range of complaints and demands, the rebels wanted Princess Mary legitimised and restored to the line of succession. They were also concerned that Henry might determine the succession by will rather than by parliament and,

Key question
How far were dynastic rebellions in Tudor England motivated by personal ambition?

worse, if he did do this, the title would 'incur to the Crown of Scotland' via his sister, Margaret.

Edward VI and Mary I

Edward VI's '**Devise**' of May 1553 also aimed to exclude Mary from the succession and was largely responsible for the Duke of Northumberland's rebellion. He wished to hold on to power and led an armed uprising in July in favour of his daughter-in-law, Lady Jane Grey. In the following year Thomas Wyatt also sought to influence the succession. He feared the consequences of Mary's planned marriage to Philip of Spain, not least the probable exclusion of Princess Elizabeth from the throne. Although the marriage agreement set clear limits on the extent of Philip's influence in England and defined conditions affecting the upbringing of any children, Wyatt and his supporters placed little trust in the Spanish prince. The rebels never admitted they wanted to overthrow Mary, which was a wise insurance policy should their uprising fail, but the prospect of having a future Spanish monarch ruling England had to be guarded against.

Elizabeth I

Getting the rights of a legitimate claimant acknowledged was one of the main objectives of a revolt facing Elizabeth I in 1569. In this case, 'the preservation of the person of the Queen of Scots, as next heir, failing issue of Her Majesty' was an important cause of the Northern Earls' rebellion, according to the Earl of Northumberland. As long as Elizabeth remained unmarried and childless and refused to acknowledge Mary Stuart's claim to the English throne, the succession was in doubt; though whether the rebellious earls wished to bring about Mary's succession prematurely is another matter. They denied treason, of course, claiming that they were 'the Queen's most true and lawful subjects', but this was to be expected. The Earl of Essex similarly denied that he wished to harm the queen when he began a rebellion in London in 1601 but he certainly wanted to endear himself to the **heir presumptive**, James VI of Scotland. If Essex could persuade the queen, by force if necessary, to dismiss her advisers and replace them with councillors such as himself, he would be rewarded as the 'kingmaker'.

'Evil councillors'

The accusation that the monarch was surrounded by 'evil councillors' and that he or she preferred to consult 'new' ministers rather than the long-established families of England was a charge frequently made in rebellions:

- In 1497 Reginald Bray and John Morton were dubbed 'evil advisers' by Cornish rebels.
- In 1525 Suffolk protesters said they were going to 'complain of the Cardinal' (i.e. Wolsey) to the king.
- In 1536 Cromwell, Cranmer, Audley and Rich were the targets in ballads and manifestos written by the Pilgrims of Grace.

Key terms

Devise
The means by which Edward disinherited his half-sisters, Mary and Elizabeth, in favour of Lady Jane Grey.

Heir presumptive
An heir who it was presumed would inherit unless an alternative claimant was subsequently born.

Key question
How common was the allegation that the Tudors were advised by 'evil councillors'?

- In 1554 Thomas Wyatt claimed, 'We seek no harm to the Queen but better counsel and councillors'.
- In 1569 the northern earls held William Cecil responsible for their revolt.
- In 1601 the Earl of Essex aimed to remove Robert Cecil, Elizabeth I's principal adviser.

The claim, that self-serving upstarts had deceived the monarch, thus appears as a justification for political disturbances throughout the Tudor period.

Each rebel leader appears to have genuinely believed that once royal advisers were removed, then wiser and more effective policies would follow. If the Pilgrimage of Grace is taken as an illustration, the pilgrims swore an oath to 'expel all **villein** blood and evil councillors against the **commonwealth** from his Grace and his Privy Council', and the rebels at York argued that 'persons as be of low birth and small reputation' had exploited their power and 'procured the profits most especially for their own advantage'. It was, of course, true that Cromwell, Cranmer, Audley and Rich were self-made men from politically obscure backgrounds. Before becoming royal councillors, Cromwell had been a merchant and one-time mercenary, Cranmer a Cambridge academic, Audley the town clerk in Colchester and Rich a Welsh lawyer. Lord Darcy was convinced that Cromwell was 'the very original and chief causer of all this rebellion and mischief', whose aim had been to 'bring us to our end and to strike off our heads', although the historian Geoffrey Elton once argued that 'it was the gentry leaders, not the commons, who singled out the hated minister of the Crown'.

Factions

It was a widely held belief that if there was no parliament and a crisis occurred, then the old nobility should be consulted. Henry VII in fact did do this, holding five Great Councils between 1487 and 1502, but by the 1530s the emergence of a few select advisers, later termed the 'privy council', eclipsed this practice and led to the formation of political **factions**. How far the Lincolnshire rising and Pilgrimage of Grace were inspired by disaffected pro-Aragonese supporters at court has been the subject of historical debate. Certainly Catherine of Aragon's supporters had links with several leading rebels caught up in the rebellion. Among the Lincoln rebels, Sir Robert Dymoke had once been her chancellor, Sir Christopher Willoughby a knight of the body and Lord Hussey chamberlain to Princess Mary. And in Yorkshire, Lord Darcy absented himself from debates in parliament concerning the Act of Succession and Sir Robert Constable fiercely opposed the divorce. Both became leading pilgrims. This Aragonese faction undoubtedly stood to lose as long as Cromwell remained in favour with the king, but their political grievances were just one of many factors that contributed to the rebellion of 1536.

Key terms

Villein
A tenant who was obliged to perform any services that his lord commanded.

Commonwealth
The 'wealth' or welfare of the common people.

Factions
A small number of like-minded people who rivalled an established and larger group for political, religious or social power.

Key question
How important were political factions as a cause of Tudor rebellions?

Essay focus

Look at Essays 1 and 2 on pages 28–33. Essay 1, paragraph 2, and Essay 2, paragraph 3, cite the Aragonese faction as a factor in causing the 1536 uprising. Do you agree that this is a valid line of argument?

Factional politics was a principal cause of the two major rebellions in Elizabeth's reign. The northern earls, Westmorland and Northumberland, in 1569, and the Earl of Essex in 1601 were in decline at Whitehall and for similar reasons. Northumberland and Westmorland, together with a handful of southern privy councillors, Arundel, Pembroke, Lumley, Leicester and Throckmorton, schemed to overthrow William Cecil, the queen's secretary. They held him responsible for ill-advised political, religious and foreign policies, and the uncertainty surrounding the succession. Central to their plan was for the Duke of Norfolk, Westmorland's brother-in-law, to marry Mary Queen of Scots, to ensure the continuity of Catholicism. When fear gripped most of the plotters they confessed all they knew and protested their innocence to the queen but the northern earls unwisely pressed on for personal reasons. Westmorland was in financial difficulties and hectored by his wife to stand up for his beliefs; Northumberland, aged 70, was no longer a political force in the north and resented seeing his wardenship of the **middle march** go to a local rival.

Political factions were also central to Essex's revolt. Suspended from the Privy Council, banned from the court, charged with treason and in financial difficulties when the queen rescinded his patent to sell sweet wine, Essex's star was falling rapidly in late 1600. 'The queen', he said, 'had thrust him down into a private life; and he could not serve with base obsequiousness.' His clients, such as the Earls of Bedford, Rutland and Southampton, still looked to him for patronage but his reputation and credit were in ruin and he was up against Robert Cecil who, as Master of the Court of Wards and Chancellor of the Duchy of Lancaster, held all the aces. His clients, like Lord Cobham, Lord Buckhurst and Sir John Stanhope, were in the ascendant and between them dominated court patronage. In Essex's opinion, these men were 'base upstarts' and 'caterpillars' who were devouring the state's resources for their own profit. Essex planned a demonstration of noble force which he believed the city of London would support and so lead to the queen readmitting him to favour. Essex gambled on his popularity and strength as a factional leader – and lost!

Key term

Middle march
The marches were the lands between England and Scotland that were divided into three and administered by wardens.

Essay focus

Look at Essay 2, paragraph 5 on page 31. It makes good use of factual details of both the Northern Earls' and Essex rebellions.

Government intervention

A final political cause of rebellion was the effects that governments had when they began to extend the power of the State into the provinces. As centralisation took hold and the Crown became more omniscient, political and legal privileges were swept away and traditional practices eroded. 'If we may enjoy our old ancient customs', Sir James Layburne of Lancashire declared in 1536, 'we have no cause to rise.' Those most affected by government intervention resided in the more distant parts of England and in Ireland, and these regions were the areas that were prepared to revolt against Tudor '**despotism**'.

Cornwall and the north of England

The Cornish had no great love for English governments and their rebellions in 1497 and 1549 were partly due to a feeling that they ought to be treated differently from the rest of the country. Similarly, the northern counties consistently complained that they were being ruled by 'strangers', that their wealth was being drained by Londoners, and the traditional nobility had a decreasing say in how the counties north of the Trent were governed. Stewardships of royal manors, custodianships of castles and the wardenships of the marches were gradually being taken out of their control and manors forcibly exchanged by the Crown. The clergy also had grievances. In the 1530s, the ecclesiastical liberties enjoyed by Ripon, Beverley and the Palatinate of Durham were surrendered to the Crown. Both the uprisings in 1536 and 1569 petitioned that a parliament should meet in the north, possibly York or Nottingham, to redress local issues, but none was held. The earls in revolt in 1569 made clear their hostility towards the central government when they proclaimed that the aim of their rebellion was 'the restoring of all ancient customs and liberties to God and this noble realm'.

Ireland

Ireland, like the north of England, came increasingly to resent interference from central government in the administration of its affairs. The Tudors had to work with key members of the Anglo-Irish nobility and manage the feuding among rival families as well as possible. Significantly for the first 50 years of this period until 1534, the Earls of Kildare had acted as the Crown's deputy lieutenants in Ireland, and there were no rebellions. Admittedly, there was considerable corruption and inefficiency but that was the Gaelic way of life, and if it was not ideal at least it worked. Between 1534 and 1603, however, five major rebellions occurred and each can be attributed to political causes:

- From 1532 Cromwell started to favour Kildare's rivals for government offices and the earl began to resent his declining influence in court circles in both London and Dublin. In September 1533 Henry ordered the earl to visit him as he doubted whether he would enforce the Reformation Acts. The earl replied by sending his wife and in the meantime began to

Key question
In what ways did government intervention in England differ from that in Ireland as a cause of rebellion?

Despotism
The government of an absolute ruler who rules without regard for the law.

Key term

Key terms

Pale
A region near Dublin that was one of the few well-governed areas of Ireland.

Martial law
Military law that replaced civil law during a political crisis.

Plantations
Lands that were confiscated from rebels and granted to English and local landlords at reduced prices.

Attainted lands
Acts of attainder were passed by parliament on traitors and their entire property and that of their family were attainted and forfeited to the Crown.

transfer weapons and gunpowder from Dublin castle to his own estates. A further demand from the king finally brought Kildare to London and once lodged in the Tower, he never left, dying there in 1534. 'Silken Thomas', his son, not surprisingly ignored similar requests to visit London, and he and five of his uncles raised 1000 men in Munster and invaded the **Pale**. Although the rebels called on the Catholic Church for support and condemned Henry's religious reforms, the uprising was primarily political in cause and intent. Thomas's objective was to expel the English administration and become sole ruler of Ireland.

- Shane O'Neill's rebellion between 1558 and 1567 was a complicated affair. He wanted to rule Ulster and was willing to murder his older brother to achieve it, but this only stirred up resentment against him. When he begged forgiveness from Queen Elizabeth, she agreed to recognise him as captain of Tyrone and 'the O'Neill', head of the clan, but he was soon intriguing with Charles IX of France and Mary Queen of Scots, and claiming to be the true defender of the faith.

- O'Neill's rising was quickly followed by two rebellions in Munster led by James Fitzmaurice Fitzgerald. In 1569 he resented attempts by Elizabeth to colonise Ireland and the imposition of **martial law** in the wake of O'Neill's uprising but he was especially aggrieved that his cousin, the Earl of Desmond, had been put in the Tower following a feud with the Butler clan. Fitzgerald also had a religious pretext, claiming that Elizabeth wanted to introduce 'another newly invented kind of religion', but the main grievance of most rebels was the growing presence of English adventurers in the new plantations and their brutal treatment of native Irish.

- Fitzgerald's second rebellion in 1579 had a more pronounced religious dimension to it, although it was fundamentally about politics. Having returned from Rome and aware of the Bull of Excommunication against Elizabeth, he saw an opportunity to rally the Catholic Irish against English rule. Before 1570 no serious effort had been made by English governments to enforce the Protestant faith; it would have been unworkable, unwelcome and unwise. Fitzgerald nevertheless played the Catholic card to good effect, but at heart lay his political animosity against the new English settlers and the Dublin administration. Munster, Ulster, Leinster and Connaught rose up in revolt, the pope gave it his blessing and 600 Spanish and Italian troops were despatched to assist.

- By the final decade of Elizabeth's reign, it was clear that political tension was gathering once more. The **plantations** in Connaught and Munster provoked ill-feeling as the new owners raised rents, claimed land to which they were not entitled, and bribed juries to obtain favourable verdicts. Government policies of compositions (taxes paid instead of military service, billeting and purveyance), establishing Protestant churches at the expense of Catholics and seizing **attainted lands** from rebels fuelled the resentment. A system of garrisons contained localised disturbances, but Ulster lay largely outside effective English rule. It is ironic that the decision to take Hugh O'Neill, the future Earl of Tyrone, away from Ireland and bring him up in the household of the Earl of Leicester should have backfired so spectacularly. When the earl returned in 1593, he was eager to be recognised as 'the O'Neill', ruler of Ulster. Between 1593 and 1594 he had come to the defence of English garrisons and officials when other clans attacked them, but in his estimation he had not been adequately rewarded and by 1595 he had had enough. What made his rebellion so different was that it signalled a nation-wide revolt against England that lasted for over eight years. His aim was blatantly political: to expel the new English settlers and Anglo-Irish administration, and to achieve independence.

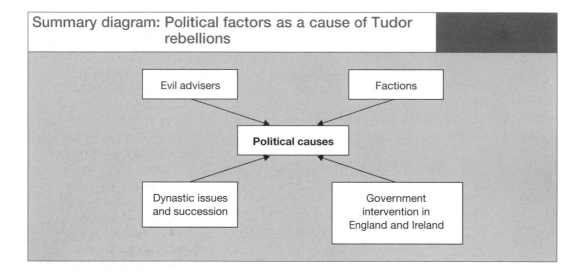

Summary diagram: Political factors as a cause of Tudor rebellions

Evil advisers

Factions

Political causes

Dynastic issues and succession

Government intervention in England and Ireland

2 | Religious causes

Religious devotion was a powerful force in convincing a man that he should rebel against the king. Although the Church upheld law and order and preached obedience to God – for surely rebellion was as much a sin as an act of treason (see Chapter 4, page 103) – some clerics nevertheless felt justified in protesting at changes to the traditional Roman Catholic faith, and in 1536, 1549 and 1569 the clergy exhorted true believers to rise up and overthrow Protestant heresy. The rebellions in eastern England in 1549 and Kent in 1554 on the other hand reflected support for the Protestant faith. Kett's rebels wanted to advance the Edwardian Reformation more effectively, while some of Wyatt's followers were anxious to preserve it in the face of Mary's Counter-Reformation. Thus, between 1536 and 1569 religious causes played a key role in a number of rebellions. In Ireland, defence of the Church, or more precisely, opposition to Protestant reforms, was the pretext for Kildare's rebellion in the 1530s and four rebellions in

Key question
Why was religious change the cause of so many rebellions between 1536 and 1569?

Elizabeth's reign, although in each case religion was almost certainly a cloak for political objectives (see pages 7–8).

The Pilgrimage of Grace 1536

The Pilgrimage of Grace is the name given to three separate uprisings that had over-arching causes and which occurred in the northern counties of England. In October 1536 uprisings occurred in the adjacent counties of Lincolnshire and Yorkshire which soon spread to most of the north of England. Both had a strong religious undercurrent. Two sets of ecclesiastical commissioners travelling through Lincolnshire had alarmed many local people: the first was authorised by the Bishop of Lincoln to investigate the condition of the parish clergy; the second was authorised by the government to close down the smaller monasteries. Each caused resentment. The rebels from Louth and Horncastle near Lincoln drew up articles requesting that their abbeys should be preserved and wanting guarantees that their parish churches would not be closed as well. They were proud of their 295-foot spire at Louth, completed in 1515, and did not trust the bishop and his chancellor to keep their hands off the church plate and ornaments.

Similar fears and rumours accompanied risings in Yorkshire. Over 100 monasteries and abbeys were scheduled to be closed and opposition to the dissolution was a dominant factor. The rebels argued that a range of social and economic services would be affected, the poor and children's education would decline, and 'spiritual information and preaching' provided by the monks would disappear. Although such anxieties and claims may have been overstated, the dissolution of the smaller monasteries did motivate many people to protest. In Lancashire, where four monasteries were closed in September 1536, monks encouraged the common people to rise up, protest at the government's religious policy, and assist them in their restoration. Even before trouble broke out in Lincolnshire and Yorkshire, it was suspected that some people in Lancashire were buying up arms.

A second concern voiced by rebel groups was that heresy was rife. A diversity of religious beliefs among the king's council and **convocation** was likely to encourage heretical ideas, which had to be stopped. Henry no doubt shared this view and had indeed drawn up the **Act of Ten Articles** in July 1536 to clarify the theological position. He would have also agreed that continental reformers such as Luther and Bucer should be identified as heretics but would have been surprised to find Rastell and St German named with them as they were both English common lawyers, and he would not condone an attack on his own archbishop Cranmer. Such allegations of heresy, however, reflected the opinions of only a minority of clerics and educated laymen, and interestingly no concern was expressed over the theological attacks on purgatory.

A third cause of protest was the government's recent assault on saints, pilgrimages and holy days, which meant a great deal to the people. At Kirkby Stephen in Westmorland, for instance, there was uproar when the priest failed to offer prayers for the forthcoming

Key terms

Convocation
The general assembly of the clergy that usually met when parliament was called.

Act of Ten Articles
This Act stressed the importance of baptism, the Eucharist and penance, and put less significance on confirmation, marriage, holy orders and the last rites.

St Luke's Day when a fair was scheduled to take place. The Durham protesters carried the banner of St Cuthbert when they marched out of their city and the rebels' decision to carry a banner of the Five Wounds of Christ was a further reminder that they were on a pilgrimage, a feature that was later repeated in the Western and Northern Earls' rebellions. English people revered their saints and enjoyed going on pilgrimages, and they were determined to preserve them. The restoration and defence of clerical privileges were also called for; people did not want to pay any more **first fruits and tenths** to the king but they were keen to restore **benefit of clergy** and ecclesiastical liberties. All of these grievances reflected the commons' and clergy's resentment at Cromwell's reforms since 1535. In particular they resented the part he and Cranmer had played in enacting the divorce and break from Rome, and they wanted the pope restored as Head of the Church, claiming that the recent Act of Supremacy was contrary to God's law.

Collectively these religious issues revealed a wide spectrum of opposition to the Henrician Reformation. Many of the changes had taken place before 1536 but the presence of government and diocesan agents in the autumn brought home to monks, priests, gentry and commons alike the reality of the 'new' reforms. Different areas had different grievances, which came to be formulated in separate articles as the uprising progressed. In Cumberland and the region to the west of the Pennines, there was resentment at **tithes** and the poor quality of many priests (a complaint reminiscent of Kett's rebellion) rather than the closure of the monasteries; in neighbouring north Lancashire and much of Yorkshire the dissolution and the restoration of the true faith were of prime concern; and in Lincolnshire, it was fear that their parish churches were going to be attacked that evoked their hostility.

Essay focus

The Pilgrimage of Grace provides a very good illustration of how different religious grievances at various levels of society, both locally and regionally, came together to produce widespread resentment. This point is well made in Essay 2, paragraph 7 on page 32, and made rather less effectively in Essay 1, paragraph 3 on page 30.

The Western rebellion 1549

The reaction of Cornwall, Devon and Norfolk to the Edwardian Reformation in the summer of 1549 demonstrates contrasting experiences and the diversity of belief in the country at that time. The Western rebellion was largely the result of religious reforms introduced in June 1549. Thirteen out of 14 articles drawn up by rebel captains at their camp near Exeter show that what they wanted was restoration not reformation, and they marched under the banner of the Five Wounds of Christ. They rejected everything that was new: the English Prayer Book, which they called 'a Christmas game', the English Bible and the revised liturgy of 1547.

Key terms

First fruits and tenths
Taxes on the first year's income of a new bishop and one-tenth of the value of ecclesiastical benefices received by the Crown after the Reformation.

Benefit of clergy
The privilege of exemption from trial by a secular court that was allowed in cases of felony to the clergy or to anyone who could read a passage from the Scriptures.

Tithes
Payments made by the laity to the parish church of one-tenth of their agricultural profits or personal income.

Liturgy
An order of church service.

Act of Six Articles
This Act upheld the orthodox Catholic faith and remained in force until 1547.

Catechism and prymer
A catechism was a book of basic religious instruction in the form of questions and answers; a prymer was an elementary book of religious instruction.

Apart from the clergy, few will have been able to read or understand the **liturgy** but they knew it was no longer in Latin, and this was unacceptable. What they did want was the return of papal relics and images, the restoration of chantries and at least two monasteries in every county, a Latin Mass that was celebrated with bread only, and a return to the **Act of Six Articles** of 1539. In this deeply orthodox region, much of the hysteria surrounding the Protestant reforms can be attributed to local priests whom Philip Nichols, a government propagandist, ungenerously called 'whelps of the Romish litter'. There was, however, no direct request to restore the papacy although the first of the Exeter articles, like those of the pilgrims in 1536, challenged the legality of secular authorities to implement religious reform. This, they argued, was the sole right of church councils.

Kett's rebellion 1549

If the Western rebellion was in defence of the old religion, Kett's rebellion was in part a protest at the slow rate of progress Protestantism was making in eastern England. Norfolk had an anticlerical tradition and by 1547 was fertile ground for a proactive Protestant reformation. The Bishop of Norwich, William Rugge, was ill-suited to achieve this – he was old and unsympathetic to radical reforms – and there was a strong feeling that the quality of ministers was not good enough to advance the reformation. The rebels wanted, they said, a better-educated and resident clergy, competent teaching of the **catechism and prymer** for children, and good-quality sermons. If the bishop could not appoint such ministers, then the parishioners would. There was also resentment at priests who indulged in the property market since they should be devoting their time to spiritual duties, not prosecuting parishioners for unpaid and unfair tithes. The daily services using the new Prayer Book conducted under the 'Tree of Reformation' on Mousehold Heath outside Norwich further testify to the rebels' religious commitment even if it was economic and social causes that had first brought them to revolt (see pages 17–18).

Wyatt's rebellion 1554

Ostensibly Wyatt's rebellion in Kent in January 1554 was caused by secular and political factors yet it also had a religious undercurrent. Significantly there were no revolts or uprisings in Mary's reign against her Catholic reforms and although it was clear that she intended restoring the old faith and had already reversed many of the Edwardian reforms by the time Wyatt plotted his revolt, he was not a reformer and his agenda was political not religious. 'You may not so much as name religion' he advised a colleague, 'for that will withdraw from us the hearts of many.' However, not everyone felt like him. Kent was a strongly Protestant county and had been in the forefront of reform since the 1530s. Many people will have been concerned at Mary's attachment to Roman Catholicism and her intention to marry Philip of Spain. There was also much local support for Protestantism in Maidstone, which supplied 78 rebels, Cranbrook and Tonbridge, and Wyatt's fellow conspirators in Leicestershire (the Duke of Suffolk), Devon (Sir Peter Carew) and Herefordshire (Sir James Croft) had Protestant leanings. Perhaps Wyatt's reluctance to play the religious card was due to his belief that xenophobia would generate greater support nationally. Invoking the Church certainly worked in some of the Irish rebellions in the later years of Elizabeth's reign but that was the Catholic Church in a country where the English were detested more than the Spanish. The English on the other hand disliked all foreigners and only a minority of Protestants would have felt that the Church and themselves were in danger so early in Mary's reign.

The Northern Earls' rebellion 1569

'Our first object in assembling was the reformation of religion and preservation of the person of the Queen of Scots.' So declared the Earl of Northumberland under interrogation in 1572. Defence of the Catholic faith, together with personal and political motives, go a long way towards explaining the origins of the Northern Earls' revolt. The leading protagonists were Catholic: Northumberland had converted in 1567, and Westmorland was born and bred a Catholic. Both men resented the newly appointed Protestant minded Bishop Pilkington to Durham, and rebel proclamations issued at Darlington, Staindrop and Richmond suggest that there was widespread Catholic sentiment. The cause of the rebellion, they declared, was 'a new found religion and heresy, contrary to God's word', which they intended 'amending and redressing'.

Many of the northern aristocratic families had retained the Catholic faith in spite of Elizabethan statutes requiring the regular attendance at church or a fine of 5p a week. Some preferred to pay the fine but others sought protection from Justices of the Peace (JPs), many of whom were Catholics themselves, and so escaped the law. Wealthier nobles and gentry of course had chapels on their estates and continued to celebrate Mass privately and only took communion once a year at Easter. For 10 years the government made no concerted attempt to enforce the **Act of Uniformity** despite the general feeling that little progress had been made in the north to advance Christianity of any kind. Sir Ralph Sadler, a privy councillor who knew the north of England well, informed Cecil in London that 'the common people are ignorant, superstitious and altogether blinded with the old popish doctrine, and therefore so favour the cause which the rebels make the colour of their rebellion, that, though their persons be here with us, their hearts are with them'.

The Earl of Sussex, President of the Council of the North, on the other hand, believed that religion was a cloak for political motives, which the earls had used to rally popular support. Recent research has also cast doubt on Sadler's claim that the old faith 'still lay like lees at the bottom of men's hearts and if the vessel was ever so little stirred came to the top'. Yet many of the rebels are known to have been sincere in their attachment to the old faith. Some like the Nortons from Ripon, the Inglebys of Ripley and Cholmeleys from Whitby had ancestors who had taken part in the

Key term

Act of Uniformity An Act that enforced the Protestant prayer book, which was first introduced in 1549, and modified in 1552 and 1559. It imposed punishments on those who did not conform.

Pilgrimage of Grace. The banner of St Cuthbert was taken out of Durham Cathedral and Francis Norton paraded with the Five Wounds of Christ, just as he had done 30 years before. And recently returned from the continent were Thomas Markenfeld and Nicholas Morton in anticipation of an armed uprising. Morton appears to have been a prime mover in warning hesitant rebels that if they did not fight there were 'dangers touching our souls and the loss of our country', and left it to them to weigh up the consequences of inactivity. It is likely therefore that many northern peasants at least revered the old customs, pilgrimages and celebration of holy days, even if they had little understanding or affection for the Mass. Of course some tenants and employees of powerful magnates and gentry had little choice in the matter and were forced to follow their masters, but 90 per cent of the known rebels were not tenants of the leaders and presumably joined in for entirely non-feudal reasons.

Essay focus

The extent to which religion was a prime cause of rebellion is examined in Essay 2, paragraphs 7 and 8, on page 32. Why do you think religion was not so important an issue in England after the accession of Elizabeth I? In contrast, defence of the Catholic faith in Ireland remained a sensitive issue and lay beneath the surface of most Irish disturbances after 1558. Why was this?

Summary diagram: Religion as a cause of rebellion in England

Year	Name of rebellion	Catholic or Protestant?	Reason	Local or regional?	Religion – main or subsidiary cause?
1536	Pilgrimage of Grace	Catholic	Reaction to the closure of monasteries and other Protestant reforms	Regional in seven northern counties	Main
1549	Western rebellion	Catholic	Reaction to a new English Prayer Book	Local to Devon and Cornwall	Main
1549	Kett's rebellion	Protestant	Demanded further Protestant reforms	Local to Norfolk	Subsidiary
1554	Wyatt's rebellion	Protestant	Fear of Catholic reformation	Local to Kent	Subsidiary
1569	Northern Earls' rebellion	Catholic	Reaction to Protestant reforms	Regional in four northern counties	Main

3 | Economic and social causes

In the majority of cases, rebellion and disorder were the product of political and religious causes, yet underlying many of the riots and disturbances that afflicted Tudor England throughout the period – some of which became full-blown rebellions – were economic and social tensions. These were the triggers that sparked off disturbances at a local level and, if not well handled, could spiral out of control and become a far more serious rebellion. In contrast, economic and social issues rarely figured overtly in Irish rebellions; and, when they did, they were inseparable from underlying political issues.

Taxation

Government taxation was the single most important cause of popular protest in early Tudor England. In this respect, it was no different from the **Peasants' Revolt** of 1381, which followed a decade of financial demands, or **Cade's rebellion** in London in 1450, after a period of heavy taxation. In 1489, 1497 and 1525 taxation was the main cause of rebellion and a contributing factor, albeit minor in bringing about the Pilgrimage of Grace and the Western rebellion. Tax collectors were often assaulted and locally people frequently claimed they were too poor or not willing to pay. In 1515 Henry VIII remitted payments from 19 Yorkshire towns and villages as they were so impoverished, and according to a survey of 1522, one-third of people in Exeter and Leicester escaped on account of poverty. Generally, around 60 per cent of the adult male population was liable for taxation, but, of course, it was only levied occasionally when there was an emergency. Ordinarily the monarch was expected to 'live of his own' and not require parliamentary taxation.

The Yorkshire rebellion 1489

In 1489 and 1497 objections came from Yorkshire and Cornwall, respectively, about having to pay a tax for a war that did not concern them. Parliament had voted Henry VII £100,000 to meet the costs of a campaign against France but the prevailing view in Yorkshire was that the tax was unfair. Traditionally, people in the south funded wars against France while the most northern counties met the cost of defending the Scottish border. Moreover, the counties of Northumberland, Westmorland and Cumberland had been exempted by the king on account of poverty. The protesters were also affected by a bad harvest of 1488 and took exception to the news that Henry Percy, Earl of Northumberland, would lead the tax commission. It has been suggested that the murder of Percy, which had sparked off the revolt, was orchestrated by the king to take over Percy's lands and gain control of the north but there is no extant evidence to support this theory. The earl was very unpopular but so was the prospect of paying taxation.

Key question
Why was taxation such a frequent cause of rebellion in the period between 1485 and 1550?

Key terms

Peasants' Revolt
In 1381, peasants in Kent and Essex led by Wat Tyler and John Ball marched on London, in protest against a poll tax and calling for the abolition of serfdom.

Cade's rebellion
Jack Cade led a revolt in Kent that briefly occupied London before being defeated in battle. The rebels were protesting at high taxes and governmental incompetence.

The Cornish rebellion 1497

The Cornish revolt arose from similar circumstances. In January 1497 parliament had voted £60,000 to fund a war against the Scots and when news reached Cornwall in May, there was widespread anger. According to Holinshed, the rebels wanted 'to punish those responsible for the tax imposed on the people without any reasonable cause'. They explained with some justification that customarily wars against Scotland were paid by a **scutage** or land tax and only by the four northern counties. Perhaps they recalled the protest in Yorkshire, and if they could get away with not paying a war tax, why not the Cornish? Two councillors were blamed: John Morton, the lord chancellor, and Reginald Bray, the king's chief financial adviser who had been responsible for finding ways of increasing revenue from the royal estate in the 1490s. In fact the 1497 parliamentary grant was an innovation. The traditional fifteenth (payable by each vill or civil parish) and tenth (payable by each borough) were levied as usual at rates that had been set in 1334, but in addition it was agreed that a further grant of £60,000 would be collected if war actually broke out and this money would be levied on individuals at rates assessed by royal commissioners. There is nothing to suggest that the Cornish rebels were protesting at the novelty of the tax, but members of parliament (MPs), gentry, merchants and clergy who were most affected would no doubt have had some misgivings. In fact war did not break out and the second tax was not collected.

The Amicable Grant 1525

On four occasions the Tudors attempted to levy taxation without parliament's consent: in 1491, 1525, 1544–6 and 1594–9. On each occasion England was at war but only once did the levy lead to rebellion. The Amicable Grant was a non-parliamentary tax which commissioners were ordered to collect in the spring of 1525. Objections to paying it were widespread for a number of reasons:

- In 1522 Wolsey had raised £260,000 in forced loans, which he said would be repaid out of the next parliamentary subsidy. This had not happened and understandably caused resentment.
- In 1523 he had tried to get parliament to vote a subsidy of £800,000 but they only offered £151,000 payable over four years. The Church was also expected to pay about £120,000.
- The Amicable Grant (which was far from amicable) made excessive demands on the laity and clergy alike. Since 1513 Wolsey had introduced tax assessments based on land, income and personal assets, and collected whichever yielded the highest tax.
- Assessments were made by government officials and so ended the principle of paying a fixed rate. The laity were now required to pay a special tax of five per cent if they were rated below £20, 7.5 per cent if rated at between £20 and £50, and 16.5 per cent if rated above £50 a year. Many of the protesters would have been paying tax for the first time at rates they could ill afford.

Key term

Scutage
Rather than fight in person for the king in times of war, tenants-in-chief could commute their feudal obligations into a tax known as a scutage or 'escuage'.

- The clergy were hit even harder. They were to pay at a rate of 25 per cent of their annual revenue or value of their movable goods worth less than £10, and 33 per cent for those above £10.
- There was a grave shortage of coin, which is why the government urgently needed to collect the tax, and rising unemployment following a fall in wool prices added to the economic distress.

Protesters in Suffolk claimed, perhaps disingenuously, that 'only for lack of work prevented them from paying'. As they explained to the Duke of Norfolk, 'since you ask who is our captain, for sooth his name is Poverty, for he and his cousin Necessity, have brought us to this doing'. It seems clear that the Grant, coming on top of recent tax demands and at a time of worsening economic conditions, triggered off the rebellion. Any suggestion that the grant may have been unconstitutional – a view put forward by some historians – did not figure in the rebels' complaints.

The Pilgrimage of Grace 1536

Of the many sets of articles drawn up by the pilgrims in 1536, only one concerned taxation. Item 14 of the Pontefract Articles requested 'to be discharged on the quindene [fifteenth] and taxes now granted by act of parliament'. This referred to the Subsidy Act of 1534. Articles presented by rebels in the West Riding of Yorkshire argued that the king was only allowed to collect taxes in defence of the realm whereas the preamble to the Act claimed that costs incurred in the defence of the realm were the same as if the country was at war and, since the country owed Henry a debt of gratitude, this debt could now be repaid in taxation. In Lincolnshire, where rebellions in 1536 first began, it may have been rumours that the tax was a prelude to further fiscal exactions, such as a tax on white meat and horned cattle, that alarmed people so much. In reality the subsidy's yield of £80,000 was comparatively small and affected only a few people, but many rebels claimed they could not afford it. Although attempts to collect taxes in peacetime would also be made in 1540 and 1553, the 1534 subsidy was the only one that provoked a popular protest.

The Western rebellion 1549

The Duke of Somerset's Subsidy Act of 1549 had a dual objective: to raise as much money as possible at a time of acute shortage, and to encourage more farmers to return their lands to tillage. To achieve these ends a tax of $1d$ (0.24p) on a sheep and $1/2d$ (0.12p) on every pound of woollen cloth was levied on pasture farmers and cloth producers. In practice the tax hit poorer peasants and tenants most of all as wealthy clothiers and sheep farmers raised their prices to offset its cost. The West Country was, of course, not the only sheep-farming region but Devon was a largely enclosed county and was affected more than most. Moreover, the tax was due to be assessed two weeks after the introduction of the English Prayer Book and so added to their list of grievances against the government (see pages 10–11).

Key question
Why were some areas of the country more affected than others by enclosures?

Key terms

Husbandmen
Small farmers or landowners of a lower social standing than yeomen.

Feodary
An officer of the court of wards.

Enclosures

The act of enclosing a field with a hedge, fence or ditch, or amalgamating two farms and enclosing them (known as engrossment) was not a major cause of rebellion but it could cause tension between landowners and tenants, provoke local disturbances and riots, and occasionally lead to something more serious. This is what happened in 1536, 1549 and 1596.

The Pilgrimage of Grace 1536

Only one of the articles presented to the 'Lords of the King's Council' at Pontefract in 1536 cited enclosure as a cause of the Pilgrimage of Grace. Item 13 called for:

> Statute for enclosures and intakes to put in execution, and that all intakes [and] enclosures since 1489 to be pulled down except [in] mountains, forest and parks.

There was much rioting over illegal enclosures in the course of 1535 and it is likely that this was a common grievance among particular northern rebels. Over 300 people at Giggleswick in Yorkshire pulled down hedges and dykes and there were riots at Fressington in Cumberland. Both areas sent rebels in the following year to attack the lands of the Earl of Cumberland, a notorious landlord who had enclosed his tenants' lands in the Eden Valley and denied them grazing rights. **Husbandmen** at Horncastle in Lincolnshire were also concerned at the encroachment of tenants' rights, although this was a minor grievance among the commons.

Kett's rebellion 1549

Kett's rebellion at first sight appears to have been caused by unlawful enclosures. Article 1 of Kett's 'Demands Being in Rebellion', published in July 1549, declared:

> We pray your grace that where it is enacted for enclosing that it be not hurtful to such as have enclosed saffron grounds [i.e. lands where saffron was grown] for they be greatly chargeable to them, and that from henceforth no man shall enclose any more.

The rebellion was triggered by a local incident between two rival landowners, Robert Kett and John Flowerdew. Both had recently enclosed their lands and Flowerdew, the county's **feodary**, was not popular in Wymondham and nearby Attleborough where rioting began. Kett, who had the presence of mind to dismantle his own fences before the locals did it for him, became the spokesman for the rebels. What had sparked this peasant revolt were allegations that landlords had been deliberately obstructing a government commission that was investigating illegal enclosures. The rebels believed that they would have the backing of the government if they were to take the law into their own hands. Similar riots and hedge-breaking occurred in Sussex, Kent, Cambridgeshire, the Midlands and south-west counties, but it was in Norfolk where riots turned to open rebellion.

Norfolk was a densely populated county, and good, flat, fertile land was scarce. Many tenant farmers in fact favoured enclosure because it denied their landlords the ancient right of **folding** their sheep and cattle on the tenants' arable fields and only opposed enclosure when they were denied this practice. This in part explains why Kett was keen to maintain enclosures where saffron was grown, a flower that produced a yellow dye used in the local cloth industry. On the other land, there was general concern at wealthy landowners, such as manorial lords who had extensive private estates, pasturing their flocks on common land, which was in short supply.

Article 3 declared:

> We pray your grace that no lord of no manor shall common upon the commons.

And Article 29 stated:

> We pray that no lord, knight, esquire nor gentleman do graze nor feed any bullocks or sheep if he may spend £40 a year by his lands only for the provision of his house.

The overstocking of common land was a widespread complaint, but one that did not necessarily infringe the law. What was unacceptable to peasants in Norfolk was that when they had turned to the law, it had let them down. In the 1540s peasants at Hingham and Great Dunham had prosecuted their landlords for encroachment but without success. Magistrates were usually landlords themselves and either knew or sympathised with the landowners involved.

1549: The 'year of commotion'

Disturbances occurred in different areas of the country in 1549 when peasants felt they could not get justice lawfully. In Somerset, for instance, disturbances occurred when open fields were converted into deer parks and at Wilton in Wiltshire peasants removed Lord Herbert's hedges that he had put up on common land. Serious riots in Sussex were only prevented when the Earl of Arundel forced 'certain gentlemen, and chiefly for enclosures' to dismantle their hedges. Only in low-lying sheep-corn areas in much of the Midlands, East Anglia, southern and south-east England might enclosure become a grievance. Some counties were more affected than others. Northamptonshire, Oxfordshire and Buckinghamshire consistently experienced disturbances. In Leicestershire, 30 per cent of land was enclosed but this was exceptional and nationally only three per cent of most seriously affected counties was enclosed under the Tudors. In most of the country, in areas of forests, fens, moorlands and uplands, enclosure was not a live issue. If enclosures were achieved by mutual consent among neighbours or if enclosures posed no threat to their livelihood, they were likely to be accomplished without objection. And in the opinion of a contemporary writer, Thomas Smith, husbandmen were just as likely to do this as the yeomen and gentry:

Key term

Folding
Allowing cattle and sheep to graze and manure the land.

Every day some of us enclose a plot of his ground to pasture, and were it not that our ground lies in the common fields, intermingled one with another, I think also our fields had been enclosed, of a common agreement of all the township, long ere this time.

The Oxfordshire rebellion 1596

As population levels started to rise in the second half of the sixteenth century, pressure on land for food and work increased, and the enclosure of common land, whether agreed amicably among farmers or enforced illegally by greedy landlords, was seen by the distressed groups as the cause of their grief. For much of this period, grain prices rose ahead of wool prices and enclosures attracted less critical attention. By the 1590s, however, private profit was replacing communal co-operation. Allegations that common lands had been fenced off, villagers denied rights of pasturage and land converted from arable to pasture lay behind the food riots in the south-west and south-east of England in 1595 and the enclosure rebellion in Oxfordshire in the following year. In 1593 the government had felt reasonably confident that restrictions on enclosing open fields, which had been in place for nearly half a century, could be lifted 'because of the great plenty and cheapness of grain'. A run of good harvests and pressure from landowners to bring more marginal and wasteland under cultivation saw new enclosures at Hampton Gay and Hampton Poyle in Oxfordshire. Three years later, four men gathered at Enslow Hill with the intention of seizing arms and artillery from the home of Lord Norris, the lord lieutenant of Oxford, and marching to London. They expected to be accompanied by many more protesters but no one else joined in. Although the Privy Council feared that similar plans existed to seize food supplies and attack gentry and their farms, no further disturbances occurred. In reality this 'rebellion' was untypical of the second half of the sixteenth century but as the **Midland Revolt** in 1607 demonstrated, it did not mean that enclosures could not be a cause of rebellion in the future.

Key term

Midland Revolt
A serious peasant uprising in Leicestershire against landlords who enclosed common fields and converted them from arable to pasture.

Key question
Why was famine not a principal cause of rebellion?

Famine and disease

On average one in four harvests in Tudor England failed and when this happened mortality rates increased. However, if there was a series of poor or bad harvests, then economic and social problems occurred as well and this could result in open rebellion. The most serious crop failures were in 1555–6 and 1596–7, but the years 1519–21, 1527–9, 1544–5, 1549–51 and 1586–7 were also periods when wheat harvests were poor. Famines usually lasted for two years before grain prices fell and food, if available, came within the budget of most people's pockets. What is interesting is that apart from the brief flashpoint in Oxfordshire in November 1596, poor harvests, dearth and the resulting famine were not responsible for any other rebellion under the Tudors. In fact good harvests occurred on the eve of rebellions in 1536, 1546–8 and 1567–9. The worst harvests in the century took place in 1555 and 1556 and coincided with an influenza epidemic that may have killed six per cent of the population, but there were no uprisings or stirrings. Nevertheless, an armed riot could readily be provoked by deprivation and hunger, and, in conjunction with other grievances, could be transformed into more aggressive and prolonged disturbances. William Cecil was in no doubt that 'nothing will sooner lead men into sedition than dearth of victual'.

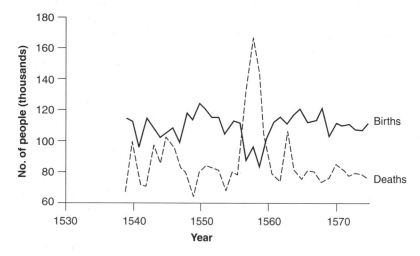

Figure 1.1: Births and deaths in England 1539–70.

Between 1485 and 1528 there were four major outbreaks of plague and the English 'sweat' was particularly virulent during this period. The 'great sweat' of 1551 is known to have killed thousands and London lost 20,000 people in 1563, Bristol suffered badly in 1565 and 1575, Hull in 1575–6 and 1582, and Norwich may have lost as many as 10 per cent of its citizens in 1579–80. It was exceptional, however, for a town to suffer a mortality and subsistence crisis simultaneously. Upland areas, where there was marginal land and often grain shortages, were rarely affected by plague or disease. Conversely towns and cities, where the population was denser, were prone to spreading contagious diseases but food supplies were generally good due to the proximity to ports and nearby areas of mixed farming. Ninety per cent of the people lived in the countryside and most were concentrated in the south-east and outskirts of London. Moreover, in times of widespread dearth and famine, starving people made poor rebels and farmers tended to stay at home to look after their cattle or to harvest their crops. In addition, the gentry and landowners, who might have led protests or uprisings, stood to gain from high prices at times of bad harvests, so the likelihood of rebellions occurring was slim. Food riots, of course, did occur in the last two decades of Elizabeth's reign: in Gloucestershire, Wiltshire and Somerset in 1586, in Kent and Essex in 1595, and in Sussex, Norfolk, Kent and the south-west in 1596, but none resulted in an armed rebellion.

Key question
In what ways did inflation contribute to the outbreak of rebellions in England?

Key terms

Entry fine
A fee paid by tenants when renewing their lease that allowed them to re-enter their property.

Inflation
A rise in prices and an accompanying fall in the purchasing power of money.

Tenants at will
Tenants who could be ejected from their land at the will of their landlord when their lease expired.

Inflation

The price rise, especially in the cost of grain, which afflicted much of the Tudor period, was not a major cause of disturbance. In the early Tudor years, population levels were only just recovering from the bubonic plague in the fourteenth century. The country's population stood at around two million in 1485. A shortage of labour meant that wages, especially for agricultural workers, were high and land rents comparatively low. Landlords had regularly granted long leases of 99 years, which by the early sixteenth century still had many years to run. Rents were usually fixed according to customary practices and although **entry fines** could reflect market conditions, they were rarely more than two years' rent. There were therefore sufficient employment opportunities in the countryside and towns and standards of living appear to have been rising. These were not conditions likely to give rise to popular unrest.

Impact of price inflation

From the 1520s onwards changes occurred. Grain prices started to rise – there was a 2.9 per cent increase by 1550 and 4.5 per cent by 1600 – wages remained static and living standards declined. As the population rose to over four million by the end of the century, demand for food, work and land increased, which served as an accelerant to **inflation**. Among those who gained were landlords who bought vacant farms at low prices, invested in trade or modernised their estates; freeholders who passed on any increase in prices to their tenants; clothiers who took advantage of the growth in the woollen cloth market and expanded their business; and speculators who invested in property, hoarded grain supplies and profited from changing economic conditions. The main losers were wage earners, day labourers, journeymen and **tenants at will**, who could be evicted without notice. These people found their wages failed to keep pace with prices, employment opportunities declined, and waste and marginal land, on which many depended in times of hardship, disappeared. These were the pre-conditions for economic and social disorder that prevailed in some parts of the country in the 1530–50s and 1580–90s, and which erupted into violence in 1536 and 1549.

Price inflation in the 1536 rebellion

Both Aske and Kett referred to the impact that inflation was having on the price of land. Unrealistically, Aske wanted the value of reed, meadow and marshland to be returned to their price in 1485. Indeed inflation was hitting the north so much that if the monasteries were to close, he claimed, 'there should be no money nor treasure in those parts, neither the tenant to have to pay his rents to the lord, nor the lord to have money to do the King service'. There was general anxiety that the dissolution would result in considerable hardship for the poor and for those dependent on charitable giving. On average as little as three per cent of monastic wealth went towards the poor but this was vital for those people who lived in almshouses and hospitals or who relied on dole money and alms. If Lancashire is taken as an example, Cartmel Priory gave 10 per cent of its income in alms and Furness Abbey housed 13 paupers and doled out £12 a year to eight local widows. Hospitality for travellers was also particularly useful to 'strangers and baggers of corn' travelling between Yorkshire, Lancashire, Kendal, Westmorland and Durham, and the government's concern to ensure there was adequate shelter and provision for merchants in the north accounts for the temporary continuation of some of the smaller monasteries. Robert Southwell, who was a Lancashire commissioner in 1537, later reflected that there might not have been a rebellion if 'some small part of the demesnes upon their suit to the Council [had been] distributed to the poor'. Unlike many monastic houses in the south, those in the north of England still played an important part in the lives of many people and, at a time of rising food prices, many poor turned to them in their hour of need.

Table 1.1: The relationship between the rapid rise in the price of foodstuffs and the comparatively slow rise in industrial products and agricultural wages between 1491 and 1570 (1491–1500 = 100 per cent)

Decade	Foodstuffs	Industrial products	Agricultural wages
1491–1500	100	97	101
1501–10	106	98	101
1511–20	116	102	101
1521–30	159	110	106
1531–40	161	110	110
1541–50	217	127	118
1551–60	315	186	160
1561–70	298	218	177

Social issues

The Pilgrimage of Grace

Among Aske's complaints in 1536 was a practice known as rack-renting. On the expiry of a lease, unscrupulous landlords had raised their rents at rates greater than the customary entry fine. In the sixteenth century the estates belonging to Henry Clifford, Earl of Cumberland, had risen eightfold and tenants unable to pay were evicted. Aske wanted the fine, known in many northern parts as a 'gressum', to be statutorily fixed at two years' rent. Henry Percy, Earl of Northumberland, had also raised the entry fines on his properties in Yorkshire although his tenants had refrained from turning against him. Excessive rents also figured among Kett's articles in 1549. Rents had increased 30 per cent since 1548 and a number of landlords had revived old feudal dues such as **castleward**. Copyholders and freeholders had also complained that they had been forced off their lands. Landlords were accused of buying land and altering tenancy conditions to their own advantage. As a result, common people were denied the right to catch rabbits and fish the rivers. The right to hunt with handguns and crossbows was also defended in Aske's articles of complaint.

Key question
Under what circumstances did landlord–tenant relations change in Tudor England?

Castleward
Tenants had once been required to defend Norwich Castle but this military service was later commuted to paying a rent.

Key term

Interestingly the gentry and lesser nobles had a social grievance of their own. In 1536 the government passed the Statute of Uses that forced landowners to keep their estates as a single block rather than divide it among several heirs or grant part of an estate to a younger son or daughter. In law only the eldest son or daughter was entitled to inherit land, and feudal dues such as **wardship** were payable to the Crown upon inheritance. In recent times, hard-pressed landowners, keen to evade these dues and wanting to partition their lands, had transferred the legal ownership of land to **feoffees** by a device known as the 'use'. Aske himself was a feoffee of two sets of estates. Cromwell was equally keen to extract every payment due to the Crown and closed this legal loophole, which angered many younger sons of nobles and gentry. They therefore found themselves fighting on the same side as the poorer commoners in 1536 but of course for different purposes.

Kett's rebellion

Economic and social issues were the principal causes of Kett's rebellion in Norfolk – 17 out of 29 of his demands were focused on enclosures, rents and landlords – but here the gentry received no sympathy from the rebels and the rebellion was as close to a class war as any in the sixteenth century. To understand this, we need to recognise that the majority of the land was held by a small number of gentry and lesser nobles. Norwich, the county town, was the second largest city in England with about 13,000 people but its principal source of employment, the worsted cloth industry, was in decline and, as demand for its material fell, unemployment levels rose. The situation in the countryside was little better. Wheat prices increased by 50 per cent in 1548, enclosures were rife and the people had lost all confidence in the governing classes to protect their welfare. In fact many of the 46 gentry and merchants who held more than 60 per cent of the land in Norfolk were JPs or had connections to local and county authorities and ensured their interests were well served. Not surprisingly the rebels wanted to return to the good old days when Henry VII reigned and to 'redress and reform all such good laws, statutes, proclamations, and all other your proceedings, which have been bid [forbidden] by your Justices of your peace, reeves, **escheators**, and others your officers, from your poor commons'.

A unique feature of Kett's rebellion was a request that 'all bond men may be made free'. Bondmen or serfs were a legacy from feudal times and few are known to have existed by the beginning of the Tudor age. The reference however may have been to tenants serving on the 40 manors belonging to the Howard family. Thomas Howard, Duke of Norfolk, and his son, the Earl of Surrey, had been arrested in 1546 and their estates administered by the Crown. Perhaps little had changed by 1549. Certainly tenants were paying high rents, **inquisition fines** were exacted and wardship levied, but this also happened elsewhere. It is far more likely that the legally minded Kett sought to eliminate an anomaly and safeguard the future tenure of all tenants in Norfolk.

The Western rebellion

Significantly the Western rebels made no complaints about enclosures or rack-renting although, like everyone else, they were concerned at rising food and wool prices which made enclosures more profitable. It has already been pointed out that their main economic concern was the novel tax on sheep and wool introduced in 1548. If their economic problems were not the same or as acute as those facing tenants and landholders in Norfolk, both sets of rebels bore some resentment towards the gentry. In Devon and Cornwall they wished to limit the size of gentry households worth 100 marks (£66) to one servant and expressed concern at how local gentry were enriching themselves by purchasing church lands. This condemnation seems little more than an attack of envy at the growing wealth of the gentry but it may also have reflected concern at the perceived loyalty shown by a servant to his lord rather than to the community as a whole. But whereas the Western rebels wanted to restore the Catholic Church and its lands to the rightful owners and had the support of local clergy and the commons, the Norfolk rebels were intent on narrowing the gap between the privileged few and unprivileged many, which seemed to be widening. Both sets of rebels, however, contained radical elements who professed a desire to 'kill all the gentlemen'. We cannot say whether this was an empty gesture or a serious threat but it served to underline the tension that existed between the commons and the gentry.

Essay focus

Look at Essays 1 and 2 on pages 28–33. Each refers to economic and social causes: very briefly in the case of Essay 1, paragraph 4, and in more detail in Essay 2, paragraph 9. Notice how Essay 2 uses factual evidence to cover synoptically five rebellions across the whole period. This is the kind of skill that you need to develop in order to synthesise developments over a long period of time.

Summary diagram: Social and economic causes

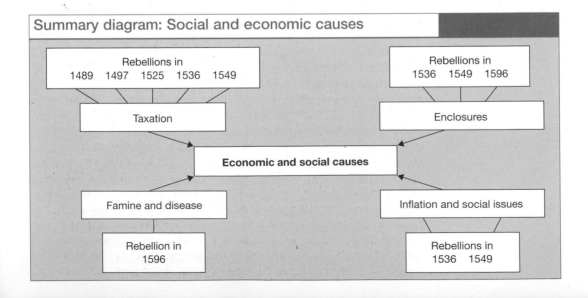

4 | Conclusion: why did rebellions occur?

Monocausal or multicausal?

It should be clear from the analysis of Tudor rebellions on the preceding pages that only a few had a single cause. Taxation, dynastic and Irish political revolts may be categorised as having predominantly one cause but most rebellions occurred for a number of reasons. Religious issues, mainly Catholics vying with Protestants, were evident in most of the uprisings in England between 1536 and 1569 but political factors were also present. Dynastic causes were most prominent in Henry VII's reign yet concern over the succession was a constant theme throughout the period and in later years assumed religious connotations. Economic and social problems were most acute in the mid-century and underpinned a host of revolts in 1549. Yet while it is the historian's task to try to make sense of events and to prioritise their causes, it should be remembered that determining the motives of rebels and their responses to developments is not an exact science.

The vast majority of rebels left no record of why they rebelled: we know that some in Yorkshire in 1536 and 1569 were forced by their landlords to take part, some were paid to join in at Maidstone in 1554 and Durham in 1569, and some at Louth in 1536 are known to have participated out of adventure. Our understanding of why rebellions began is not helped by 'official' accounts sponsored by the government. For example, in 1554 John Proctor claimed in his official *Historie of Wyates rebellion*, that the rebels were solely motivated by xenophobia, which is precisely what Mary and her advisers wanted people to believe. Catholicism must not be seen to be under attack yet it is apparent that a number of rebels were Protestants, some of the gentry saw rebellion as a way of enhancing their political prospects at court and in the county, while unemployed cloth workers who participated had their own social and economic grievances. One cause alone, no matter how 'official' an account may be, does not explain this rebellion.

The role of rumour

Rumour undoubtedly played a key part in bringing about a rebellion. Fear, and the anger which it engendered, lay behind many revolts. In Yorkshire in 1536 people believed that their parish plate and jewels were going to be seized, their churches destroyed, taxes imposed on christenings, marriages and burials, and laws passed prohibiting the eating of white bread, geese and chickens. And once an uprising began, news spread to neighbouring areas and triggered further disturbances, often out of solidarity with their fellow commons. In 1549 stories circulated the south-west of England that babies would only be baptised on Sundays, which would put the soul of a dying child in peril, and in King's Lynn in Norfolk it was alleged that gentlemen's servants had 'killed poor men in their harvest work and also killed women there with child'. Rumours once begun were hard to stop and quickly proved infectious. Fear that Spain would take over the country if Philip married Mary was translated into fact in Kent and Devon on the eve of Wyatt's rebellion. Over 100 Spaniards armed with '**harness, arquebuses and morions, with matchlight**' were reported to have occupied Rochester in the dead of night and it was rumoured in Plymouth that they planned to rape all the women in Devon.

Uncovering the motives

What was recorded in the rebels' demands and in the subsequent depositions and confessions of leaders reflects the interests of the literate minority who may or may not have been speaking on behalf of the majority of those who took part. And of course they may have been lying! What remained of the Earl of Essex's declining reputation took a further knock when he later confessed that he had lied under examination. When we try to assess the relative importance of a particular cause in bringing about a rebellion, we should perhaps ask 'importance to whom?' To the gentry, clergy, lawyers or commons?

If we take the Pilgrimage of Grace as an illustration, the tenants on Clifford's estates in Westmorland were mainly concerned about the unfair rents and entry fines levied by the earl. In Cumberland the Penrith rebels were most concerned at endemic thieving and robbery. In northern Lancashire, disturbances were inspired more by the threatened closure of monasteries but people in the south of the county felt less concerned and none of them joined the rebellion. Across the Pennines on the Percy estates in Yorkshire and Durham, tenant–landlord relations were not an issue, and instead peasants joined their landlords in protesting at a range of government policies. At the same time, none of the peasants would have had the slightest interest in the Statute of Uses or the high fees charged by feodaries and escheators. These were the concern of lawyers and gentry. And only the most erudite of theologians would have been in a position to demand the condemnation as heretics of continental reformers such as **Melanchthon and Oecolampadius**, but this is what the Lincolnshire clerics insisted Aske should do when he presented his articles at York. Nevertheless, there was much common ground between the different groups and areas of disturbance from which rebels were recruited. 'Each professed to be a rising of the commons', writes Michael Bush, 'each was similarly marked by a concern for both the Faith of Christ and the Commonwealth; each hated the government for being extortionate and heretical.'

Underlying issues and short-term causes

Historians should also try to separate underlying issues, which may go back a long way, from short-term causes that usually trigger rebellions. At times this is feasible although there are difficulties in attempting such an analysis. Rebellions caused by religious reforms, for example, can usually be traced back to the reform itself. The presence of commissioners in 1536 surveying the smaller monasteries in the northern counties led to an immediate reaction, and four days before the new Prayer Book was due to be

Key terms

Harness, arquebuses and morions, with matchlight
Body armour, long-barrelled handguns, metal helmets, and fuses to ignite the arquebuses.

Melanchthon and Oecolampadius
Philip Melanchthon was a moderate Protestant who succeeded Luther as the leader of the German Reformation. Johannes Oecolampadius was a leading Swiss Protestant who implemented reforms in Basel in the 1520s.

used in Bodmin and the day after it was first used at Sampford Courtenay in June 1549, violence broke out in the West Country. The dissolution of the chantries, on the other hand, should remind us that not all religious reforms evoked immediate popular revolts. The Act of 1547 was implemented in the spring of 1548 but no rebellions occurred in spite of their universal popularity until the following year, and then only in the western counties.

Social and economic factors often took a long time before they had an impact on society. Population levels had been steadily rising since the end of the fifteenth century though their real effects were not felt until the 1540s. Pressure for work and demand for food were added to the increasing shortage of land, all of which contributed to the rising cost of living. Contemporaries, looking for immediate causes, understandably focused on enclosures and sheep and blamed the Subsidy Act and enclosure commissions of 1549. In fact, whether or not a revolt broke out usually depended on local conditions and other unrelated factors. Thus there were riots and disturbances in 27 English counties in the summer of 1549 but only in Devon and Cornwall and Norfolk and Suffolk were there prolonged rebellions. Most riots were local incidents and were suppressed by town and county authorities before they got out of hand. The decline of feudalism, especially in the north of England, has been seen as an underlying issue in the Northern Earls' revolt yet particular political and personal factors that triggered the uprising were not present elsewhere in the north. It seems, therefore, that attempts to distinguish between long-term underlying issues and more immediate causes of rebellions can throw light on the interplay of different factors. However, they are also likely to produce a simplistic analysis of a very complex event.

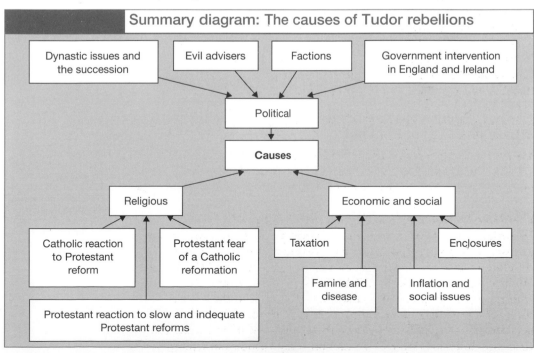

Summary diagram: The causes of Tudor rebellions

Further questions for debate

1 Were 'evil councillors' simply scapegoats for unpopular government policies?

2 How important were factions as a cause of rebellions?

3 To what extent was religion a cloak for politically motivated rebellions?

4 How far were economic and social causes of rebellion inter-related?

5 What difficulties face the historian in trying to discern the real motives of English and Irish rebels?

One way in which you will improve your essay technique is by drafting essay plans. Choose two of the above questions and write plans in the form of notes and/or diagrams. Different strategies suit different students but the plans should outline your main arguments, any relevant supporting evidence and how key ideas are linked synoptically.

Advice on answering essay questions on causation

There are two main types of essay question on causation: questions which begin 'Assess the role of … /the importance of … factor x in causing rebellions' and those that ask 'How far … /to what extent … was rebellion caused by factor x?' In the essays that follow, the focus of the question is 'factions'. To secure the highest marks, you need to evaluate the part played by factor x in terms of its overall contribution as a cause of rebellion. In practice this means examining with specific examples how factions caused rebellions and analysing its relationship with other causes, i.e. was it a consistent cause and was it a major or an indirect factor? It is important that you show that you have understood any links and connections between various causes and that you can synthesise developments over the whole period so as to demonstrate the concepts of continuity and change over time.

Read each of the following essays carefully. Each essay was written in one hour and without the use of notes. Note any strengths and limitations and compare your views with those of the assessor. Marks should be awarded for each of the two assessment objectives described in the tables at the end of the book (see pages 142–3).

Essay 1: Assess the role of factions as a cause of rebellions in Tudor England

1 The rebellions in England during the sixteenth century were because of many reasons. These included religious reasons, socio-economic problems, and also political factions. However, I would argue that there were different peaks in the century which would be politically motivated, and in other parts of the century, it would be economic problems or religious problems.

2 Having said that, political factions were a prime motivator in many of the rebellions. Perkin Warbeck and Lambert Simnel are classic examples of the Yorkists vs Lancastrian problem in the earlier part of the century, during Henry VII's reign. The Aragonese faction may have been behind the Pilgrimage of Grace in Henry VIII's reign and Wyatt's rebellion in 1554 was also motivated by political differences. Wyatt

1 The essay suggests that political factions were one of several causes, which is a direct start, but in separating politics from economic and religious issues, the student seems set on a monocausal analysis.

and the rebels objected to the marriage of Mary and Philip of Spain. They thought England would become a mere outpost of Spain's empire. They thought England would be overrun by Spaniards. The Revolt of the Northern Earls also had political grievances. They essentially wanted to remove Elizabeth from the throne and put Mary Queen of Scots there instead. Essex also had lost out at court and his rebellion in 1601 was largely due to political factions.

3 However, religion was also a huge reason why people rebelled. In fact, after the reformation in 1536, it always had the churches in England who would be against the monarchy, e.g. during Protestant reigns – save Kett's which was a Protestant rebellion during a Protestant period – like Edward, there would be a Catholic rising like the Western Rebellion, and vice versa. The Western is a classic example of a religiously motivated rebellion – it was nicknamed the Prayer Book Rebellion. They wanted the mass to be back in Latin, and religious texts to be accessible to the public (they were only allowed for the priests to interpret). The Pilgrimage of Grace also had religious reasons for the rebellion. They wanted the monasteries and abbeys restored, and also had demands about how the priests acted. However, it is thought that the Pilgrimage of Grace used religious reasons as a 'cloak' for political motives; demands such as the removal of Cromwell and other leaders of the reformation from office featured prominently above others.

4 Economic and social reasons were, I'd argue, the reason that people decided to rebel. I don't think the peasants would revolt if life was going well – but I don't think it was the reason for rebellion. However it does seem that Kett's rebels had severe problems with their lives at the time. Rent prices had doubled to keep up with rising inflation. They were not allowed in some parts of the country to hunt and even some rivers were banned. Kett is just one of the rebellions which had economic as part of their demands – most of them featured it at least once. However, it could be said that the rebels were just pushing their luck and seeing how far they could go.

5 Therefore, I think that at certain times during the century (e.g. before 1536 and the Reformation), political factions were the main reason for unrest. However, there were other parts of the century where religious problems were the main grievances (e.g. 1549–70), or economic. However, I do believe that there was a crossover, and that a rebellion was never the result – more likely it was a combination.

Assessment for essay 1

Knowledge has been relevantly deployed at a very modest level but with some inaccurate, unclear and disorganised sections. Communication is mostly satisfactory. **[Level IV: 10 out of 20 marks]**

There is a satisfactory understanding of key concepts (causation) and focuses on the question set. Demonstrates limited synoptic links and partial coverage; several statements lack explanation and development. **[Level IV: 20 out of 40 marks]**

The overall mark of 30 is on the Grade D/E boundary. To raise the grade, further evaluation of each cause is needed, together with more examples and cross-referencing. Most paragraphs require more explanation and development. The paragraph dealing with factions is very limited in its development and the economic and social section is particularly thin in its synthesis and coverage.

Essay 2: Assess the role of factions as a cause of rebellions in Tudor England

1 Factional politics was the standard procedure of the Tudor courts. Given that the nobles who were 'out of favour' with the monarch would lose patronage, wealth and influence, it is hardly surprising that factions have been identified as playing a large role in Tudor rebellions. Also, given that there was nearly always an 'in' faction, factional politics may be said to have been a consistent cause of rebellion throughout the period. However, there were evidently rebellions that did not involve the nobility and courtiers or where commoners outnumbered the nobility, and clearly faction was not the cause of these rebellions. Therefore, it will be argued that factions were only one cause of Tudor rebellions, and possibly not even the most important one.

> 1 This is a focused and promising start. The student explains what is meant by 'factions', raises the idea of consistency (continuity and change over time) and suggests that faction is only one of several causes to be considered.

2 When Henry Tudor took the throne in 1485, it marked the end of a long power struggle between rival factions – the House of Lancaster and the House of York. It is hardly surprising that Henry experienced several attempts in his early years of his reign from the Yorkist faction to usurp his throne. In 1486–7 Lambert Simnel was supported by leading Yorkists such as John Earl of Lincoln as a pretender to the throne. Simnel attempted to impersonate the Earl of Warwick, and Henry only narrowly defeated these Yorkists at the battle of Stoke in 1487. Similarly Perkin Warbeck imitated the younger of the two Yorkist princes in the Tower, Richard, between 1491 and 1497. His Yorkist connections are further seen as he had been in the employment of Sir Edward Brampton, a Yorkist sympathiser. Thus factions certainly were the sole cause of these two early rebellions as they were instigated and supported by Yorkists seeking to regain power, and both pretenders were financially backed by Margaret of Burgundy, a die-hard Yorkist. However, even after the Tudor dynasty was established, factional conflict remained a consistent cause of rebellion.

> 2 Good blend of factual knowledge and argument centred on Yorkist factions behind the Simnel and Warbeck rebellions.

3 Although the Pilgrimage of Grace in 1536 has often been thought of as a religious revolt, revisionist historians have put forward the view that the out-of-favour conservative faction (Darcy and Hussey, for example) used religious motives as a cloak for their own political

3 Excellent use of specific examples backs up the interplay between political factions and religious causes, though the Catholic and Aragonese element in the Pilgrimage of Grace could have been further developed.

4 Sound synoptic links are evident here. It would have been useful to know who was at the heart of the Marian faction. Of course, the writer begs the question whether Wyatt was part of a political faction.

5 Good cross-referencing to the Pilgrimage and nature of factional politics in 1569 and 1601.

6 Refers to Edward's reign and makes an interesting point about rival court factions. Could have compared this situation with Essex; Warwick succeeded in his coup, Essex did not.

gain. Their dislike and jealousy of the men of low birth such as Cromwell, Audley and Rich, who currently had the king's ear, can certainly be seen in the Pontefract Articles which called for their removal. Similarly, historians have noted that the pilgrims 'capture' of Pontefract castle was little more than a charade, with Darcy practically handing it over for the rebels' use. Therefore, it seems likely that the out-of-favour faction used their power and resources to support this rebellion. In addition the pilgrims' prelude, the Lincolnshire rising, featured both Willoughby and Dymoke at its centre. Both had lost power at court and in the county, and Willoughby in particular resented the Duke of Suffolk's growing control over his cousin Katherine and, as a result over his money, power and status.

4 In Mary's reign, Wyatt launched a rebellion motivated in a way by faction, as he resented the imminent influence of Spanish councillors at the court who, he believed, would attempt to exert more power once Philip was married to the queen. This is further supported by the fact that Wyatt used anti-Spanish propaganda to gain popular support. Not only would English nobles suffer but, he claimed, the Spaniards would impose tax burdens and embroil England in Spanish foreign conquests. Therefore, Wyatt's revolt, which had its origins in Kent, was launched against Mary and her advisers at court who seemed to be favouring this Spanish faction. In this respect, the antipathy towards factions surrounding Mary was very similar to the complaints raised by the pilgrims in 1536.

5 Elizabeth's reign saw two factional rebellions. The revolt of the northern earls in 1569 again saw the northern gentry rise up against the 'in' faction in Whitehall. This time their nemesis was William Cecil. Similarities with the Pilgrimage of Grace are many: the nobility again but this time perhaps less subtly have been accused of using the Catholic faith as a cloak for their motives and, like the pilgrims, the earls demanded a return of political power to the north – a northern parliament and a reformed Council of the North in York. This would ensure a restoration of the earls' influence in the government of the northern counties and reverse a downward slide in their financial and political fortunes. Finally, Essex's rebellion of 1601 was a rather feeble but blatantly factional revolt against Elizabeth and her political adviser Robert Cecil. Essex had been banned from court, lost his monopoly on sweet wines and seen his rival Cecil rise to prominence. This revolt was Essex's attempt to restore his influence.

6 Faction was certainly a consistent cause of rebellion in Tudor England. A notable exception may be seen in Edward VI's reign but this can be explained by the fact that the two prominent factions, those who supported Somerset and those who looked towards his rival Warwick, were strongly represented in the Protectorate council, which enabled them to exercise as much power as they wished. Never

the less, disputes were still possible, as may be seen in Warwick's coup over Somerset in 1549.

7 Clearly ordinary people were not motivated by factional politics. They must have been driven to rebellion by other causes, and one of these was religion. Although a conservative faction might have masterminded the Pilgrimage of Grace, the people who supported it were definitely motivated by their outrage at Henry's break from Rome, the dissolution of the smaller monasteries and the anticipated attack on their parochial goods. These issues were reflected in the demands outlined in the Lincoln, York and Pontefract Articles. Furthermore, the rebels' banner was that of the Five Wounds of Christ and several priests became rebel captains, and abbots and monks also joined the ranks of the rebellion. Moreover, the 'Great Captain' Robert Aske, always maintained that religion was the main cause of this mass demonstration. Another religious uprising occurred in Devon and Cornwall in 1549. This was so overtly Catholic, with its demands against changes such as Edward's Protestant Book of Common Prayer and the dissolution of the chantries, that it was named the Prayer Book rebellion. Religion was its principal motive for many people and several priests participated including Robert Welsh, vicar of St Thomas' near Exeter. Similar to the Pilgrimage and Western rebellion, the Northern Earls' revolt of 1569 gathered popular support by advocating religious motives and marched behind the same banner of Christian unity. Once the rebels reached Durham Cathedral a Catholic mass was celebrated and Protestant bibles and prayer books destroyed. Although the Earl of Northumberland maintained in his confession that the restoration of Catholicism was their main aim, it seems more likely that in this case the earls were seeking to gain as much popular support as possible to achieve their own restoration as power brokers in the north.

> 7 Important paragraph that assesses rebellions in which religion was a principal cause and aware of multicausal nature of most rebellions. Good synoptic cross-references.

8 There is no denying that religion was a divisive force; indeed, after the Reformation some rebellions had Protestant motives. Kett's rebellion, for instance, held Protestant services at the rebel camp on Mousehold Heath and called for an improvement in the quality of preachers and residential incumbents in their diocese. In Wyatt's revolt, which was ostensibly driven by factional politics, there is the possibility that some of the rebels were motivated by religious grievances against Mary. Eight out of the 14 leaders were protestant and much support for the rising came from Maidstone in Kent, the area from where many of Mary's martyrs were to come. Religion therefore became an important source of discontent after Henry VIII's break from Rome but as a cause of rebellion, its importance waned as Elizabeth's reign progressed, and religious stability was maintained by her moderate Religious Settlement.

> 8 Considers Protestant influences and sets religion in the context of the whole period, thus demonstrating continuity and change.

9 A final cause of rebellion was social and economic. The Yorkshire and Cornish rebellions in 1489 and 1497, respectively, were both the result of attempts by Henry VII to impose war taxation on

9 Good, concise evaluation of economic and social issues behind five rebellions.

unreceptive counties. Further rebellions in 1525, 1549 and 1596 also resulted from economic hardship. The Amicable Grant for instance was a reaction to excessive taxation and disturbances in the spring and summer of 1549 that saw camps established in more than 27 counties reflected opposition to enclosures, inflation and extortionate rents imposed by many gentry. Similarly the Oxfordshire rising of 1596 was caused solely by food shortages, unregulated enclosures and runaway inflation. These disturbances had nothing to do with factions and everything to do with economic survival.

10 Addresses the issue of continuity and change, consistency and relative importance of different causes. Very good conclusion.

10 In conclusion, I think that faction was the most consistent cause of rebellions in Tudor England. It can be seen that throughout the period, and even where religious motives were stated, men with power and resources lay behind the revolts, often using religion as a propaganda tool for their own political purposes. However, notably for the commoners, religion was an important cause in the middle of the period though not in Henry VII's reign nor towards the end of Elizabeth's reign. Finally, in times of economic distress, the rebellions against taxation, enclosures, rack-renting and food shortages, particularly in the 1520s and 1540s, show that poverty could be enough to make people rebel. However, this was clearly not the most important cause throughout the period as some rebellions occurred when there was economic stability, for example Wyatt's rebellion in 1554 and the Northern Earls' revolt in 1569. Conversely, in the 1590s when there was considerable social and economic discontent and a rebellion was planned in Oxfordshire by disgruntled artisans and servants, only four men turned up. This leads me to conclude that factions were the most consistent cause of rebellion, and also the most important as people with financial as well as political resources were capable of launching a threatening rebellion.

Assessment for essay 2

Uses a wide range of accurate and relevant evidence, appropriate historical terminology, coherent structure and communicates accurately [Level IA: 19 marks out of 20]

Shows a very good understanding of key concepts in their historical context. Consistently focused on the question, with a very good level of analysis and supporting judgement. Very good synthesis and synoptic assessments of the whole period. [Level IB: 34 marks out of 40]

The overall mark of 53 is a comfortable Grade A. To attain an A*, the essay needs to be more overtly synoptic especially in the first half of the argument when factions are assessed. For instance, paragraphs 2, 3, 4 and 5 provide a chronological assessment of various factions and only in 5 are synoptic and comparative points made. Cross-references to any similarities and differences could have been usefully made in paragraphs 2, 3 and 4.

2 The Nature of Rebellions

OVERVIEW

This chapter examines the frequency and nature of rebellions in Tudor England and Ireland under the following headings:

- Objectives, duration and location
- Leadership
- Strategy and tactics
- Organisation
- Size, support and frequency
- Irish rebellions
- Conclusion: success or failure?
- An assessment of two A2 essays: Grades A and C

The chapter will compare and synthesise different rebellions in respect of their objectives, location and duration, their leaders, their strategy and tactics, their organisation, support and size, and explain why some types of rebellion were more frequent and others less frequent during the Tudor period. Finally, it looks at the minority of rebellions that achieved some of their objectives and the overwhelming majority that ended in defeat. Why were some rebellions more successful than others?

Note making

Read through each section before you start to make notes. Identify the main points, decide on your headings and select one or two examples as your illustrations. Notes should be concise, clearly set out and fully understood.

1 | Objectives, duration and location

Objectives

Tudor rebellions can be divided into three broad categories:

- dynastic rebellions that aimed to overthrow the monarch
- demonstrations against government policies
- Irish rebellions that sought to gain independence from England.

Key question
Did the objectives of a rebellion usually change or remain the same in the course of the uprising?

Dynastic rebellions

The desire to remove the monarch was most evident in the disturbances of 1486, 1487 and 1497 when Yorkist claimants, pretenders and sympathisers wanted to overthrow Henry VII and, if the opportunity arose, to assassinate him. Half a century later Mary Tudor was the target of Northumberland's revolt when he aimed to prevent her from ascending the throne. Subsequent dynastic rebellions, however, were less clear-cut in their objectives, and it seems likely that as the rebellions developed, the leaders changed their objectives or, in some cases, concealed their aim to overthrow the ruler. Wyatt, for instance, could not have realistically expected Mary Tudor to cancel her marriage to Philip of Spain in 1554 simply on account of his opposition, and in all probability he planned to put Princess Elizabeth on the throne. Similarly the Northern Earls in 1569 initially intended releasing Mary Queen of Scots from her house arrest, marrying her to the Duke of Norfolk and forcing Elizabeth either to abdicate (which seems unlikely) or to recognise Mary as her heir presumptive. Once it became clear that the rebels could not get to Mary, the rebellion turned into a demonstration of northern opposition against Elizabeth's religious and political policies. Finally, Essex's rebellion in 1601 had mixed and wavering motives from the outset. The earl may have considered assassinating the queen but it is more likely that his main objective was to overthrow the political regime in power and by a show of strength, force Elizabeth to appoint him as her principal adviser. In practice, none of these rebellions succeeded; indeed, few came close to realising their goals.

Anti-government demonstrations

A more frequent type of rebellion, and one that occurred throughout the period, was popular demonstrations against government policies and councillors who were held responsible for them. Protests against taxation took place in 1489, 1497 and 1525. On each occasion England was at war or preparing for war, but the objective of rebellion was not to frustrate the government's foreign policy but to get unpopular taxes rescinded. Social and economic issues also lay behind many disturbances in 1549. In East Anglia and the south-west of England, people wanted the government to do something about high food prices, recent taxes on sheep and wool, and unregulated enclosures. Oxfordshire was the scene of anti-enclosure riots in both 1549 and 1596, although stopping enclosures was only one of several rebel objectives. Perhaps nothing stirred people more to rise up and rebel than the changes to the Catholic Church and faith. The major rebellions that occurred in England in 1536, 1549 and 1569 were primarily a reaction to Protestant reforms implemented by Henry VIII, Edward VI and Elizabeth in the quarter century following the **break from Rome**. A common theme runs through each of these rebellions: discontented Catholics believed the only way they could redress their grievances was to take to the roads and lanes, protest in numbers and, if necessary, fight and die for their beliefs.

Key term

Break from Rome
The name given to Henry VIII's separation of England from the Roman Catholic Church by a series of parliamentary Acts culminating in the Act of Supremacy of 1534.

Irish rebellions

The third type of rebellion only occurred in the final decade of the period in Ireland but political matters had been coming to a head for over half a century. Ever since the 1534 Kildare rebellion, when Henry VIII decided to transfer the administration of Ireland to English councillors, resentment had been growing from Anglo-Irish families and Gaelic clans alike. Rebellions in 1558, 1569 and 1579 owed much to opposition to English policies – political, religious, economic and cultural – all of which coalesced in the 1590s into a national uprising. Its overt objective was to expel the English administration from Ireland and preserve the Catholic faith, notionally on behalf of the Irish people, but privately O'Neill, its leader, desired political power for himself. In this respect, his rebellion was similar to that of the English northern earls: they claimed to be defending the true faith from heresy when in reality their main objective was to recover political and social pre-eminence in the northern counties.

Duration

At some stage in the course of the Tudor period almost every English county and every Irish province experienced a rebellion. At first sight there does not appear to be a pattern to either their duration or their location. In some cases, most notably in the spring and summer of 1549 when some 27 counties reported major riots, the protests lasted only a few days and were dealt with before they escalated out of control. On other occasions, rebellions could run for several weeks and in the case of Ireland many years before they were suppressed. On closer examination, however, a general trend can be discerned: the greater the distance from the seat of government, the more troublesome was the area and the longer a rebellion tended to last. In Ireland, for example, the Dublin administration invariably had to wait for instructions from London before countermeasures could be put in place and then the financial and military resources were rarely equal to the task of dealing with a rebellion effectively. Thus, the Munster rebellion in 1569 took four years to suppress and O'Neill's national rising in 1595 was not subdued until 1603.

In England, disturbances in the south-west and northern counties might last two or three months on account of the slow and erratic communications, which impeded the ability of the government to act decisively, and local magnates failing to deal with a rebellion before it got out of hand. Certainly some rebellions such as the Pilgrimage of Grace, Western and Kett's took a long time to suppress because governments underestimated their seriousness or failed to make them a priority. Rebellions that began in or near to London, on the other hand, lasted but a short period of time. Rebels needed to strike quickly and take control of the government before troops could be raised against them. Thus, Wyatt's rebellion lasted 18 days but only one day was spent trying to enter the city; the Earl of Essex in contrast was in revolt for less than 12 hours.

Key question
Why did some rebellions take longer to suppress than others?

Key question
To what extent were disturbances common occurrences in particular parts of the kingdom?

Location

In general, most major disturbances and rebellions occurred in the more distant parts of the kingdom, namely the northern and south-western counties, East Anglia and the provinces of Ulster and Munster in Ireland. Wales was exceptional in that it experienced no rebellions in the course of the period (see Chapter 4).

Pro-Yorkist areas

In the early years of Tudor rule, areas that had been popular with the Yorkist kings were likely to present difficulties and Lovel in Yorkshire and the Stafford brothers in Worcester in 1486 tried unsuccessfully to rouse these areas against the king. Yorkshire was again the scene of a more serious disturbance in 1489 when the Earl of Northumberland was murdered supervising a tax commission on behalf of the king.

South-west England

The south-western counties, on the other hand, had no dynastic axe to grind: they simply resented government interference in their daily life. The county of Somerset was renowned for its truculent attitude. It contributed most of the rebels that marched to Blackheath in 1497 and proved unwilling to supply troops to suppress a rebellion in Devon in 1549. Cornwall, in particular, had a strong cultural tradition and resisted innovations or intrusions in its political affairs. The Celtic language was widely spoken by commoners in the sixteenth century and contributed to Cornwall's geographical isolation from much of England. Above all, Cornishmen resented the English. In his *Description of Cornwall*, written in the late sixteenth century, John Norden claimed that the Cornish seemed to 'retain a kind of concealed envy against the English, whom they yet effect with a kind of desire for revenge for their fathers' sakes, by whom their fathers received the repulse'. In 1537 the dean of Exeter cathedral, Dr Simon Heynes, remarked that the region was a 'perilous country', an observation confirmed by the outbreak of two rebellions in 1497, disturbances at Helston in 1548 when the archdeacon of Cornwall was murdered, and the Prayer Book rebellion of 1549, which originated in the south-west.

Customary practice

In some cases, rebel leaders aware of their heritage, shrewdly selected the same town, even the same meeting place, which had been the site of earlier disturbances. Areas of open land were ideal meeting places for large crowds to gather. The Cornish rebels of 1497 chose Blackheath for their encampment just as Wat Tyler and John Ball had done in 1381 and Jack Cade in 1450. In Oxfordshire, the 1596 rebels met at Enslow Hill where anti-enclosure protesters had gathered 50 years before. Some rebels congregated outside their local church. The Prayer Book demonstrators of 1549, for instance, assembled outside Bodmin church, as had their ancestors in 1497 when they protested at

Figure 2.1: Tudor England and Wales.

Henry VII's war tax. The county of Norfolk also had a long
tradition of rebellious activity. In 1381 east Norfolk rebels attacked
local gentry as part of the Peasants' Revolt, and further riots
occurred against enclosures in 1525 and the gentry in 1540. Rebels
who camped at seven locations in the county in 1549 were
therefore following a well-established pattern of behaviour.

Influence of local magnates

Particular areas of the country were prone to disorder if the relationship between the leading magnate and the people was fraught or unresponsive. If it was mutually beneficial, as in Hampshire where the Earl of Southampton was a prominent landowner, in Lancashire where the pro-Tudor Derby family dominated county politics and in Sussex where the Earl of Arundel kept effective control, few disturbances of any note occurred. But if the magnate was absent, as in the case of John Russell of Devon in 1549, who as Lord Privy Seal spent most of his time in London, or there was a political vacuum due to the demise of a powerful family, such as the Courtenays in Cornwall and the Howards in Norfolk, trouble was likely to take some time to die down. Ireland posed similar difficulties for English governments once the Kildares ceased to hold their customary office of deputy lieutenant. The absence of a paternalistic administration at county and regional level thus removed a key layer of political cohesion between rulers and subjects and rendered these areas potential flashpoints.

London

In the case of politically motivated rebellions such as Simnel, Warbeck, Wyatt, the Northern Earls and Essex, their objective was to reach Whitehall, the seat of central government in London. Most, with the exception of Wyatt and Essex, fell a long way short. Warbeck, for example, on landing in Cornwall from Scotland only got as far as Taunton, 160 miles from London. Wyatt, who started his rebellion in Kent came close but was repelled at Ludgate, three miles from the city, while the Earl of Essex, who had the distinct advantage of beginning in the Strand in central London, got as far as Fenchurch Street before retreating by river back to his house. The capital in fact was consistently loyal to the Tudors and never rallied to a pretender, illegitimate claimant or would-be usurper.

Principal towns and cities

In the case of protest marches, rebels targeted county and diocesan towns to stage their demonstration. These objectives entailed far shorter journeys than marching to London, which was a key factor in retaining a large following if harvests were due to be collected, rebels fed and paid, and long distances overcome. In 1549 the Cornish rebels, for instance, walked 50 miles to Exeter, and Kett travelled 10 miles from Wymondham to Norwich. These were far more manageable distances than the 100 or so miles that Aske and his supporters would have covered in 1536 before arriving at Doncaster.

The Cornish tax revolt of 1497 was unusual in that as many as 15,000 rebels decided to take their grievances to London, some 250 miles away. It is hardly surprising that as the march entered its fourth week, thousands of rebels deserted the cause and returned to their farms in time for the June harvest. The Amicable Grant protesters in 1525 similarly intended walking 50 miles from

Lavenham to London to confront Wolsey with their complaints and appear only to have been stopped by someone removing the clapper from the church bell, which would have been the signal to commence the march. In all other demonstrations against Tudor policies, the county town was the focus of protest. Few welcomed these insurgents. How local authorities reacted to the challenge often determined the length of the rebellion as well as its course. Rebels needed food, supplies, weapons and popular support. If they were denied these, as at Exeter in 1549, their days were numbered; if the city co-operated and even assisted, as at York in 1536 and Norwich in 1549, the rebellion could be sustained until it was resolved by arbitration or force.

Summary diagram: Objectives, duration and location

Objectives	Duration	Location
• Overthrow the government	Hours	Pro-Yorkist areas
• Remedy grievances	Days	South-west England
• Increase Irish independence	Weeks	Customary practices
	Months	Local magnates
	Years	London, towns and cities

2 | Leadership

Royal claimants

Leadership was clearly an important factor in determining how much success a rebellion was going to enjoy. Ideally, dynastic revolts needed to be led by a **prince of the blood** or royal claimant. This explains the potency of Simnel's rebellion in 1487 since he not only claimed to be the Earl of Warwick, Richard III's oldest nephew, but was also supported by the Earl of Lincoln, another of Richard's nephews, and the self-styled 'white rose' of York. Similarly in the 1490s, Warbeck claimed he was the Duke of York, and 60 years later Edward VI and the Duke of Northumberland championed the cause of Lady Jane Grey, the great-granddaughter of Henry VII. Legitimacy was vitally important however. If Henry VII had some difficulty dealing with the pretenders Simnel and Warbeck because his own claim to the throne was somewhat shaky, Northumberland was always likely to fail in his bid to topple Mary Tudor, the legitimate daughter of Henry VIII.

Nobility and gentry

The nobility and gentry were the natural leaders in society and played key roles in most Tudor rebellions. In Ireland the leading rebels were earls such as Tyrone, Kildare and Desmond, who used their position as head of a clan to mobilise large numbers of supporters. Some English nobles like Lovel in 1486, Audley in 1497, Lumley and Latimer in 1536, Dacre in 1570 and Essex in 1601 also put themselves at the head of a revolt or led a company

Key question
Did rebel leaders share any common characteristics?

Prince of the blood
A prince who was a blood relation of the monarch.

Key term

of rebels against the monarch. Others like Hussey and Darcy in 1536 and the earls of Northumberland and Westmorland in 1569 assumed leadership more reluctantly and later claimed (in the cold light of defeat) that their social inferiors had pressed them into action. It should be recognised, however, that it was a convention for nobles and gentry to deny that they had given their support willingly and to claim instead that they and their families had been forced to participate.

Any protest that aspired to authority and legitimacy needed a noble as its leader. The Cornish in 1497 looked to Lord Audley, an impoverished Somerset peer, whose father had once been treasurer of England but was dismissed by Richard III and never trusted by Henry VII. The Yorkshire rebels in 1536 similarly besieged Lord Darcy in his castle at Pontefract to enlist his support, if not his leadership. As the period advanced, however, the Tudor nobility became less inclined to indulge in treasonous activities and instead rebel leaders tended to come from the gentry, lawyers and clergy. There were no nobles in Norfolk to whom rebels might turn in 1549, and Robert Kett, a minor landowner, assumed command. It was a Yorkshire gentleman, Sir John Egremont, who led the anti-tax demonstrations in 1489, and the revolts in Lincolnshire and the Pilgrimage of Grace were notable for the large number of county gentry who either supported or led rebel groups. The sheriff of Lincoln, for instance, Sir Edward Dymoke, his associate Sir Christopher Willoughby, and Sir Robert Bowes, Sir Ingram Percy and Sir Stephen Hammerton were all gentry captains of their troops. The lay leaders of the Western rebellion, Sir Humphrey Arundell, John Winslade and John Bury, were also minor gentry on the fringe of county politics, and Sir Thomas Wyatt, who led the Kent rebels in 1554, was a courtier and former sheriff.

Clergy

The clergy, on the other hand, rarely led a revolt. Rebellion against a divinely anointed ruler was a sin as well as an act of treason, although rebelling against a usurper could be justified, as several Irish bishops claimed in 1487. Nevertheless, in regions where the Catholic faith was deeply entrenched, such as Cornwall, Lincolnshire, Durham and parts of Lancashire and Yorkshire, the clergy were prepared to stand shoulder to shoulder with their community, and from time to time assume leading roles in a rebellion. Thus in 1536, the abbots of Kirkstead, Furness and Barlings, and the vicars of Louth, Brough and Brayton, supported the Lincolnshire and Pilgrimage revolts; and the vicars of St Clare, St Uny and Poundstock all travelled to Exeter with the Cornish rising of 1549. It is even possible that the vicar of St Thomas, Exeter, was the most significant figure in uniting the Devon and Cornish rebels.

Lawyers

Since the main objective of most rebels was to bring their grievances to the attention of local authorities, it is quite understandable that men with legal experience and social standing in the region emerged as leaders. Thomas Flamank from Bodmin (1497), Thomas Moigne, the recorder of Lincoln (1536) and William Stapleton in the East Riding of Yorkshire (1536) all took a prominent part in their rebellions, but the most celebrated lawyer to lead a revolt was Robert Aske, who headed the Pilgrimage of Grace. As attorney to the Earl of Northumberland, a cousin of the Earl of Cumberland and a respected lawyer in Yorkshire and London, Aske had all the attributes of an outstanding leader. Not surprisingly his contemporaries dubbed him 'the Great Captain' and several minor nobles and gentry deferred to his leadership.

Commoners

With the notable exception of the 1549 revolts, few rebellions were led by commoners or could hope to have much success if they were. Most of the rebel leaders in 1549 came from the ranks of the commons. Kett, for instance, was a tanner by trade and Thomas Underhill, who appears to have started disturbances at Sampford Courtenay in Devon, was a tailor. The Oxfordshire rising of 1596 was organised by local servants and tradesmen – millers, masons, weavers, bakers – and headed by a carpenter, Bartholomew Steer. They failed to attract any substantial support and the rising collapsed within hours of its start. On the other hand, the Amicable Grant revolt of 1525, which was led by husbandmen, urban artisans, weavers and rural peasants, owed its success to its size and to the sympathy it received from members of the king's council.

Leadership qualities

There was no single quality that made a good leader. Age was clearly of some importance. Simnel was too young and the earls in 1569 were too old. Warbeck, on the other hand, was 25, Wyatt 33 and Kett 57 years old at the time of their uprisings. Legitimacy and social standing were obviously key factors but so too was the capacity to employ the right strategy and tactics, and demonstrate good organisational skills. Leading a rebellion was an enormous responsibility: the consequences were usually fatal and the larger the host and longer the revolt, the more the qualities of the leader were tested. It is for these reasons that historians have generally regarded Aske and Kett as the outstanding English rebel leaders and Hugh O'Neill the most effective Irish leader during this period. These men were able to unite disparate factions, command thousands of troops in a disciplined manner and keep Tudor authorities on tenterhooks for a considerable period of time.

All rebellions needed men who were physically strong and intimidating, and some craftsmen and labourers figured among the leaders. Michael Joseph, who led the Cornish rebels into battle at Blackheath, was a blacksmith; Nicholas Melton, the captain of Louth rebels in 1536, was a cobbler; and Robert Welsh, vicar of St Thomas, who led the rebel host at the siege of Exeter in 1549, was a well-known wrestler. These were charismatic figures in their communities and must have been an inspiration to others.

Similarly, a man with military experience was always an asset in times of crisis. Arundell, who became the Cornish leader in 1549, had fought for Henry VIII in France, and Wyatt, who had been a military strategist to the king, put his theories into practice against Mary Tudor in 1554. These men were used to commanding troops and leadership came naturally to them.

What seems apparent therefore is that some men were born leaders and some had leadership thrust on them. At first most disturbances started with the lower ranks of society – craftsmen, artisans, labourers and peasants – who looked to their superiors, often men with legal and clerical backgrounds, to lead them and articulate their complaints. Before long in most cases the gentry assumed control, either willingly or under duress (as many claimed). Only occasionally, and usually for selfish and feckless reasons, lesser nobles got involved, but the heads of noble families and the aristocracy remained steadfast in their loyalty to the Tudors.

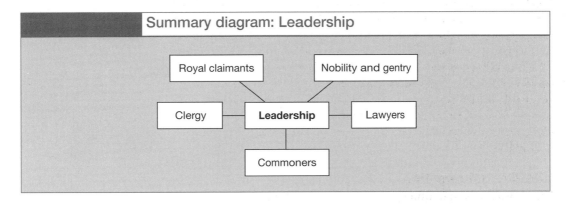

Summary diagram: Leadership

3 | Strategy and tactics

Dynastic rebellions

Key question
How did Tudor rebellions compare in respect of their strategies and tactics?

The **strategy and tactics** deployed by rebel leaders varied from rebellion to rebellion. If the prime objective was to overthrow the monarch, first he or she had to be drawn out of the capital and either forced to abdicate or killed on the battlefield. Until London had been seized, no rebel leader could claim victory and, as Londoners stood by legitimate rulers, the odds in favour of a successful coup were not good. To achieve their ends, dynastic rebellions therefore needed to have an alternative and *bona fide* claimant ready to rule: the Yorkists had pretenders as well as genuine claimants, Northumberland championed Lady Jane Grey, Wyatt favoured Princess Elizabeth, the northern earls wanted Mary Stuart and Essex looked to James VI of Scotland. In each case their tactics entailed raising noble and gentry support, enlisting foreign diplomatic and military aid, and putting pressure on the incumbent ruler to yield. Simnel and Warbeck landed in Lancashire and Cornwall, respectively, with the expectation of raising troops from disaffected counties before marching on

Key term

Strategy and tactics
Strategy is an overall plan and management of troops designed to achieve an objective; tactics are the means by which the plan is carried out.

London. In practice they each only raised 4000–5000 troops and failed to advance beyond Nottinghamshire and Somerset, some 150 miles from the capital. Wyatt and Essex had the advantage of starting in or near to London. Wyatt was a good strategist but a poor tactician. He understood the need to have nation-wide support but delayed his entry into London when time was of the essence. Essex, in contrast, had an uncertain strategy and no clear tactics. Disorganised from the start, his revolt quickly disintegrated into chaos.

Protests against government policies

Demonstrators against government policies and ministers adopted a different strategy. These protests were essentially peaceful and, in the opinion of the participants, justified. Their strategy was to raise as much popular support as possible, acquire the backing of gentry, clergy and nobles, and pressurise the authorities to respond to their requests (or, in the case of the Western rebels, their demands). Grievances were presented as articles to the Crown's representatives and once these had been submitted, there was little more that a rebel host could do but wait for a reply. All demonstrations claimed to be peace-loving and few rebel leaders relished the prospect of military confrontation, but beneath the surface of most revolts was the implicit threat of social violence.

If the revolts of 1536–7 are taken as an example, hundreds of gentry and lesser nobles appear to have been intimidated by the commons and forced to participate. The Abbot of Jervaulx recounted that he was threatened with beheading if he did not surrender his abbey; Marmaduke Neville claimed that his wife and goods were at risk if he refused to join in, and Sir Roger Cholmeley was told his house would be looted there and then. At Horncastle, William Leach informed the sheriff of Lincoln that he must 'be sworn to do as we do, or else it shall cost you your life'. Outside a mob of 100 men waited for his answer. Fear clearly induced many men to enlist. Aske claimed that he was 'persuaded' and Lord Darcy yielded Pontefract castle when 3000 rebels approached. Barnard castle similarly fell, as did the towns of Lincoln, Hull, York, Lancaster and Durham, ostensibly to save the citizens from unnecessary bloodshed. According to Thomas Moigne, the main reason why he and other Lincoln gentry agreed to become captains was to enable him to 'do the most good amongst his own neighbours in the staying of them [the commons]'. This may well have been true though Henry VIII did not believe him and Moigne paid for his involvement with his life.

The Lincolnshire rising and the Pilgrimage of Grace may have been exceptional cases on account of the scale and duration of the disturbances but the tactic of intimidation can also be found in the 1549 rebellions. The Western rebels kidnapped local gentry, detained passing merchants and put the sheriff of Devon under house arrest. In Suffolk four magistrates were imprisoned at Melton and in Norfolk Kett's captains held and humiliated any gentry who would not co-operate. Sir Roger Wodehouse tried to persuade rebels on Mousehold Heath to disperse by bribing them with three carts of food and drink only to be chased, imprisoned and have his provisions seized. Thomas Gawdy MP, Richard Catlyn and other gentry were chained and fettered and placed in the front line as battle-shields at Dussindale. Violence against the upper classes was however a rarity. It is hard to judge whether the Oxfordshire rebels of 1596 were serious when they spoke about murdering seven local landlords who had enclosed nearby fields but it could explain the reluctance of serving men to join them.

When violence did occur, the victim was usually a figure of hatred and the source of local anger. In 1489 it was the Earl of Northumberland, Henry VII's sheriff of Yorkshire who was responsible for collecting an unpopular war tax; eight years later the target was the provost of Penryn, the collector of a war tax in Cornwall, who escaped to Taunton before being murdered in the market place. In 1536 Dr John Raynes was hacked to pieces by an angry mob and another innocent man was hanged. In 1549 William Hellions was cut down at Launceston when he tried to buy off the rebel host with a cartload of provisions and, in the same year in Norwich, Kett's rebels captured an Italian mercenary and hanged him from the city walls. Nevertheless, apart from these isolated incidents and the fatalities of armed conflicts, we can believe the peaceful intentions of most rebels. The Cornishmen in 1497 wished 'to do no creature hurt'; the Lincolnshire rebels claimed they were 'true and faithful subjects' and the Western protesters declared 'God save king Edward, for we be his, both body and soul'. Pulling down a hedge, pillaging a deer park, or destroying Protestant bibles and ransacking a bishop's library were physical, even symbolic gestures of righting a wrong, while disrupting local communications and stealing supplies from the gentry were considered to be valid tactics in achieving the rebels' goal.

Laying siege to county towns was a standard tactic in most uprisings. Apart from securing the support of several thousand citizens, a successful rebellion looked to win over the mayor, aldermen and sheriff whenever possible. Their involvement also gave the protest added strength and respectability and increased the rebels' bargaining power when dealing with the government. Camps of rebels became a common sight in 1549, the 'year of commotions', when thousands of demonstrators encamped in open fields and heaths outside city walls. Exeter on three occasions – twice in 1497 and again in 1549 – repelled rebel sieges, and Carlisle in 1537 and 1570 refused to submit to rebel leaders. Some county officials, however, cracked under the strain and opened their gates: Taunton (1497), York (1536), Lancaster (1536), Norwich (1549) and Durham (1536 and 1569) all yielded to violent threats. Only a minority of mayors, for example, Wells (1497), Lincoln (1536), Torrington (1549) and Bodmin (1549), openly supported the protesters. And Thomas Codd, mayor of Norwich, fraternised rather too readily with Kett's rebels on Mousehold Heath to believe his later claim that he did it to protect the welfare of his fellow citizens.

A common way of alerting people that something important was going to happen was to ring the church bells, light beacons and post notices on village halls and church doors. Such tactics kept people informed and maintained the unity among rebel groups. Robert Kett held daily council meetings at his camp. Robert Aske issued badges to the pilgrims who adopted the Five Wounds of Christ as their banner. It was the traditional cry of religious conformity in the face of heresy and chosen by rebels in 1549 and 1569, and all pilgrims swore an oath of allegiance 'to be true to God, the king and the commons'. This novelty bound the rebel host together and most of the rebels in 1536 took it. Swearing an oath was an important element of rebel propaganda; so too was utilising the printing press. Ballads and seditious rhymes were composed, letters and circulars published, and posters nailed to church doors claiming that the Catholic faith was 'piteously and abominably confounded'.

Irish rebellions

The strategy and tactics of Irish rebellions were not dissimilar from those found in modern guerrilla warfare. English landowners and Anglo-Irish government officials were prime targets of attack and the inhospitable terrain, particularly in Ulster and lands to the west and south of the Pale around Dublin, made combating rebel troops very hard. The Irish wisely avoided military confrontations unless an English army was outnumbered or caught isolated, as occurred at Yellow Ford in 1598 when English troops suffered heavy losses. If the Irish rebels faced defeat or capture, the leaders 'disappeared' into the more remote regions of Ireland where few Englishmen dared to venture. Of course, English rebels similarly escaped to the mountains of Wales, the Lake District and Scotland or to the moors of south-west England, but in Ireland rebels often survived to continue their fight several months later. James Fitzgerald, for instance, evaded capture in 1573 after four years of intermittent hostilities, only to resurface in 1579 and renew his rebellion in concert with his cousin the Earl of Desmond. Such tactics proved very frustrating for loyalist commanders who might win a skirmish but rarely won a battle. And unlike English rebellions, Irish revolts were altogether more violent, brutal and protracted.

Summary diagram: Strategy and tactics

Type of rebellion	Strategy	Tactics
Dynastic rebellions	Raise an army and overthrow the ruler	Gather widespread support prior to fighting a battle
Anti-government protests in England	Pressurise the authorities into remedying grievances	Popular demonstrations and intimidation of officials and local leaders
Irish rebellions	Disrupt the Dublin administration	Attack English landowners and officials through the use of violence and guerrilla warfare

Key question
What organisational difficulties faced rebel leaders?

Key terms

Muster
To summon soldiers for an inspection.

Richard II
In 1399 Henry Bolingbroke had seized the Crown from Richard II. The re-enactment of Shakespeare's play (written in 1595) reminded Londoners that the deposition of Elizabeth I would not be unprecedented.

4 | Organisation

Once a rebellion was underway its effectiveness depended on how well the leader held together its different social groups, disciplined its members and organised its infrastructure – enlisting and paying troops, requisitioning food and equipment, detailing daily **musters** and keeping rebels informed of general developments. Little is known about the day-to-day affairs of most rebellions but where evidence has survived, it is clear that the quality of organisation varied considerably.

Poorly organised rebellions

Some rebellions were poorly planned from the start and got progressively worse. In 1569 the Earl of Northumberland left himself insufficient time to call on his own tenants in Yorkshire and failed to appreciate how long it would take to march from Durham to Tutbury in Staffordshire in order to release Mary Stuart from captivity, or indeed realise that she had been moved 30 miles further south to Coventry. Moreover, when he and the Earl of Westmorland came to pay 1000 footmen at North Allerton, they could only raise £20 between them. Six hundred potential troops deserted there and then. The Simnel rebellion was another badly organised uprising. The presence of 2000 German mercenaries and 40 Irish nobles with their 'wild' tenants deterred many English from joining the rebel army as it progressed south from Lancashire.

The Western rising had problems of a different kind among its ranks. Not only was there animosity between the Cornishmen and Devonians, there was tension between the peasantry, clergy and gentry. Hints of social radicalism were apparent when some of those in the Clyst camp outside Exeter wanted to 'kill all the gentlemen', but nothing further transpired. Significantly, the nine captains who commanded the siege comprised three Devon gentry, three Cornish gentry and three commoners. However, when the rebels' final petition was presented to the Crown, it contained no reference to any economic grievances, and it was these that really mattered to the peasants.

On the face of it, there seemed to be little wrong with the organisation of the Oxfordshire rising in 1596: the ringleaders spent a great deal of time planning their moves and determining when and where it would take place. Unfortunately secrecy was not high on their agenda and a fair-weather colleague alerted his lord of the intended rising. The rebels' choice of Enslow Hill, which was where a revolt had been staged in 1549, made their arrest fairly predictable and the attempted rebellion was defeated before it could start.

Essex's rebellion fared little better. He too had advertised that he was going to do something dramatic – he even hired a troupe of actors to perform Shakespeare's *Richard II* on the eve of the rebellion – and when it began, he expected Londoners to rally to his cause. Instead most stood and watched his assembly pass by in bemusement. Once he had failed to enlist the support of the mayor and sheriff of London whom he mistakenly thought would back him, he decided to retreat. Unfortunately, he had no exit strategy and, finding Ludgate blocked, was forced to withdraw in total disarray.

Well-organised rebellions: 1536 and 1549

Not all rebellions were disorganised affairs. Indeed, those led by Aske and Kett are noteworthy precisely because of their excellent organisation. Aske had the unenviable task of trying to manage more than 30,000 followers from a variety of social backgrounds and geographical regions who were pursuing different objectives. Recruits were mustered into companies according to their district, town or village, which meant that most men knew each other at least by sight and were able to elect a captain to represent and lead them. The captains met each day, received instructions from Aske as to where they would be going and attended regular council meetings with other captains. Villages usually elected one captain, towns as many as four. Each recruit was given a badge, a supply of food and wages, and took the pilgrim oath of good behaviour. While some companies raided churches and abbeys, most appear to have been well disciplined. For instance, when 8000 rebels approached York, Aske arranged that half would camp outside the city while the rest would accompany him and all paid for their board and lodging.

Aske kept firm control of the majority of the pilgrims but those rebels who came from regions to the west of the Pennines proved more difficult to manage. There was moreover, as in other disturbances, tension between the gentry leaders and the commoners. For instance, 300 representatives from all counties north of the river Don assembled near Doncaster in November 1536, while the rest of the host waited at Pontefract. Forty pilgrims were selected to parley with the Duke of Norfolk, and Aske then returned to the main body of rebels to explain what had been discussed. Most of the commons feared that the gentry were going to betray them, as had happened at Lincoln earlier in October. Although they were given assurances to the contrary, later events proved their suspicion was not misplaced.

Robert Kett was the undisputed leader of his rebellion in Norfolk and demonstrated how to marshal a peaceful protest of at least 16,000 rebels for nearly seven weeks. Camps of protesting rebels were set up in many English counties in the summer of 1549 but we know most about the one that Kett organised on Mousehold Heath, outside Norwich. The community occupied Surrey Place, a mansion on the heath, and he ran the camp like a model local government. One of his objectives was to show that he and his colleagues could manage business affairs as well as the gentry or government officials. Each of the 24 **hundreds** in the county that contributed rebels elected two governors to sit on an advisory council, courts of justice imposed disciplinary fines and punishments, and proclamations and warrants were issued. For instance, when seeking supplies, a warrant undertook that 'no violence or injury be done to any honest or poor man', and this

Hundreds
Norfolk, like most counties, was divided administratively into hundreds.

Key term

promise of decent behaviour appears to have been upheld. He sent out search parties to keep the camp supplied with food and beer, negotiated with the mayor of Norwich to purchase general provisions and gunpowder and arranged for artillery to be brought from the coast. Twice a day prayers were taken by a minister, Thomas Conyers, under the **Oak of Reformation**. Even when the rebels attacked the city and held it for a week before retiring to their encampment, discipline was maintained. A garrison was established in the cathedral grounds, aldermen and constables were appointed, citizens conscripted as night watchmen, and the city gates, castle and guildhall guarded. Significantly no one was killed until royal troops and foreign mercenaries arrived to recover control of the city.

Key term

Oak of Reformation An old oak tree on Mousehold Heath outside Norwich.

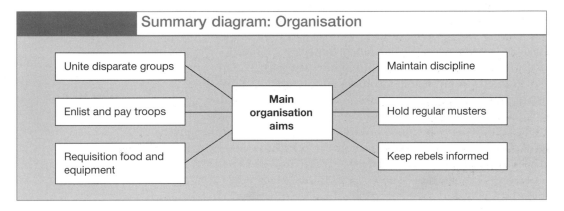

Summary diagram: Organisation

Unite disparate groups

Enlist and pay troops

Requisition food and equipment

Main organisation aims

Maintain discipline

Hold regular musters

Keep rebels informed

Key question
Why were some rebellions larger than others?

5 | Size, support and frequency

Size

Rebellions came in all shapes and sizes. Although it is impossible to be certain of exact numbers, Tudor rebellions seem to have ranged from as small as four rebels in the 1596 Oxfordshire rising to as many as 40,000 in the 1536 Pilgrimage of Grace. Most disturbances gathered a few thousand supporters; some saw their numbers increase as the rebellion progressed, while the majority fluctuated as circumstances changed. The Cornish rebels of 1497, for example, may have grown in size from a few thousand to 15,000 as they travelled east through Devon, Somerset, Wiltshire, Hampshire, Surrey to Kent, but by the time they reached Blackheath an estimated 5000 rebels had deserted. The Pilgrimage was another rebellion in which numbers varied in the course of two months. Some of the 30,000 rebels who occupied Lincoln in October 1536 left to join the Yorkshire movement but as different groups targeted particular towns, the numbers in individual rebel parties ranged from 3000 at Hull to some 20,000 at York. By the time various dissident groups had converged on Pontefract under the leadership of Aske, there may have been as many as 40,000 rebels. After 1536 rebellions in both England and Ireland were smaller affairs. Perhaps as many as 16,000 protesters descended on Norwich in 1549, Wyatt had around 3000 supporters in Kent, some 6000 followed the northern earls and Essex mustered no more than 300 men. Irish rebellions generally comprised a few hundred men at most and O'Neill's national uprising of 1595 was exceptional in that he was able to rally more than 6000 troops.

Support

Noble and foreign support

Key question
What was the most valuable kind of support a rebellion might receive?

Although the size of a rebel host was clearly a problem for the authorities, not least because royal armies took a while to assemble and even then they might be smaller, of far greater concern was the nature of the support a rebellion might receive. The most serious revolts were those that attracted noble and foreign interest. Nobles were the natural leaders in society; they could call on their own servants and tenants to fight for them, they had the finances to fund an army and they had access to military equipment. Foreign-sponsored rebellions presented a different kind of threat. Troops were often battle-hardened mercenaries and the English authorities could not be sure when and where they might strike. Fortunately, in most cases promises of foreign assistance failed to materialise but the prospect of foreign troops landing in England gave a rebellion added potency.

Rebellions of this nature mostly occurred at the beginning and end of the Tudor period, and sought to overthrow the monarch or alter the line of succession. Henry VII faced three rebellions involving English nobles, two of which were backed by foreign powers. Lovel and the Stafford brothers were unable to get enough support from their **retainers** in 1486 before Henry suppressed their conspiracies but Simnel and Warbeck each attracted Irish interest and a small number of English nobles intent on dethroning the king. Simnel had the greater support that ranged from Irish nobles and bishops to English nobles and clerics and German mercenaries, who were funded by Margaret of Burgundy. Warbeck's support came from disaffected Yorkists keen to remove Henry, from merchants unhappy at trade **embargoes** with Flanders, and from renegade Scottish, Irish and Flemish adventurers. Also caught up in the conspiracy were two powerful English nobles, Lord Fitzwater, steward of the royal household, and Sir William Stanley, Henry's step-uncle and lord chamberlain. Significantly, Henry appears to have nipped noble treason in the bud: when Warbeck finally landed in Cornwall, he gathered mainly 6000 Cornish miners, artisans and farmers – none was a noble or gentleman.

Key terms

Retainers
Nobles retained servants in their households who might be used as private armies.

Embargoes
Trade restrictions such as those imposed on Burgundy in 1493.

Each of the dynastic rebellions that occurred in the second half of the period had noble involvement and several hoped for some degree of foreign commitment. The Duke of Northumberland in 1553 had the support of aristocrats like the earls of Oxford and Huntingdon, and lords Grey and Clinton in his attempt to overthrow Mary, but significantly more nobles rallied to her defence and most of Northumberland's army of 2000 deserted when a confrontation seemed likely. Wyatt in the following year had expected the Duke of Suffolk and his brothers in Leicestershire, Sir James Croft in Herefordshire and Sir Peter

Carew in Devon, as well as French troops, to support his uprising in Kent but none transpired. Instead Wyatt had to rely on the county militia and gentry like Sir Henry Isley, Sir George Harper and Thomas Culpepper, all former sheriffs, and a host of minor gentry and their tenants. Significantly only two leading Kentishmen, Lord Abergavenny and Sir Robert Southwell, were openly loyal to the government.

Thomas Percy and Charles Neville, the earls of Northumberland and Westmorland, also failed to attract any major noble family to their cause in 1569. None rose in Lancashire, Cheshire or Cumberland, and even some of Neville's tenants were reluctant to get involved. Again the rebellion rested on mainly disaffected Catholic gentry but the belief that a Spanish army under Alva was preparing to give them military support remained wishful thinking. Essex in 1601 had more noble support than any other rebellion. The earls of Southampton, Sussex and Rutland, lords Cromwell, Mounteagle and Sandes, and 12 deputy lieutenants of their counties gathered in London with their servants and retainers. Nevertheless, in spite of soliciting Scottish and Irish aid, Essex received no external help, nor did he get any support from the mayor, sheriff and city of London. An Irish earl or clan claimant eager to acquire an earldom always led rebellions in Ireland but most of their support came from their tenants and Catholic clergy, who were loyal to their landlord and faith and opposed to all things English. It was a situation that Spain tried to exploit in 1580 and 1601 when it sent troops to assist revolts in Munster.

Commoners

Revolts that were demonstrations against government policies often attracted support from a range of lower social groups. Few attracted noble or gentry interest and some, like the Amicable Grant and Oxfordshire rising, solely consisted of commoners. In 1525 as many as 4000 rural peasants, urban artisans and unemployed people gathered in Sudbury and Lavenham, Suffolk. It is important to realise, however, that although no nobles or gentry led the revolt, royal councillors and the Archbishop of Canterbury sympathised with the complaints and similar anti-tax protests were voiced in other parts of the country. The Oxfordshire rising, in contrast, had neither sympathy nor support from the landed gentry and nobility, and without their financial backing and involvement, the rebellion had no hope of success. In fact even most of the servants of the gentry who had considered giving support to the rebels lost their nerve when the uprising began. Some 30 men were rounded up and all were found to be local workers and tradesmen.

Variety of social groups

Exactly the reverse happened in the other large-scale demonstrations of the period. The Cornish rebellion of 1497 not only had a peer, a lawyer and a blacksmith at the helm, it was backed by 44 parish priests, several abbots, monks and local gentry. As such it was a formidable assembly. When it reached Somerset, 22 gentry, four sheriffs, three MPs and four abbots were among the 4000 rebels who enlisted, although the majority who joined were urban artisans and peasant farmers. Fifty-two years later, a similar protest was launched in Cornwall against a new English prayer book; it too had the same broad cross-section of support that included at least eight priests, several JPs, two mayors, gentry such as Arundell and Winslade, and a large number of farmers, labourers, artisans and itinerant unemployed. Significantly it attracted no noble support. Kett's rebellion also had no major landowner in its ranks. Its support came from small tenant farmers, lesser gentry, rural workers and unemployed craftsmen, many of whom joined the revolt once the city of Norwich had fallen.

The rebellion that reflected the greatest degree of social variety was the Pilgrimage of Grace. Among the leading nobles were younger sons and relatives of the four major northern houses – Stanley, Neville, Percy and Clifford – including Sir Ingram and Sir Thomas Percy, Lords Darcy and Hussey, George Lumley, son of Lord Lumley, and John Neville, Lord Latimer, and his younger brother Marmaduke. Although several revolts against religious reforms and economic and social conditions were started in 1536 by lower orders and parish clergy, leadership and control soon passed to the gentry and the more politically important families. The Dymokes and Willoughbys, for example, ultimately led the Lincolnshire rising but it began in Louth at the hands of 'Captain Cobbler' and the local clergy.

What made the Pilgrimage of Grace unique, however, was the high-profile involvement of the commons, clergy, gentry and lesser nobles at every stage of the revolt. Many became captains of the nine host armies under the overall leadership of Aske. Of course, it is impossible to say who enlisted voluntarily and who was forced to join and lead the rebel hosts. Many gentry like Sir Christopher Hilyard, John Hallam and Robert Bowes in Yorkshire later claimed they were threatened but most had ulterior motives in accounting for their involvement. The Willoughbys in Lincolnshire, for instance, resented the Duke of Suffolk's acquisition of family lands, Sir Ingram Percy of Alnwick had been disinherited, and Lord Darcy of Pontefract was out of favour with the king. All claimed they supported the pilgrims under duress but it was widely reported that once the rebellion had begun, the gentry were 'first harnessed of all others'.

Frequency

Most English rebellions occurred at the beginning of the period when the Tudor dynasty was very vulnerable. Henry VII faced five serious revolts, three of which aimed to overthrow him. The summer of 1497 was a particularly critical time. England was at war with Scotland, Henry had to fight the battle of Blackheath to suppress the Cornish rebellion and Warbeck was laying claim to the throne. The Spanish ambassador to the Imperial court may

Key question
Does an analysis of English rebellions suggest any patterns of frequency?

have been exaggerating when he wrote that 'the whole kingdom was against the King', but he was closer to the mark when he claimed that 'had the king lost the battle he would have been finished off and beheaded'. As the Tudors became more secure, alternative claimants died out and people grew accustomed to their rule. At the same time, the politically important groups, the nobility, gentry and yeomen, saw the benefits of allying with the ruling family and turned away from rebellion as a means of solving their problems. Instead issues of major concern came to be aired and often resolved at court, in council and in parliament. Thus, after 1570 Elizabeth faced only one rebellion of note, and this lasted less than 12 hours. Of course, she did have to contend with numerous plots on her life, notably Ridolfi, Babington and Throckmorton, but none grew into a rebellion. Ireland, on the other hand, gave Elizabeth a lot of trouble. There she had to deal with more rebellions than any of her predecessors due to a combination of factors that are considered below (see page 55).

In contrast, most of the disturbances that faced Henry VIII, Edward VI and Mary I between 1536 and 1554 were principally a reaction to their religious and economic policies. Undoubtedly 1549 was the worst year when between June and August some 27 English counties experienced revolts or longer periods of rebellion. Riots and disturbances continued to be reported in the early 1550s but the frequency had peaked in terms of both size and extent. Mary Tudor, for example, faced only two serious revolts, one of which enabled her to secure the throne from Lady Jane Grey, while Elizabeth was confronted with just one serious rebellion in the north of England in 1569.

Reasons for the decline in the frequency of rebellions

A number of reasons, some of which are developed more fully in Chapter 4, may be offered to explain this decline in the frequency of rebellions:

- Most of the dynastic and political factors that had underpinned Yorkist rebellions began to lose their impetus as the Tudors systematically removed pretenders and claimants. As late as 1541 Henry VIII was still eliminating members of the Pole family, who were descended from the royal house of Plantagenet, but thereafter there were no more scions of the House of York lurking in the political woodwork.
- The Reformation was a source of provocation to many Englishmen and religious issues in 1536 and 1549, and to a lesser extent in 1569, lay behind armed rebellions. The Elizabethan Church Settlement of 1559, however, was a moderate policy that satisfied most religious groups. Moreover, the government and the Church wisely held back from strictly enforcing its terms. If no offence was given, then it was hoped that none would be taken, and so it proved. After 1549 religion ceased to be a major issue worthy of a rebellion.
- Social and economic problems, which could be a frequent source of discontent, peaked in the 1540s. Although difficulties

remained for the rest of the period, issues such as enclosures, engrossments, excessive taxation, hyper-inflation and poor tenant–landlord relations, all abated.

- A major factor that prevented the outbreak of disturbances in the second half of the century was the measures taken by Mary and Elizabeth. In particular, the poor and unemployed were helped rather than punished, JPs and lords lieutenant kept a closer eye on local tensions and endeavoured to overcome potential difficulties before they got out of hand, and people were encouraged to resolve their problems by peaceful means such as arbitration, litigation and parliamentary bills rather than by acts of lawlessness and violence.

As a result of these developments, many of which did not operate in Ireland, rebellions in England became less frequent in the course of the period.

Essay focus

Compare how the essays tackle the question of frequency on pages 60–4. Each essay refers to the role of the nobility but Essay 1, paragraph 2, fails to link this to developments before and after 1549, whereas Essay 2, paragraph 4, is far more focused and synoptic. Similarly, Essay 1, paragraph 4, cites religious and social/economic reforms, whereas Essay 2, paragraphs 3 and 5, explains these reasons more fully. Essay 2 supplies additional reasons in paragraphs 2 and 6, thereby demonstrating a wider range of explanations. It is important that examples are drawn from the whole period to show continuity and change in developments over time. These are key elements in a synoptic study.

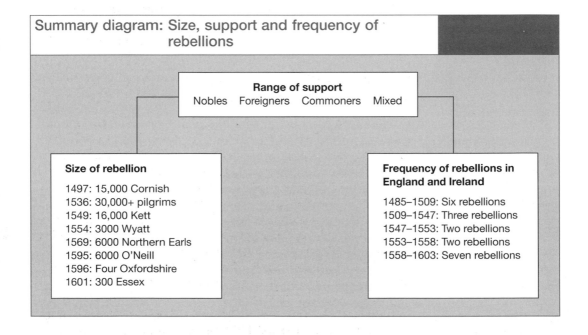

Summary diagram: Size, support and frequency of rebellions

Range of support
Nobles   Foreigners   Commoners   Mixed

Size of rebellion

1497: 15,000 Cornish
1536: 30,000+ pilgrims
1549: 16,000 Kett
1554: 3000 Wyatt
1569: 6000 Northern Earls
1595: 6000 O'Neill
1596: Four Oxfordshire
1601: 300 Essex

Frequency of rebellions in England and Ireland

1485–1509: Six rebellions
1509–1547: Three rebellions
1547–1553: Two rebellions
1553–1558: Two rebellions
1558–1603: Seven rebellions

Key question
In what respects did Irish rebellions differ in their nature and frequency from English rebellions?

6 | Irish rebellions

It has often been claimed that during this period rebellions in Ireland were quite different from those that occurred in England:

- There were differences in scale and duration. Most Irish disturbances lasted several years and, like bushfires, no sooner had one been put out than another started up. The scale of fighting also increased in the course of the period. Sir Edward Poynings, Henry VII's lord deputy of Ireland in the 1490s, tried to defend English interests in the Pale with some 400 troops; a century later the Earl of Essex took 17,000 men and Lord Mountjoy 13,000 troops to combat O'Neill's rebellion. English soldiers were usually better trained and equipped but until the 1590s the Tudors consistently underestimated the nature of the problem confronting local garrisons and the amount of money needed to keep effective control. In practice, if an Irish chieftain was determined to resist English rule, there was little that could be done to stop him.

- Although all Irish leaders pledged their loyalty to the English monarch, they were not averse to acting dishonourably when it suited them. The Earl of Kildare, for instance, backed the pretender Simnel before swearing allegiance to Henry VII, and made little attempt to apprehend Warbeck when he landed in Ireland. Similarly, the Earl of Desmond spent five years in the Tower of London but it still did not prevent him from taking part in the Geraldine rebellion of 1579. And if a truce was signed between leaders, as O'Neill and English commanders agreed in 1596 and 1599, it was simply regarded as a device to buy more time. In effect, Irish rebellions were most likely to end when the clan leader was killed, and even this could not be guaranteed. As Lord Grey discovered in 1579, no sooner was Fitzgerald killed than Desmond took his place and prolonged the rebellion for another four years.

After 1534, three factors affected Anglo-Irish relations and influenced the nature and course of rebellions in Ireland:

- Henry VIII ended generations of Irish aristocratic rule and seriously destabilised relations between English governments and Irish subjects and between Irish and **Gaelic clans**. For the first time English-born officials were appointed to key administrative posts as lord deputies, lieutenants, treasurers and chancellors. The Crown no longer had an Irish family, such as the Kildares, to safeguard its interest, and rival clans, like the Butlers, O'Neills, O'Mores, O'Connors and O'Donnells, felt less intimidated and more willing to break the law.

- Once Henry became King of Ireland in 1541 rather than 'Lord of Ireland', his relationship with Gaelic chiefs changed. They were now obliged to 'surrender' their lands, renounce their traditional customs and have their lands 'regranted' according to English usage. Attempts by Henry and later Tudors to **Anglicise** the Irish led to fierce resistance that soon developed

Key terms

Gaelic clans
Some native and older Irish families spoke Gaelic and were distinguished from the families of Norman descent and more recent immigrants who spoke English.

Anglicise
To make English.

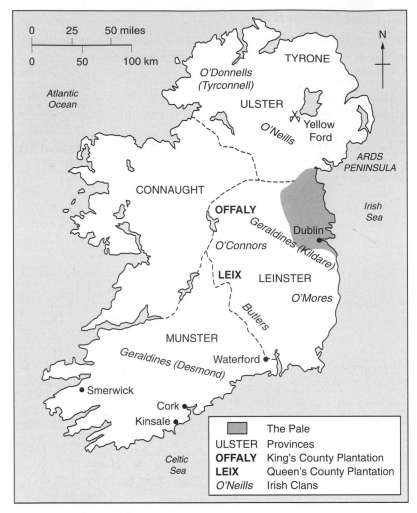

Figure 2.2: Tudor Ireland.

into a more general and national resentment. Gaelic tribes defended their language, laws and customs, and resented attacks on their culture as much as incursions on their lands by 'new' English colonists and absentee landlords.

- Many 'old' English families resented attempts by the Tudors to introduce a Protestant reformation. Although Elizabeth had no desire to provoke the Irish over religious matters and deliberately discouraged her bishops from sending over Protestant evangelists, after her excommunication in 1570 Roman Catholic missionaries arrived in Ireland from the continent intent on whipping up anti-English sentiment. This religious zeal was indeed a feature of the Geraldine and O'Neill rebellions, and reminiscent of Catholic **firebrands** operating in the Northern Earls' revolt in England in 1569.

Firebrands
People who cause unrest.

Key term

Summary diagram: Irish rebellions		
Key features • Scale • Duration	→ **Irish rebellions** ←	**Turning points** • Direct rule • Anglicisation • Reformation

7 | Conclusion: why were some rebellions more successful than others at achieving their objectives?

How can success or failure be measured? It is not enough to say that a rebellion was a success if particular grievances were brought to the government's attention, unless those grievances were redressed. Nor is it acceptable to claim that a rebellion was successful if some of its lesser grievances were corrected but the more important issues were ignored or left unresolved. For a rebellion to succeed, it had to fulfil its principal objectives. In this respect, none of the dynastic rebellions achieved their goal and only Mary succeeded in removing the government *in situ*, namely Northumberland and Lady Jane Grey. Indeed rebellions were always going to fail as long as the government held its nerve. Only one rebellion that involved the commons achieved its objective – the withdrawal of the Amicable Grant – and this was precisely because several councillors alerted the king to the likely consequences if he did not comply. Apart from the wide geographical spread of opposition, resistance in London was too close to the government for comfort. Of course, Henry VIII had the neat let-out of being able to blame Wolsey for the problems that precipitated the revolt and so the government emerged with credit and the king enhanced his undeserved reputation for generosity.

Other demonstrations resulted in some satisfactory resolutions (see Chapter 3, pages 88–90). The Yorkshire and Cornish tax rebellions of 1489 and 1497 discouraged Henry VII from making any further novel demands. Protests against religious changes in 1536 may have deterred Henry VIII from implementing further Protestant reforms and the repeal of the Statute of Uses, which was one of the pilgrims' requests, occurred in 1540. The Edwardian government also made concessions. It responded to the 1549 rebellions by repealing the Subsidy Act, passing Enclosure and Tillage Acts, and enacting poor law legislation, all of which was designed to assist the commons in a constructive and benevolent manner. Complaints by northern rebels in 1536 and 1569 led to changes in the composition of the Council of the North, and concern raised by the Oxford rebels in 1596 saw the Privy Council restore land under tillage and initiate prosecutions against illegal enclosures. Only one rebellion resulted in the overthrow of a leading politician. Ironically it was the Duke of Somerset who, of all Tudor ministers, wanted so desperately to help the rank and file in times of economic and social crisis. Yet his overthrow was less the objective of any rebellion but more the result of gentry and privy councillors reacting to his inept policies and failure to suppress widespread revolts. This occurrence was exceptional; in general, rebellions failed to achieve their main objectives.

Reasons for success or failure of rebellions

There are several explanations why most rebellions failed:

- Successful rebellions needed strong and effective leadership, and this feature was not always present. Often the best leaders were the gentry, lawyers and yeomen rather than their social superiors, the nobility and clergy, and the lack of support from these two groups largely explains why rebellions failed.
- The government deployed a strategy of playing for time, offering pardons to all but the ringleaders, and agreeing to discuss grievances on condition that the rebels dispersed (see Chapter 3, pages 71–3). Once this occurred, no matter what government promises were made, the likelihood that the rebels' complaints would be addressed was slim. Tudor rebellions are littered with examples of betrayal by the authorities. The Lincolnshire rebels implored Aske in Yorkshire not to bargain with the Duke of Norfolk as earlier the Duke of Suffolk had duped them and their rising had accomplished nothing. The Western rebels likewise suspected a deal was going to be done when gentry leaders met Devon JPs outside Exeter in 1549. Similarly Kett was discouraged from holding private talks with the Earl of Warwick as his supporters feared he might be tempted to make a deal. The authorities knew that the longer a rebellion continued, the more likely it would end in failure. The possibility that rebels would quarrel, desert or betray their cause increased as food supplies ran out and living conditions deteriorated. Rebels also needed to consider the welfare of their families who they had left behind, farmers had to harvest their crops and, if a royal army was known to be approaching, the possibility of death on the battlefield was not a welcome proposition.
- Unlike political rebellions, which could only be successful if the monarch was defeated or killed in battle, and at Stoke (1487), Blackheath (1497) and Cambridge (1553), the thrones of Henry VII and Mary were at risk, most protesters tried to avoid a military confrontation. Aske in 1536 wrote to rebels at Clitheroe Moor ordering them not to fight the Earl of Derby's troops and, even though he had a following of some 40,000 at Pontefract, Aske had no wish to do battle with the Duke of Norfolk's troops assembled nearby. Both Arundell at Exeter and Kett at Norwich felt the same way but once a royal army had gathered enough men, such that its commander believed victory was certain, there was only going to be one winner. Lack of funding for rebels resulted in inadequate cavalry, weapons, ammunition and supplies, whereas government troops could bide their time until they were ready to attack. If foreign mercenaries supplemented the latter, as occurred at Clyst and Dussindale in 1549, the more hardened professional army was likely to prove victorious.

- Rebellions failed on account of their provincialism. Most aimed to resolve local grievances and had no desire to link up with other disaffected areas or to broaden their appeal. Only on one occasion were rebels known to have made contact with protesters some distance away when the Exeter rebels made overtures to demonstrators in Winchester, Hampshire, in July 1549, but the latter was discouraged from marching to their assistance. Understandably the government felt more anxiety the nearer a rebellion got to London, and this increased the rebels' chances of success. In practice, however, only the Cornish revolt in 1497, Wyatt's rebellion in 1554 and Essex in 1601 came within striking distance of Whitehall. In each case, the government withstood the challenge, loyal troops dispersed the insurgents and the insurrections ended in failure.

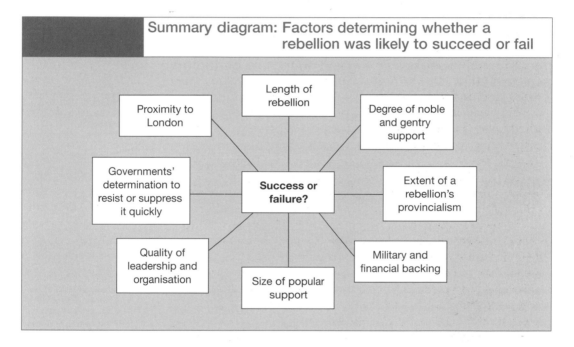

Summary diagram: Factors determining whether a rebellion was likely to succeed or fail

Further questions for debate

1 Why were some areas of England and Ireland more prone to rebellions than others?

2 How does an analysis of the strategy and tactics of Tudor rebellions help to explain their limited success?

3 Assess the role of landed groups in supporting and opposing rebellions in England and Ireland.

4 Assess the relative importance of leadership, organisation and support in explaining the failure of most rebellions.

5 Explain why there were fewer rebellions in England during Elizabeth's reign than in the years between 1485 and 1558.

Choose two of the above questions and write plans in the form of notes and/or diagrams. Your plans should outline your main arguments, any relevant supporting evidence and how key ideas are linked synoptically.

Advice on answering essay questions on historical turning points

In the essays that follow, the focus of the question is on the frequency of rebellions and why 1549 may be considered a turning point in the Tudor period. You need to explain and analyse what preceded and succeeded this year to show change and continuity over time. You need to assess and explain several reasons to show that you have understood the links and connections between various developments, thereby showing that you can synthesise ideas and concepts.

Read each of the following essays carefully. Each essay was written in one hour and without the use of notes. Note any strengths and limitations and compare your views with those of the assessor. Marks should be awarded for each of the two assessment objectives described in the tables at the end of the book (see pages 142–3).

Essay 1: Why did 1549 mark a turning point in the frequency of rebellions in England during the period from 1485 to 1603?

1 1549 was a year of dreadful disturbances throughout England. It marked a turning point for the frequency of rebellions for a number of reasons. Firstly rebellions after this point tended to have a lack of noble support or have dynastic aims, there was an increase in the involvement of gentlemen and yeomen in the administration and leadership of towns and villages. There was also a loss of religion as an issue and an increase in the ability to satisfy the poor, certainly in Elizabeth's reign.

2 The near anarchy of 1549 marked a turning point for the noblemen. The beating to death of Lord Sheffield by the rebels in the Kett's rebellion is just one example of how the nobility were further motivated towards the Crown. This ultimately created an increase in polarisation between rich and poor. However the increase of nobility supporting the monarch meant rebellions could be put down easily. Before this date there was numerous support of noblemen for rebellion, particularly in the reign of Henry VII. 1486 showed a rebellion of a nobleman in Lord Lovell and the Stafford brothers, trying to increase their power. Lambert Simnel was also supported by Lovel and by the Earl of Lincoln, who had supported Henry VII at Bosworth and helped him secure victory there. The Irish noble, the Earl of Kildare also supported rebellion. Numerous other examples include Stanley supporting Warbeck (1491–7) and Lord Audley supporting the Cornish rebels in 1497. Moreover noble support for rebellion was also maintained in the reign of Henry VIII in the Amicable Grant where nobles were quick to report rebellion but slow to stop it. The Pilgrimage of Grace (1536) contained supporters such as Lords Hussey and Darcy. Moreover, after the 1549 rebellions, the nobility failed to support rebellion. For instance in 1569 only two nobles were involved in the Northern Earls' rebellion – Northumberland and Westmorland – and Elizabeth was supported by many nobles such as

1 A focused start that outlines several reasons.

2 Some sections could be better expressed but most of the material needed to be used as an explanation why nobles after 1549 tended not to support rebellions. Some errors also, e.g. Lincoln did not support Henry at Bosworth; Lord Dacre was also involved in the Northern Earls' revolt.

the earls of Sussex and Rutland. In fact the only other nobles to engage in rebellion after 1549 were the Wyatt plotters (Lord Courtenay), who didn't even manage to get his rebellion in Cornwall off the ground, and the Essex rebellion of 1601, which only had 300 supporters and lasted all of 12 hours. Furthermore, the lack of noble support ties in with the absence of dynastically aimed rebellions, showing again that 1549 was a turning point in the frequency of rebellions.

3 This paragraph is not clearly focused on the demands of the question. It does not explain why there were fewer dynastic rebellions after 1549.

3 The rebellions of Henry VII's reign contained numerous attempts at dynastic rivalry, shown in the rebellion of Simnel in his attempt to seize the throne at the Battle of Stoke (1487) and Warbeck (1497). With the exception of the Elizabethan plots after 1549, there were no dynastically aimed rebellions, unless Wyatt (1554) was indeed trying to get Elizabeth or Lady Jane Grey on the throne, although he said he was rebelling against Mary's proposed marriage to Philip of Spain. The fact that the motives of rebels changed also ties in with the lack of dynastic rebellions.

4 A strong section on socio-economic changes but too much of the evidence is asserted.

4 1549 marked a turning point in the different causes of rebellion. In 1549 we see the last rebellion that was really motivated by religion: the Western rebellion. After the short reign of Mary, there was religious stability for nearly 50 years. The rebellion of the Northern Earls in 1569 could be seen as a rebellion motivated by religion, however this is unlikely and it is much more likely that the rebellion was caused by the nobles' dwindling power. Moreover 1549 also marked a turning point in the absence of social and economic rebellions. Before this date there were many taxation rebellions such as in 1489 in Yorkshire (rebelling against taxes to pay for a French war), in 1497 in Cornwall (rebelling against taxes to pay for a Scottish war), and in the Amicable Grant rebellion of 1525 (again rebelling against taxes for a war with France). Other multi-causal disturbances reflected grievances against tax, such as the Pilgrimage of Grace (1536) against the 1534 subsidy and the Western rebellion (1549) against a sheep tax. Moreover the 1549 Kett's rebellion was the last to gain support for social and economic conditions against enclosures and rack-renting. The lack of support for social and economic issues was shown when only a handful of rebels supported the Oxfordshire rising in 1596. Furthermore there were less frequent rebellions motivated by this because of Elizabeth introducing poor law acts, culminating in the 1597 Act, which enabled the government to more readily manage the poor.

5 Makes a valid point but the explanation (the gentry's allegiance to county administration) needed to be more fully developed.

5 1549 also marked a turning point in the fact that yeomen and other landowning men were less motivated to rebel. Before this date, it had been the landowning class who had led rebellion, as shown in Robert Aske leading the Pilgrimage of Grace (1536) and Robert Kett leading Kett's rebellion (1549). Local priests and gentlemen also led the Western rebellion. After this date fewer men of this sort wanted to rebel because they had more duties in the administration of local towns. Elizabeth created more MPs, JPs and lieutenants. Indeed the

only rebellion caused by landowners after 1549 was led by Wyatt and he failed to muster much support.

6 In conclusion 1549 marked a turning point in the frequency of rebellions because there were so many before this date, and so few after. The most predominant reason for this was the decline of noble support and the increase in gentlemen and landowners supporting the Crown. Moreover the frequency changed because people became more loyal to the monarch. This was shown when Mary flattered her people with praise when seeking their support against Wyatt.

> 6 A fair conclusion though the reference to Mary is not a good example.

Assessment for essay 1

Uses relevant evidence but there are some inaccuracies; uses relevant historical terminology. A structured answer, generally well communicated. [Level III: 13 marks out of 20]

Satisfactory understanding of continuity and change and focus on the question set; but explanations are uneven in development – some assertions. Assesses several relevant factors but makes limited synoptic judgements over the whole period. [Level IV: 23 marks out of 40]

The overall mark of 36 is worth a low Grade C. To raise the grade, the answer needed to be more focused on explanations. These should be fully developed with knowledge used synoptically.

Essay 2: Why did 1549 mark a turning point in the frequency of rebellions in England during the period from 1485 to 1603?

1 The widespread disturbances of 1549 indicated a turning point in the Tudor period and after this time we can see a decline in the frequency and threat of rebellions. The main reasons for this change were the growing security of the Tudor dynasty, the Elizabethan Church Settlement of 1559, the changing attitude of the ruling elite and the changes which Tudor governments put in place.

> 1 A concise and focused start.

2 In the first half of the period, the Tudors had to deal with numerous pretenders and claimants, each seeking to overthrow them by acts of rebellion. Henry VII had to deal with Lovel, the Staffords, Simnel and Warbeck, imprison Warwick and Suffolk and, for much of his reign, combat Yorkist threats to his throne. Henry VIII also took steps to eliminate dynastic threats by executing Suffolk and surviving members of the de la Pole family between 1538 and 1541. Indeed the Pilgrimage of Grace may have triggered him into acting in this way even though the rebels were not actuated by a desire to overthrow him. However when Edward VI ascended the throne, there were no more rival claimants and rebellions after 1549 would be of a different nature.

> 2 This offers a sound synthesis of dynastic problems preceding 1549.

3 Secondly, a major cause of rebellion between 1536 and 1549 was the Protestant changes introduced by Henry VIII and Edward VI. These were directly responsible for the Pilgrimage of Grace and Western rebellions, as well as minor disturbances in 1547–48. However, largely due to the moderate religious policies implemented by Elizabeth after 1559 Catholics had less reason to rebel. Only in 1569–70 did

> 3 Though this paragraph provides a clear comparison of religious developments before and after 1549, the nature of the Elizabethan church after 1559 could be contrasted more fully with the theological reforms of 1549 that provoked rebellion.

disturbances occur in the north of England, and this region rebelled for political rather than for religious reasons. Significantly, equally conservative areas such as the West Country, Hampshire and Lancashire did not stir. Thus the Prayer Book rebellion of 1549 marked a turning point in the frequency of religiously motivated rebellions.

4 Very good paragraph. The main point is clearly made, and relevant examples covering the whole period are synoptically linked and explained.

4 Thirdly the widespread disorder among the commons during the 'camping time' and Kett's and the Western rebellions showed the nobility and gentry how potentially threatening the commons could be. This would have worried them especially as much of the anger was directed at them. Landowners were disliked by Kett's rebels for unlawfully enclosing land and a slogan of the Western rebels was 'kill the gentlemen'. The events of 1549, therefore, provoked a change. Earlier in the period the ruling elite had often led or played a major part in rebellion for example Lord Lovel and the Stafford brothers rebelled in 1486, Lords Darcy and Hussey were involved in the Pilgrimage of Grace in 1536 and the leader of the Yorkshire rebellion in 1489 was Sir John Egremont. After 1549 however the nobility and gentry were more allied with the government and only rebelled when they had nothing to lose, as was the case for the Earls of Northumberland and Westmorland in 1569 and the Earl of Essex in 1601. Not only were the ruling elite unlikely to rebel but they were able to help control the lower orders. This meant that in the later years of the period rebellion was less frequent and also less threatening as they often could not gain support. For example, in 1554 four simultaneous risings were planned at various locations across England and Wales, however due to lack of support only Wyatt in Kent was able to go ahead. Also the fact that the ruling elite would not get involved meant that rebellions like the Oxfordshire rising in 1596 had only commons' support and found it difficult to recruit more men. Just four rebels were involved in this rising.

5 Government responses to rebellion are well assessed and explained. Focus remains on the nature of 1549 as a turning point.

5 The events of 1549 also opened the eyes of the government to the potential threat of widespread resistance. This fear of popular disorder is clearly shown by the harsh punishment of the Oxfordshire rebels, who were tortured and executed despite having posed very little threat. The government therefore introduced policies to reduce the risk of rebellion. Immediately after 1549 Somerset who was a weak leader was replaced by Northumberland who took a much more hard-line approach to religious reform and was generally seen as a stronger leader. He proved himself by putting down some of the 1549 disorders. The policies that most reduced the risk of rebellion however are clearly seen in Elizabeth's reign. One change was that the state had taken responsibility for the poor whereas previously the ruling elite had taken responsibility. The Statute of Labourers (1563) helped to stabilise the labour market and strengthen the economy while poor laws of 1572, 1576 and 1597 demonstrated the desire of the Crown to help the deserving poor. This also reinforced the polarisation of the rich and poor, which was naturally occurring, and meant the ruling elite was less likely to get involved in rebellion. At the same time, real

progress was made to alleviate the suffering of unemployed and poor subjects, who turned to the church, town and state for assistance, rather than seek to bring their complaints to the attention of the authorities by demonstrations and rebellion.

6 Also post-1549, the ruling elite was more allied with the government. Henry VII had first rewarded his loyal nobles and Crown servants with long tenures in office and this steadily built up an affinity between the monarch and his subjects. This feature was reinforced by the Crown offering them positions of power, such as JPs or lords lieutenant in the counties, and it was continued when Henry VIII granted monastic lands to his nobles, gentry and court servants. This disposal of royal patronage meant that the nobility and gentry came to develop a vested interest in supporting the government, and the longer the Tudors remained on the throne, the less likely the gentry and political elite would participate in rebellion. By Elizabeth's reign, there were few nobles and even fewer gentry willing to risk their family fortunes as well as their lives by supporting rebellion. On the contrary, they had a real desire to see domestic peace and stability continue indefinitely. If local issues arose, the gentry were encouraged to voice them via their MP in parliament. In this way, economic and social grievances, which had given rise to rebellions in the period before 1549, came to be raised, debated and even acted upon democratically in the parliaments after 1549. Not all complaints were resolved but discussion rather than demonstration seemed to be the way forward.

> 6 Good synoptic explanations.

7 In conclusion, I think that 1549 marks a turning point in the frequency of rebellions mainly because of the changing attitude of the ruling elite, which resulted in the growing polarisation between the rich and poor. This was also encouraged by the government's actions and had the result that rebellions in the later years of the period had only commons' support.

> 7 A fair summary of the key arguments.

Assessment for essay 2

Uses accurate and relevant evidence and a range of appropriate historical terminology. Answer is clearly structured, coherent and well communicated. **[Level IA: 19 marks out of 20]**

Very good level of understanding of key concepts; answer is consistently focused on the question; very good level of explanation and synthesis of the whole period supported by a range of accurate factual details. **[Level IB: 33 marks out of 40]**

The overall mark of 52 is a clear Grade A. The essay displays the key requirements of a very good answer. It is consistently focused, synoptic and informative. To gain a Grade A*, an analysis of or reference to some of the tax revolts is required since these were a characteristic of rebellions in 1489, 1497, 1525, 1536 and 1549 but not thereafter.

The Impact of Disturbances on Tudor Governments

OVERVIEW

This chapter looks at how Tudor governments responded to rebellions and the changes that resulted from them:

- How did the Tudors deal with rebellions? Strategy, tactics, fate of the rebels
- The effects of rebellions on government and society: Crown servants, religious developments, policy changes, Ireland, foreign affairs
- Conclusion: were Tudor governments ever seriously threatened by rebellion?
- An assessment of two A2 essays: Grades A and D

At first sight we might expect disturbances to have had little impact on government and society. Few administrations were likely to make concessions to rebels, and so appear vulnerable to further demands, and almost all rebellions ended in failure. Yet upon examination, it is evident that changes did take place. Sometimes they happened immediately; more often they occurred over a period of time but nevertheless owed their origin to a rebellion. Governments understood that if they were to reduce the likelihood of future disturbances, then it was sensible to consider why a rebellion had occurred and whether policy changes were needed.

Note making

Use the headings and sub-headings as the framework for your notes. Once you have read a section, begin to extract the appropriate information and examples, ensuring that you first understand the significance of the material and how it might be used to answer an essay question.

1 | How did Tudor governments deal with rebellions?

Strategy

Key question
How did rulers find out about and act on information concerning rebellions?

Consult advisers

As soon as the government discovered there was trouble in the kingdom, talks were held between the monarch and a select group of councillors to decide on the best course of action. Henry VII consulted one or more of his most trusted household servants, and occasionally convened a meeting of nobles in a Great Council. This is what occurred in February 1487 when the king first heard that Simnel was planning to invade England. Henry VIII, on the other hand, left the strategy of combating rebellion to his council and principal ministers – Wolsey in the 1520s and Cromwell in the 1530s – but insisted on being kept informed. A major criticism that was levelled against the Duke of Somerset in 1549 was that he did not regularly consult or heed the advice of the Privy Council on how to deal with rebellion. Both Mary and Elizabeth, on the other hand, relied on their secretaries and councillors to determine the strategy and suppression of rebellions: Elizabeth was well served and all disturbances in England were effectively handled but Mary received conflicting advice during Wyatt's revolt. When London seemed open to attack in January 1554, the council began to panic. According to Renard, the Imperial ambassador and Mary's confidant, the council was 'quarrelling, taking sides and blaming one another'. Some suggested they should enlist the help of Imperial troops, while others, notably Gardiner, urged the queen to leave the city. Her decision to stay saved her throne and almost certainly her life.

Information gathering

When a rebellion broke out, governments needed to find out as much as possible about its size, location and nature. Did it threaten the life of the monarch or was it a protest against government policies, and were any nobles or gentry involved? Getting reliable information was never easy and delays in communication sometimes explained apparent inactivity and unwise decisions by councillors as they waited on the latest news. For example, when Henry VIII heard that Sawley Abbey had been reoccupied by monks in 1536, he wrote to the Earl of Derby ordering him to execute the abbot, monks and rebel captains, without appreciating that the earl, who was heavily outnumbered and some distance from the abbey, was in no position to carry out the order.

The Duke of Somerset faced a similar communication problem in 1549. In trying to decide the right strategy to deal with the Western rebellion that was occurring some 200 miles away, he had to rely on out-of-date reports. Thus on 26 June he wrote to the Devon JPs that they should try to persuade the ringleaders to return home and use as an argument the rebels' unnatural behaviour, the dangers they were causing national security and the need to adopt lawful remedies for their grievances. If the JPs failed (which was a near certainty), they were to try to prevent a large assembly from gathering, to raise troops from local gentry and await reinforcements in the shape of Lord Russell. What Somerset did not know was that by this stage, three JPs had already tried and failed to reason with the rebels, most local gentry had either joined the rebellion or gone into hiding, the combined size of the rebellion exceeded 6000, the Cornish and Devon protesters had joined forces and they were already camped outside Exeter.

Most of the Tudors employed spies, secret agents and informers to find out what was happening and to forward intelligence reports, sometimes from inside rebel camps or within the conspirators' circle. Henry VII's agents tracked rebels who had escaped from the battle of Bosworth, such as the Stafford brothers and Lord Lovel. These rebels had first taken sanctuary in Colchester Abbey before fleeing west to Worcester and Yorkshire respectively, but Henry's agents followed them. The Staffords were tracked down to Culham church near Oxford where they were arrested, while Lovel was forced to leave the country after his abortive uprising in Yorkshire. Elizabeth came to rely heavily on Francis Walsingham's gathering of intelligence. He employed over 50 agents at home and overseas who enabled him to detect conspiracies, identify and arrest suspects and reduce the likelihood of rebellions from occurring. The ineffectiveness of continental schemes to stir up domestic rebellions after 1572 owed a great deal to his vigilance.

Henry VII also had an extensive network of spies in various European courts who kept him informed of the pretenders' whereabouts and who their supporters were. For instance, men like Sir Edward Brampton in Flanders and Sir Robert Clifford, who infiltrated Yorkist circles in England, supplied the king with vital information about Warbeck. It was principally due to secret intelligence that Henry discovered the treason of Sir William Stanley and arrested him in 1495 before he could join up with the pretender. Attached to many **bonds of allegiance** that Henry imposed on suspected rebels were conditions that obliged them to inform the council if they heard any seditious information, and this requirement may well have deterred individuals from further involvement and enabled the king to gather useful intelligence.

Key term

Bonds of allegiance Financial and legal penalties were imposed on rebels and on anyone of doubtful allegiance.

Essay focus

Look at Essays 1 and 2 on pages 97–101. Both refer to the nobility who helped to suppress disturbances, but note that Essay 2, paragraph 2, gives more examples, including references to Ireland. It is all too easy to overlook the Irish rebellions but they should be used to illustrate both similarities to and differences from rebellions in England.

Role of the nobility

Once news was confirmed that a rebellion had broken out, letters were written to JPs and sheriffs of a disturbed region ordering them to deal with the problem. Nobles and councillors who held estates or lived in the vicinity of the disturbance were only called upon to restore order if the JPs proved to be ineffectual. This is what occurred in Suffolk in 1525 when the Amicable Grant protesters threatened to march on London. The Dukes of Norfolk and Suffolk assumed command and successfully dealt with the rebellion. It was in the nobles' interests to contain the unrest and the government certainly did not expect the disturbances to spread to neighbouring areas or to get out of hand.

Lincolnshire rising

Ten years later a more serious uprising occurred in Lincolnshire. On 5 October 1536 the Privy Council first learned that 20,000 rebels were preparing to converge on the county town of Lincoln. Worse, the sheriff Sir Edward Dymoke, the mayor Robert Sutton, several leading gentry like William Willoughby, and an MP Vincent Grantham had out of sympathy or fear also joined the rebels. Henry VIII's response was to command Lord Hussey, the most senior peer in the county, to raise his tenants and deal with the rising. The king was naturally alarmed to discover that the elderly lord had first considered mediating with the rebels and then, on failing to raise enough loyal men, had fled to the safety of Nottingham. Again it fell to the dukes of Suffolk and Norfolk to suppress the rising but due to the number of rebels involved, the Earl of Huntingdon in Leicestershire and the Earl of Shrewsbury at Sheffield were also requested to stand by.

Duke of Somerset's handling of rebellions

A similar situation occurred in 1549. The Duke of Somerset first heard that there were disturbances in Devon and Cornwall in June but he considered the problem to be an isolated incident that could be dealt with locally. Unfortunately the absence of a powerful privy councillor and major landowner in the south-west proved a serious weakness that he had not foreseen. Lord John Russell, who had estates in Devon, was the High Steward of the Duchy of Cornwall and Lord Privy Seal but spent most of his time in London. The most powerful Cornish landowner was Sir John Arundell, a former privy councillor, but out of favour with the Protestant regime. In any case, he was living at his country house in Dorset. The onus for dealing with the risings in Devon and Cornwall therefore fell to the sheriffs, JPs and local mayors, but they were simply not strong enough to contain the rebellion.

The Duke of Somerset decided to send Sir Peter Carew, a former sheriff of Devon, and an experienced soldier to persuade the rebels to disperse, but this proved to be a disastrous decision. Carew was impetuous, lacked diplomacy and was a devout Protestant. When he tried to reason with the Catholic rebels at Crediton, one of his men set fire to a barn and thereafter the rebels believed the gentry intended to 'spoil and destroy them'. What had started as a local protest against the new prayer book had quickly become something much more serious.

In the same year, it was the Lord Lieutenant of Norfolk, the Marquis of Northampton, who was ordered to deal with Kett and his rebels. As in Devon and Cornwall, there was no resident privy councillor in Norfolk, the prominent Howard family was in disgrace and none of the leading gentry was willing to take a stand against the rebels. Moreover the sheriff, Sir Edmund Wyndham, had no troops with which to threaten the host and had retreated to the comparative safety of Norwich castle.

Elizabethan Privy Council

Elizabeth's council took prompt action when disturbances occurred in north Oxfordshire in November 1596. Earlier that year, the Privy Council had alerted all sheriffs, lords lieutenant and JPs of probable food riots, and told them to be on the look out for gangs seizing grain and food supplies. The Oxfordshire county gentry had been informed of a possible plot to attack Sir Henry Norris's house and four men were arrested before the revolt gathered momentum. Essex's rebellion of 1601 was similarly dealt with before it got out of hand. The Privy Council knew that Essex was planning something dramatic: either a coup, which would entail seizing the queen and capturing the Tower and its arsenal, or a demonstration of noble force in the city. The sheriff and Lord Mayor of London therefore took appropriate defensive action. They ordered the closure of the city gates, heavy artillery from the Tower was prepared and the Earl of Nottingham deputed to draw up sufficient cannon to blast a hole in Essex's house if he resisted arrest. When Essex saw that his attempted revolt failed to get the backing of Londoners, he submitted without a fight.

Henry VII's personal supervision

Unlike other Tudor rulers, Henry VII dealt with most serious disturbances himself. He appointed Sir Giles Daubeny to lead his forces against Simnel, the Cornish rebels and Warbeck, and on each occasion the king was present in the field or heading towards the rebels' camp when they dispersed. Henry was unsure whom to trust and only relied with certainty upon his closest advisers and men who had been with him in exile. Sir Richard Edgecombe, Controller of the Household, and Sir William Tyler, Keeper of the Jewels, were therefore sent to apprehend Lovel in the North Riding of Yorkshire in 1486. A year later, when **commissions of array** were issued to defend the more troublesome areas of England that might support Simnel, Henry relied on nobles who had fought with him at Bosworth and a handful of ex-Ricardians whom he was prepared to trust: the Earl of Northumberland secured the far north, the Earl of Oxford watched over East Anglia, the Earl of Derby reported upon south Lancashire and the Duke of Bedford held the Welsh borders. When Yorkshire broke into revolt in 1489 and the Earl of Northumberland was

Key term

Commissions of array
Authority given by the Crown to nobles to raise troops.

murdered, Henry assembled a force even larger than the one that had fought at Stoke, and the rebels fled as the royal army approached York.

The Cornish rebellion of 1497 also required a military solution but was altogether a more threatening affair. When Henry first heard that a large group of rebels was marching towards London, he expected the leading families in the south-west and south of England to deal with it. At the time his attention was directed towards Scotland and the threat of war presented by James IV in support of the pretender Warbeck. Already a royal army was heading north although its designated commander, Daubeny, was still in London. News that the Cornish rebels had been able to pass through Devon, Somerset, Wiltshire and Hampshire without any noble resistance alarmed the king. Henry acted decisively. He moved from London to Woodstock and then to Wallingford before gathering troops at Henley, well out of range of the rebels. He also recalled Daubeny and wrote to Edmund de la Pole in Oxfordshire, Rhys ap Thomas in south Wales and the Earl of Oxford in Norfolk to raise as many men as possible. It was these men who defeated the rebels at the battle of Blackheath.

Ireland

The Tudors treated Ireland like the northern counties. The council in Dublin received its instructions from London and military aid might come from England but the Crown's representative, the Lord Deputy, had no JPs, only a sheriff and local nobles to call on as his first line of defence, and they were not always willing to help. Moreover, he rarely had sufficient resources to deal with disturbances. Until 1534 there was only a small garrison of around 700 troops in the Pale near Dublin and although this number was periodically increased, reaching 2000 in the 1570s, there were never enough troops to deal with rebellions if they broke out simultaneously in different provinces.

The principal strategy was to defend English interests and areas under English rule and to play for time. Elizabeth preferred diplomacy to military solutions: it was cheaper and might pave the way for long-term solutions. Her treatment of Shane O'Neill illustrates this point. In 1558 Shane murdered his half brother when he heard that Mary Tudor had conferred the earldom of Tyrone on him. On Elizabeth's accession, she invited Shane to London but he refused to come until 1561 when she accepted his confession to the murder and to causing rebellion in Ulster. In return Elizabeth recognised him as Captain of Tyrone and Lord of Tyrconnel. In 1563 she went so far as to acknowledge him as 'The O'Neill', unwisely ignoring the sound advice of Sussex, her Lord Deputy in Ireland, who warned, 'If Shane be overthrown, all is settled; if Shane settle, all is overthrown'. On his return to Ireland, Shane continued to disregard the law: he raided the lands of rival clansmen, kidnapped hostages and dabbled in high treason. In 1566 Elizabeth finally abandoned her attempts to reconcile him and turned to a military solution.

Key question
How did the Tudors
seek to combat
rebellion?

Key term

De facto
By deed, as opposed
to *de jure*, 'by law'.
Henry VII
descended from an
illegitimate line and
based his claim to
the English throne
on the fact that he
had killed the
alleged usurper,
Richard III, in
battle.

Tactics

Buy time

Tudor governments had limited resources at their disposal: they
had no standing army, no police force and, at times, very little
money. Their main weapon was their claim to be legitimate rulers
(at least *de facto* if not *de jure*) and the fact that they had been
anointed with holy oil and so derived their authority from God.
Anyone who fought against them would therefore be condemned
as a sinner as well as a traitor. All governments stressed the need to
uphold order and used a range of tactics to persuade rebels to
disperse. In essence, governments sought to buy time until they
had enough troops to call the rebels' bluff, and then and only
then did they consider fighting a battle.

Governments wanted to avoid violent confrontations: the
outcome was uncertain and always expensive whether in terms of
finance or casualties. It was common for pardons to be offered to
rebels if they would first disperse and this tactic certainly weakened
the morale of some rebels and reduced their numbers. Rebels at
Stoke, Blackheath, Clyst St Mary and Dussindale were all offered a
general pardon on the eve of battle if they surrendered, and a
royal herald on two occasions in 1554 gave Wyatt's rebels a chance
to go home in peace. Moreover, endemic disorder reflected badly
on any administration. Most governments saw no mileage in
negotiating with rebels: it was a sign of weakness and would only
serve to encourage future rebel leaders. Yet confrontations had to
be skilfully handled and, as Wolsey discovered to his cost,
circumstances could easily spiral out of control.

Wolsey and the Amicable Grant

Wolsey received reports in the first week of April 1525 that a small
number of people were refusing to pay the Amicable Grant. At
first the king's minister took an uncompromising stance towards
reluctant taxpayers and sympathetic commissioners. He told the
Lord Mayor of London, Sir William Bailey, 'beware and resist not,
nor ruffle not in this case, for it may fortune to cost some their
heads', and Lord Lisle was threatened with execution if he failed
to collect taxes in Berkshire. When the Duke of Suffolk reported
that protesters were becoming more vociferous, Wolsey advised
stiff retribution and accused the duke of being oversensitive.

By 25 April 1525 it was clear that Wolsey's bullying tactics were
not working. Henry may well have seen for himself the growing
discontent in London, and informed the Lord Mayor and
Aldermen that the Amicable Grant would be halved. However,
none of the commissioners outside London was informed and
soon there were reports of hundreds of protesters gathering in
Kent, Warwickshire, Essex, Norfolk and Suffolk. When some 4000
protesters gathered at Lavenham in Suffolk, it fell to the dukes of
Suffolk and Norfolk to handle this crisis. And they had a problem.
Suffolk's army of retainers was much smaller than the rebels'
forces and he was unsure of the reliability of his own men. He

informed Wolsey: 'They [his retainers] would defend him from all perils, if he hurt not their neighbours, but against their neighbours they would not fight.' While he waited for Norfolk to join him with more troops, Suffolk tried to contain the rebellion by destroying bridges 'so that their assembly was somewhat letted [impeded]'. On 11 May Suffolk and Norfolk heard a deputation of 60 rebels at Bury St Edmunds, warned them of the heinous consequences of rebellion and finally succeeded in persuading them to submit before anyone died.

Essay focus

Essay 1, paragraph 3 on page 97, analyses the Amicable Grant very simplistically; in contrast, Essay 2, paragraph 4 on page 100, shows how the rebellion can be used to illustrate the role of diplomacy. In order to score high marks, you must explain and evaluate your examples and not just assert them as evidence.

Henry VIII and the Pilgrimage of Grace

Henry VIII and Cromwell took the same hard line in 1536 when they faced rebellions in Lincolnshire, Yorkshire and other northern counties. The size of rebel armies and the involvement of nobles, gentry and clergy so alarmed the king that he allowed the Duke of Norfolk to negotiate with them on condition that they agreed to go home. More than two weeks passed before Norfolk and Shrewsbury had enough troops to advance north of the Trent. Their 8000 men, however, were dwarfed by over 30,000 rebels waiting at Pontefract castle. Norfolk decided to arrange a truce with the gentry, promise whatever was needed to disperse their army and, once the leaders were separated from the rank and file, pacify the disaffected areas in revolt. The king favoured a military solution from the outset but bowed to Norfolk's more diplomatic approach. Moreover, the duke had assured Henry that 'whatsoever promise I shall make unto the rebels (if any such be the advice of others make) for surely I shall observe no part thereof for any respect of that other might call mine honour'. When he met the rebels' spokesmen on 27 October, he only talked to the gentry and nobles and Darcy later reflected how the commons feared they might be betrayed 'because we tarried a while about the entreaty'. Norfolk had succeeded in stemming the advancing rebels, separating the rank and file from the leaders, and escorted four of them to Windsor to meet the king.

Henry's tactic now was to stand firm and browbeat the emissaries into submission. He refused to discuss their petition which he found 'general, dark and obscure', he rejected pleas to reverse his policies which he claimed had been misrepresented, and he told them to go away and clarify their grievances before arranging a second meeting with Norfolk. It was not what the rebels wanted to hear. Moreover, their representatives were kept waiting in London for over three weeks and many of the commons and several gentry suspected they might not return. A meeting between 40 pilgrims and Norfolk finally took place on 6 December 1536 when the duke promised that a parliament would resolve the issues behind the rebellion, there would be no more monastic suppressions and the rebels would receive a general pardon. Aske accepted the terms, tore off his badge, and declared, 'We will wear no badge nor sign but the badge of our sovereign Lord'. The rebel captains followed suit and the rebellion was over – or so they thought. In fact Henry spent the next month gathering information, interviewing the gentry and nobles involved in the uprising and deciding what to do about the north.

Somerset and the Western rebellion

The Duke of Somerset's response to the news early in July 1549 that Exeter was under attack was to send a series of letters to the rebel camp urging them to desist, offering them a free pardon if they did and dire punishment if they did not:

- A proclamation dated 11 July threatened to forfeit their land and property with the intention of creating 'a terror and division among the rebels themselves', but it had no effect.
- On 12 July he pardoned any guilty of 'riotous assembly' if they made a 'humble submission'. None did.
- On 16 July another proclamation pardoned submissive rioters but future offenders were threatened with martial law. There was still no reaction.

Somerset, perhaps unwisely, had not only promised to listen to the rebels' grievances, he even guaranteed to let the leaders sit on committees to implement reforms. He may have been sincere in his intentions since he did read the rebel grievances and, in the case of the Western rebels, believed they had acted 'rather out of ignorance than of malice' but his fellow councillors begged to differ. William Paget consistently criticised his leniency and both Herbert and Warwick favoured swift repression. Pre-emptive action had worked in Oxfordshire, Leicestershire and Kent, where rioters were summarily executed, and they pressed Somerset to send troops to Devon and Norfolk. He preferred conciliation and for several weeks ignored their advice.

Propaganda

Propaganda was widely used by governments in trying to persuade rebels to give up and return home. Cromwell employed a team of writers to condemn rebellion in 1536 and one of them, Richard Morrison, attacked the rebels in his pamphlet *A lamentation in which is showed what ruin and destruction cometh of seditious rebellion*. 'Obedience is the badge of a Christian man', he declared. Henry himself replied to the Lincoln Articles on 10 October rejecting their petition and ordering them to disperse. They were, he said, 'one of the most brute and beastly of the whole realm', and he warned that Suffolk was gathering a 100,000-strong army which he would command. This was a wild exaggeration. Later that month, the king, in response to the Pilgrimage of Grace, penned *Answers to the Rebels*, in which he defended his policies and ministers, and ordered Morrison to hit them with some choice words. His *Remedy for Sedition* condemned disobedience in the body politic and he asked rhetorically, 'when every man will rule, who shall obey?' Unfortunately, it had little if any impact on Aske and his supporters.

Essay focus

Essay 2, paragraph 3 on page 99, develops the concept of obedience and deference to a legitimate authority – see also Chapter 4, pages 103–7. Of course, we will never know for certain the extent to which people were affected by government and church propaganda.

The Edwardian government in 1549 also undertook a lively propaganda campaign both during and after the summer disturbances. Thomas Cranmer attacked the Western rebels' religious ignorance and brazen effrontery, and compared them to magpies and parrots that 'be taught to speak and yet understood not one word what they say'. Philip Nichols, a Devon Protestant, was commissioned to write a lengthy criticism of the rebel articles, which he condemned on moral and religious grounds. One of the more skilful pieces of propaganda was John Cheke's *The Hurt of Sedition*, in which he compared the conduct of Exeter and Norwich. The citizens of Exeter, he declared, were to be commended because 'being in the midst of rebels unvitteled, unfurnished, unprepared, for so long a siege did hold out the continual and dangerous assault of the rebels'. In contrast the people of Norwich were censured, and their behaviour 'white livered' because they had 'sought more safeguard than honesty, and private hope more than common quietness'. Significantly, the mayor of Exeter was later knighted whereas the mayor of Norwich was obliged to explain his co-operation with Kett's rebels.

Writing polemics against rebellion of course had only a limited impact; few could read and rebels were not interested in lessons on morality. Perhaps the circulation of court propaganda did more to buttress the morale of the government than alter the views of rebels. Governments also used speeches and sermons to persuade rebels to disperse, though these too had only a limited impact. When Russell arrived at Honiton in east Devon to confront the Western rebels, he took with him a handful of preachers whom Somerset advised should proclaim the Gospel to the rebels. The decision to send Protestant preachers to assuage Catholic rebels seems at best wildly optimistic and, of course, their words were roughly received.

Somerset also sent preachers to appeal to rebels at their camp on Mousehold Heath, near Norwich. Robert Watson, a Protestant, tried to appease the rebels and, although they shared his theological views, they were not prepared to listen to platitudes about duty and obedience. Archbishop Cranmer saw the need to broaden the message and prepared sermons to be read in parish churches that emphasised the sin of rebellion. He declared, 'If they [the people] will be true gospellers, let them be obedient, meek, patient in adversity and long-suffering, and in no wise rebel against the laws and magistrates'. This may have had some effect after the rebellions had ended but cut no ice with the rebels at the time. As Matthew Parker, a young Cambridge scholar, discovered when he visited Kett's camp, the rebels were in no mood to be placated or lectured into submission, and he narrowly escaped being captured.

Pre-emptive measures

Governments from time to time also applied political pressure to undermine rebels and so weaken their cause. Henry VII in particular took pre-emptive measures against any suspects before they became too dangerous. In 1487 a papal bull that excommunicated all rebels was translated, printed and publicly proclaimed by the clergy. He produced the same papal condemnation on the eve of the battle of Stoke and at Blackheath and many rebels surrendered rather than risk eternal damnation. At Easter 1487 the real Earl of Warwick was paraded at St Paul's and introduced to visiting ambassadors to convince them that Simnel was an impostor, a proclamation ordered all rumour-mongers to be pilloried, and the king made two significant arrests. The estates of the queen mother, Elizabeth Woodville, were seized and she was confined to a nunnery, and her son by a former marriage, the Marquis of Dorset, was put in the Tower. This was a judicious move. Both had a history of intrigue and Henry was aware that a Yorkist, the Earl of Lincoln, was leading the rebellion. To combat the subsequent threat of Warbeck, pressure was put on diplomats to deny him political support wherever he went in the 1490s. Charles VIII of France expelled him and his supporters, Kildare in Ireland was persuaded to renounce him, trade sanctions were imposed on Burgundy until he was ejected, and James IV of Scotland, after playing host between 1496 and 1497, expelled him when Henry threatened to go to war.

The king was equally busy domestically. In the summer of 1493, he went to Warwickshire to inform potential trouble-makers that there was no future in supporting Warbeck. Fifteen counties were under suspicion and investigated by commissioners. When Desmond offered his support in Ireland in 1494, Henry deprived him of his office of Constable of Limerick castle and put his arch-rival in his place. In January 1495 Clifford had discovered the names of several English nobles and gentry willing to back the pretender. Among them were Sir William Stanley, the Lord Chamberlain and the king's step-uncle, and Lord Fitzwater, Steward of the Household. In all 14 men were attainted and four executed, including Stanley. When Warbeck did try to land in England in 1495, Henry's men were waiting. Fifty-one were caught and hanged, and a further 150 put on trial. For his part, Henry preferred to be on the move. He visited the Midlands, travelled to Stanley's lands in the north-west, before returning to Nottingham. Ever vigilant, Henry was never outwitted.

Mary also demonstrated the virtues of a pre-emptive strike. Her councillors first heard whispers that there was a conspiracy to depose her in December 1553. The council acted speedily. They interrogated Edward Courtenay and identified Carew, Suffolk, Croft and Wyatt as the main leaders. Circular letters were sent to the relevant counties in January 1554 denouncing the plot and local authorities took preventive measures. The sheriff of Devon garrisoned Exeter, which so alarmed Carew that he fled to France; the Earl of Huntingdon searched for Suffolk in the Midlands, which discouraged others from joining him; and Croft lost his nerve and disappeared into North Wales. By late January the council seemed to have the situation largely under control. Only Wyatt remained a problem.

Elizabeth also acted decisively when required. She first heard rumours at court in the summer of 1569 that several disgruntled nobles were plotting to bring down her chief secretary William Cecil, secure the succession of Mary Stuart, and marry Mary to the Duke of Norfolk. Elizabeth acted quickly. Norfolk was denied permission to marry and nobles such as Arundel, Pembroke, Lumley and Leicester all disassociated themselves from an alleged plot. In November Norfolk sent a letter to his brother-in-law, the Earl of Westmorland, forbidding him from starting a revolt in his name. When news reached the queen that a rebellion had broken out, she took further steps to safeguard her throne. Norfolk was lodged in the Tower, Mary was moved 30 miles south to a new location near Coventry, and the President of the Council of the North, Sussex, was ordered to suppress the uprising.

Ireland

Tactics in handling rebellions in Ireland were similar to those employed in England. Rebels were offered pardons and promises, rival clan chiefs were encouraged to assist the Crown through offers of reward, and steps were taken to raise a sufficiently large loyalist army, while most commanders tried to avoid a military confrontation. Wet marshy terrain, poor communications, problems in recruiting troops and the increasing hostility of native Irish towards the English, all contributed to the government's difficulties. Unlike in England, Irish rebellions had to be treated like wars of attrition that could last for several years and still end without a satisfactory outcome. The Munster rebellion went on for four years and Fitzmaurice eluded capture, the Geraldine rebellion lasted for nearly five years, even though Fitzmaurice was killed within weeks of its start, and the national rising of Tyrone, which lasted for more than eight years, only ended when the earl reached a deal with the Lord Deputy.

Raise troops

The decision to raise troops was not taken lightly and, in several cases, governments delayed giving the order for a variety of reasons. First, paying troops was an expensive business and if the men were not paid they became as much of a threat as the rebels themselves. Somerset, for instance, faced the prospect of having to suppress revolts and rebellions in over half of all English counties in the summer of 1549 as well as waging war against Scotland. Not only was the Treasury short of money, Somerset was short of soldiers. From the outset he was more concerned about disturbances in Oxfordshire, Buckinghamshire, Berkshire, Cambridge, Hertfordshire and Lincolnshire, which were much closer to London. As a result, he had to deploy his troops prudently, which explains why the two major rebellions in Devon and Norfolk took so long to suppress and why he was the only ruler to employ foreign mercenaries.

Second, the government relied on the nobility and gentry to provide retainers for their army but this brought hazards. Licences were required to hold more than a reasonable number of retainers and if any noble put his men in armour and prepared to fight without first receiving a royal commission, he knew he was technically committing treason. This dilemma faced Henry VIII's commanders in October 1536. The Earl of Shrewsbury knew that he was likely to be called on to serve the king and in his keenness to appear as patriotic as possible and raise a large retinue mustered troops in anticipation, writing to his friends 'to get as many able men as ye can make, well horsed and harnessed'. The Earl of Huntingdon, on the other hand, preferred to wait for official authorisation. In fact Henry seriously underestimated the size of the rebel host in comparison with the small number of loyalist troops available to his commanders. He bragged that at least 40,000 would soon arrive from the Midlands and Wales when in practice the Duke of Suffolk had half this number and many of his men were poorly equipped.

Troop shortages: Henry VII and Simnel and the Cornish rebellions

A shortage of troops was a perennial problem. In every rebellion where rebel armies were drawn up, at some stage their numbers exceeded that of the Crown.

Henry VII was fortunate in that he had six weeks in which to prepare for battle against Simnel's forces and the king showed his skill at military organisation. He set up his command at Kenilworth castle in Warwickshire. From there he could deal with an invasion from either the east or west of England, or quickly return to London if necessary, while he was busy raising money to pay for retainers, urging nobles to muster as many men as possible, and sifting intelligence reports from his agents. When he finally prepared for battle at East Stoke in Nottinghamshire, he had the cream of the English aristocracy with him: a duke, five earls, a viscount, four barons and their retainers numbering 15,000, perhaps twice the size of the rebel army. In contrast 10 years later, Daubeny was unable to prevent the Cornish rebels from reaching Blackheath because he had insufficient men and held back until he was joined by Rhys ap Thomas, the Earl of Oxford and the king himself.

Henry VIII and the Pilgrimage of Grace

Henry VIII was caught by surprise in October 1536. No sooner had he detailed the Duke of Suffolk to scale down his military operations in Lincolnshire than news reached the council that the

East Riding of Yorkshire was in revolt. Plans for royal troops to assemble in Bedfordshire to deal with the earlier rising had been cancelled and there was word that further revolts had broken out in Richmond and Lancashire. Worse, Henry heard that many gentry and some lesser nobles had defected to the rebels or gone into hiding. Not until 13 October does Henry seem to have realised just how serious was the situation. At last letters were issued commissioning nobles to raise armies and the Duke of Norfolk was told to take as many men as he could, join the Earl of Shrewsbury and hold a line of the river Trent. The king had a number of problems. One was that he did not know whom to trust. He always doubted the honesty of Lord Darcy, which was confirmed when he surrendered Pontefract castle to the rebels. He also had his doubts about the Earl of Derby although these proved groundless. Second, more than two weeks were to pass before Norfolk and Shrewsbury had enough troops to advance north of the Trent.

Western rebellion

In 1549 Lord Russell faced worse odds when he arrived at Honiton in east Devon to deal with the Western rebellion. He had with him a retinue of some 300 men but ranged against him were 6000 rebels. In the course of the next few weeks, he raised some 2000 soldiers but since most of the gentry in nearby counties were unwilling to volunteer their services, all he could do was wait for reinforcements and hope that the besieged city of Exeter could hold out. He had to wait over five weeks. Finally at the end of July, Wilton appeared with 400 English troops and some 1400 German, Swiss and Italian mercenaries, whom Somerset originally planned on sending to Scotland. Only then was Russell prepared to risk a battle. A similar situation arose in Norfolk. Once Somerset recognised that a military solution was the only option, he decided to send an army under the Marquis of Northampton. He was accompanied by two privy councillors, two peers, a secretary of state, five JPs and leading Norfolk gentry, which Somerset deemed strong enough to deal with the rebels, but Northampton was only given 1500 troops. He had no trouble entering Norwich because the rebels had withdrawn to their camp a few hundred metres away but his army was outnumbered 10 to 1. It only took one day of fierce fighting before he decided to leave for the safety of Cambridge and await reinforcements. Not until 24 August did the Earl of Warwick with 7500 troops appear in Norfolk with Northampton in tow and together they reoccupied the city.

Wyatt's rebellion

Mary's council in 1554 believed they had reduced the threat from Wyatt and his co-conspirators to a manageable size but his sudden appearance at Rochester, Kent, with 2000 men revealed the frailty of the government's position. The queen in fact compounded her problems by insisting that the Duke of Norfolk should lead her army. Although a veteran of many military campaigns, the duke was now over 80, uninspiring and unable to discipline his 500 'whitecoats', most of whom deserted to Wyatt's army. Worse, neither the sheriff of Kent nor the principal landowner in the county, Lord Abergavenny, was able to raise many men. As rebel forces were reported to be gathering in several towns, Mary also learned that hordes of London trained bands had changed sides. In this crisis she revealed her Tudor character. She bought time by twice offering Wyatt a truce to negotiate with the rebels and appointed lords Pembroke and Clinton to raise an army. On 1 February she played her trump card. She spoke to a crowd at the Guildhall, declared that she would only marry Philip with her council's consent and called on the assembled citizens to support her. Her speech had its desired effect as Londoners rallied behind their legitimate ruler. London bridge was blocked, other crossing points were damaged and barricades were thrown up around the city. When Wyatt tried to enter London on 7 February, some 40 men died in the fighting. Pembroke repelled the attack and Wyatt surrendered, unwilling to sacrifice any more of his supporters.

Northern Earls' rebellion

Sussex, President of the Council of the North, realised that he faced a difficult task when he heard that the northern earls were in revolt in 1569. He could raise 400 cavalry and a small number of county militia of doubtful reliability but ranged against him were 1600 cavalry and 3400 infantry. Ralph Sadler, Chancellor of the Duchy, underlined the problem when he informed Cecil in London:

> If we should go to the field with this northern force only, they would fight faintly; for if the father be on this side, the son is on the other; and one brother with us and the other with the rebels.

Elizabeth, perhaps alarmed at the potential unrest indicated by early reports from the north, exaggerated the dangers of a lawless mob that had been enlarged by vagrants and **masterless** men. Parliament duly responded by voting more money to pay for a very large army but it took time to assemble. By December 1569 Sussex had gathered 12,000 troops in York, Lord Hunsdon was preparing to move south from Newcastle with a small army and Lords Warwick and Clinton were collecting 10,000 men to the south. These royal forces under the command of lords lieutenant far outnumbered the rebels and when Sussex started to move towards them, they fled north into Scotland. Only Lord Dacre continued to resist until Hunsdon killed or captured 500 rebels at Carlisle in 1570.

Key term

Masterless
Adolescents who were not apprenticed to a master or an employer and so were more likely to be itinerant and ill-disciplined.

Irish rebellions

Raising troops to deal with rebellions in Ireland brought its own problems. In time troops were based in garrisons in the Pale, Ulster, Munster and Leinster but they were never sufficient to deal with large-scale disturbances, and lord deputies had to rely on recruiting Irish volunteers and the retainers of clan chiefs:

- Sir William Skeffington raised 2300 in 1534, which was enough to defeat Silken Thomas, but only after 14 months of attrition.
- Elizabeth sent 700 troops under Edward Randolph in 1566 to establish a garrison in Ulster, but Lord Deputy Sidney depended

mainly on the earls of Kildare and O'Donnell to bring about the defeat of Shane O'Neill.

- Lord Wilton's army of 6500 in 1580 was more than enough to suppress the Geraldine rebellion, and demonstrated that when the government in London put its mind to tackling the Irish problem, well-led professional forces could achieve a decisive result. His troops captured Smerwick from Irish and Spanish rebels and rounded up the ringleaders.

- The national uprising of the 1590s, however, proved the biggest test for Elizabeth. England was at war with Spain and there were serious domestic problems such as runaway inflation, food shortages, rising unemployment and recurrent plague. Elizabeth was aware of the strategic importance of Ireland – Spain had landed troops before and Philip intended assisting Irish rebels again – but suppressing rebellions was an expensive business and in the 1590s both money and men were in short supply. As a result, the scale of Tyrone's rebellion was allowed to grow. By 1596 it traversed all four Irish provinces and the size of rebel armies exceeded 6000, which was far too large for Elizabeth to defeat. Moreover, her frequent change of political leaders in Ireland – seven in eight years – did little to ease the situation. Not until 1599 was a force of 17,000 sent under the command of Essex. This would have been large enough to combat the revolt if he had deployed the troops effectively but he proceeded to divide his army, putting half in garrisons and sending the rest into the provinces, without ever forcing Tyrone to submit. By 1603, when Tyrone finally surrendered to Lord Mountjoy, more than 30,000 English troops had been sent to Ireland.

The fate of the rebels

Not all rebellions ended in battles even if both rebel and government forces had troops in the field. The overwhelming desire of all concerned was to avoid military confrontation; life may have been nasty, brutish and short but there was little point in bringing it to a premature end. There are therefore numerous examples of rebel leaders backing away from confrontation:

Key question
Why did the overwhelming majority of rebels escape unpunished?

- Warbeck arrived at Taunton in 1497 with about 6000 men mainly from Cornwall but soon realised that he had walked into a trap. The Earl of Devon waited at Exeter, Willoughby de Broke gathered ships at Portsmouth to block any escape by sea, Daubeny started to gather troops and Henry prepared to move west from Woodstock. Rather than risk battle, Warbeck fled at the approach of Daubeny's army.

- A military confrontation also seemed likely in October 1536 when rebel pilgrims in Lancashire called on the Earl of Derby's army to settle their differences at Clitheroe Moor. When he heard about this, Aske wrote hastily to the rebels urging them not to break the truce he had negotiated and the Earl of Shrewsbury ordered Derby to disband. Derby complied and there was no battle.

- On 14 July 1553 the Duke of Northumberland decided to confront Mary and try to defeat her in battle. The 2000 men he took with him to Cambridge, however, were never going to be enough, and his problems increased when some of them deserted. The critical moment came on 18 July when the Earl of Oxford, Lord Lieutenant of Essex, defected. Next day, the Privy Council declared for Mary, and the Lord Mayor and Aldermen of London followed suit. Though Northumberland could still count on the earls of Huntingdon and Warwick, the Marquis of Northampton, and lords Clinton and Grey, he decided the game was up.
- Similarly in 1554, having seen a number of friends killed at Ludgate, Wyatt surrendered to the Earl of Pembroke's troops rather than risk a full-blooded battle in the streets of London.
- The northern earls in 1569 also lost heart when confronted with the prospect of fighting a pitched battle even though they could muster over 5000 men. Instead they took a chance at trying to evade the gathering royal armies: Westmorland succeeded but Northumberland was captured in Scotland.
- Finally, 30 years later the Earl of Essex held back from engaging royal troops in central London after failing to get past Ludgate.

Military casualties

Battles were fought only when rebels refused to surrender. It was not the government's wish to fight its own subjects, although this was necessary from time to time. When battles did occur, casualties were usually high. Some 4000 rebels, mainly Irish and German mercenaries, were killed at East Stoke in 1487 and over 1000 Cornish rebels died at Blackheath in 1497. More than 700 of Sir Francis Bigod's supporters may have fallen when they attempted to storm Carlisle in February 1537 and a further 800 rebels were taken prisoner at the hands of the Duke of Norfolk. Heavier casualties were reported in 1549. According to an eyewitness, John Hooker, at least 4000 men fell at the battles of Clyst St Mary and Sampford Courtenay. In Norfolk, the Earl of Warwick made his intentions clear as soon as he entered Norwich in August 1549: when Kett turned down another offer of pardon, Warwick hanged 49 prisoners, and at nearby Dussindale, the rebels suffered an estimated 3000 casualties at the hands of the royal army strengthened by 1400 Swiss and German mercenaries. The last rebellion in England to witness heavy casualties occurred when 500 of Lord Dacre's 3000-strong rebel army were killed or captured at Naworth near Carlisle in February 1570.

Few battles were fought in Ireland. Most rebellions consisted of skirmishes between clans and frequently ended with the murder of one of the leaders. Sometimes military clashes did occur, as in 1567 when Shane O'Neill's rebels were defeated in Ulster, Cork was relieved in 1569 and Spanish troops were beaten at Smerwick in 1580 and again at Kinsale in 1601. The battle of Yellow Ford in 1598 was exceptional in so far as the English commander, Sir Henry Bagenal, commanded 4000 troops and still suffered a heavy defeat.

Essay focus

Essay 2, paragraph 6 on page 99, makes good use of a wide range of factual evidence to show how the government applied force to deter future disturbances. By referring to examples across the Tudor period, you should be able to show that for the most part governments behaved consistently in their treatment of rebel armies.

Trials and retribution

The extent to which governments sought justice, vengeance or a mixture of both varied from ruler to ruler. Some like Henry VII and Mary were notably lenient; others such as Henry VIII and Elizabeth could be quite vindictive. Those rebels who indulged in treason knew that the penalty was death but not all rebels were subsequently executed. In Ireland in contrast, English officers treated rebels with contempt and many of the punishments were excessive and barbaric.

Henry VII

Henry VII assessed each rebellion on its merits and dispensed justice accordingly. Sir John Conyers, for example, who was suspected of being involved in the Lovel revolt and was a major officeholder in Yorkshire, lost his stewardship of Middleham and had a £2000 bond imposed; and the Abbot of Abingdon, who had secured **sanctuary** for the Stafford brothers, faced a 3000 mark bond of allegiance. Imposing **bonds and recognizances** was a favoured policy of the king, which was widely employed in the months leading up to the battle of Stoke. In February 1487, for instance, a large Sussex contingent including the mayor of Winchelsea was bound over for sums up to £1000. In the aftermath of the battle, Henry travelled around the Midlands and north of England before returning to Warwickshire, and finally London. He needed to thank those who had been loyal – some 70 men were knighted – and to punish or threaten any who had not. In general he was anxious to appease his northern subjects and avoided excessive reprisals. Thirty-three gentry had their lands attainted and fines were paid by several Yorkshire gentry and clergy between 1487 and 1489. Henry's preferred punishment, however, was to bind men under surety of good behaviour, and bonds up to £1000 were quite common. More unusual was the treatment given to lords Scrope of Bolton and Masham, who were bound over for £3000 each, and Sir Edmund Hastings for £2000; in addition each faced a spell in prison. Although they had not fought against Henry, the king felt they had been sympathetic towards the rebels and he was not yet ready to trust them.

Most of the ringleaders of the Yorkshire and Cornish tax revolts were rounded up, tried and executed but the rank and file rebels were allowed to return home and await the king's judgement. In the case of Yorkshire, some 1500 men were pardoned and only six were executed, including John Chamber, the leader of the revolt. The tax, however, was not collected. Henry spent three years

Sanctuary
A place that provided a haven for outlaws. Every parish church, cathedral and monastery had the privilege to offer sanctuary, although in practice certain crimes such as treason were rendered ineligible.

Bonds and recognizances
Bonds were written obligations binding one person to another (often the Crown) to perform a specified action or to pay a sum of money; a recognizance acknowledged that someone was bound to fulfil a commitment.

investigating the Cornish rebellion, interrogating those involved as well as the gentry who failed to halt the eastward advance, before determining the fate of the rebels. Eventually heavy fines were imposed on both active and passive suspects, most of whom came from Somerset and Cornwall. Over 4000 people in Somerset, mainly small tradesmen and craftsmen but also several monks and abbots, were fined in 1500. Bridgwater, Taunton, Wells and Bruton paid £1400, and ex-sheriffs Lutrell and Speke, £100 each. In Cornwall, a huge fine of £14,000 was levied on the county as a whole and families such as the Trefusis, Godolphins and Trewynnards were bound over to keep the peace.

In October 1497 Henry visited Wells and Exeter with an escort of 10,000 troops to reassert his authority in the area. Many of the officials in Wells were later fined or had bonds of loyalty imposed but at Exeter, the city was presented with a sword and ceremonial cap of maintenance for its loyalty during the crisis. Perhaps wisely the king did not visit Cornwall. The county was reportedly 'still eager to promote a revolution if they were in any way provoked', and significantly none of the bodies slaughtered at Blackheath was sent home for burial. Only in 1504 was Henry willing to draw a line under the rebellion: 24 attainders were passed on the leading rebels and 38 received a royal pardon. The king forgave those who had subsequently shown their loyalty to the regime, but he was still determined to squeeze lands and fines out of the guilty.

Henry VIII

Thomas Wolsey intended showing the ringleaders of the Amicable Grant no generosity: they had given him so much grief and must pay for their crime. Eighteen ringleaders were therefore taken to London to await trial. He wanted revenge as, in his opinion, it would be 'convenient for the king's honour and our estimations' and called for the indictment of a further 525 men on charges of riot and unlawful assembly. The leading rebels duly appeared before Wolsey in Star Chamber where he reprimanded them for their treasonous activity and then, no doubt to their surprise, freed them. Either he realised how impoverished they were (which is what he declared) or he was forced to release them by the king (which is what Wolsey's critics claimed) and the rebels returned to Suffolk with 90 pieces of silver as compensation paid by the prison keeper on Wolsey's instructions. It was a bizarre end to an episode that brought no credit to either the king or his chief minister.

Henry VIII showed his vindictive side when he determined the fate of the rebels involved in the Lincolnshire, Pilgrimage and Bigod's rebellions. The king left no doubt as to his intentions when he told the Duke of Norfolk in 1537 that the accused in Carlisle and York were to be tried by commissions without a jury and a summary verdict without appeal announced. Although the Duke professed he was 'unlearned in the law', he nevertheless justified the use of martial law. 'If I should proceed by indictments', he informed Cromwell, 'many a great offender might fortune be found not guilty.' Anyone who was involved in the recent troubles or who was suspected of knowing something had to take an oath disclosing the names of the rebel captains, and these were then arrested and sent to London for interrogation. The king had also instructed Norfolk to hang any monks who had repossessed their dissolved monastery and he identified those rebels he wanted to question personally. Seventy-four men were executed in Carlisle and surrounding villages. In Lancaster, the Earl of Sussex executed the Abbot of Whalley and four monks, four canons from Cartmel, and 19 husbandmen. In Lincoln, Sir William Parr arrested 12 ringleaders and sent them to London, and sentenced 34 others to death, including Sir Thomas Moigne, the Abbot of Kirkstead, 14 monks and six priests. Further trials took place in May in York and Lincoln in the absence of the accused where juries were carefully selected and loyal subjects urged to convict.

Lords Darcy and Hussey were tried by a special court of peers in London and executed. Darcy had failed to distance himself from the pilgrims and Hussey had simply not tried hard enough to stop the Lincolnshire rising. Robert Aske, the Percy brothers, George Lumley and gentry, like Sir Robert Constable and Sir John Bulmer, were judged to have been in contact with Bigod and so broke their pardon. Nicholas Tempest and Stephen Hammerton, on the other hand, admitted helping monks return to their abbeys. All the accused were executed in the summer of 1537. In total 46 were hanged as a result of the Lincolnshire rising and 132 from the Pilgrimage of Grace and Bigod's rising. However, not everyone brought before the courts was found guilty. Fifty-six rebels were pardoned and a few were acquitted by sympathetic juries. Nevertheless, while the vast majority of the nobility and gentry escaped death, the clergy was less fortunate. All 20 clerics tried at Lincoln in March 1537 were executed, whereas only 14 out of 67 laymen were given death sentences. Henry expected his clergy to set an example to his lay subjects and if they did not, then he made an example of them.

Edward VI

Once Lord Russell and his colleagues, William Herbert and Lord Grey, had suppressed the Prayer Book rebels at Sampford Courtenay, Edward VI's Privy Council was determined to silence the western counties once and for all. Russell was ordered to execute 'the heads and stirrers of rebellion in so diverse places as you may to the more terror of the unruly'. Over 100 rebels were hanged in Devon and Somerset towns and Sir Anthony Kingston, the Provost Marshal, imposed martial law in Cornwall. Among his victims were eight priests. The ringleaders were sent to London, housed in the Fleet prison, and in January 1550 Arundell, Winslade, Bury and Holmes were executed. Six other leaders were pardoned with the exception of Robert Welsh, vicar of St Thomas, who was hanged on his own church tower in Exeter dressed in his Catholic vestments and decorated with popish ornaments. The Edwardian government was equally determined to punish Kett and his rebel captains. The ringleaders who survived the battle of Dussindale were tried and executed, some under the Oak of Reformation, others on the city gallows. Kett was taken to the Tower, held for six weeks, tortured, tried, convicted and returned to Norwich to hang from the city walls in December 1549.

Mary I

Mary's response to Northumberland's revolt was to show leniency towards the rebels. Only a handful were punished: Northumberland and two of his close associates, Sir John Gates (vice chamberlain) and Sir Thomas Palmer (captain of the guards), were executed, and Lady Jane Grey, her father and Northumberland's sons were imprisoned. Mary was similarly generous towards most of Wyatt's rebels in 1554. More than 1000 rebels were indicted, but 600 were pardoned and, of 480 convicted of waging war against the queen, only 71 were executed. Among the victims were Wyatt, Suffolk and his brother, and Jane and her husband. Renard, the Imperial ambassador in London, reassured Philip of Spain that the rebellion was really a minor religious disturbance and that Englishmen looked forward to the forthcoming wedding, but behind the scenes investigations into the revolt continued. The Privy Council was divided over the extent of Princess Elizabeth's and Courtenay's involvement. Some Catholics, like Rochester, Waldegrave and Englefield, wanted to put her on trial; others, like Paget, Arundel, Pembroke and Sussex, came to her defence. After several weeks' deliberation, the government decided to place her under house arrest at Woodstock while Courtenay was confined to Fotheringay castle. Both detainees were released in 1555: Elizabeth returned to court and Courtenay went into exile in Venice. Throughout the spring of 1554 arrests were made, fines levied, and pardons granted. Most of those held in the Tower were not released until January 1555 but the queen and her council were less concerned at exacting revenge and more interested in winning over the hearts and minds of the people.

Elizabeth I

Elizabeth was far less forgiving towards rebels. Once victory was secured over the northern earls, she demanded revenge. Sussex and Hunsdon were encouraged to take raiding parties into Scotland, where they burned 300 villages and sacked 50 castles. The Earl of Northumberland went into hiding but was eventually captured and ransomed to the English for £2000 in 1572, and then executed. Martial law was declared and many innocent parties appear to have been caught up in the aftermath. Dacre and Westmorland evaded capture but 700 rebels were arrested and about 450 hanged. Nevertheless, George Bowes, who was one of the officers required to exact punishments, acted more discriminately and claimed that he had only hanged 81 out of 256 tried in Darlington and Richmond. Most of those who died were commoners. The gentry and lesser nobles, on the other hand, had their lands attainted and castles seized.

The severity of punishments meted out to the Oxfordshire rebels in 1596–7, however, merits an explanation. Five ringleaders were taken to London, interrogated by the Lord Chief Justice and other Privy Councillors, imprisoned for six months, tortured and then sentenced to death for making war against the queen. In June two rebels – Bradshaw and Burton – were hanged, drawn and quartered; the fate of the others is unknown. On four occasions the council ordered the Lord Lieutenant of Oxford to make extensive arrests even though he believed no more than 20 men were involved. As a result many innocent men found themselves in London prisons. Clearly the council over-reacted out of fear that the Oxfordshire rising was part of a larger conspiracy or that a similar incident might occur elsewhere. In a climate of suspicion and uncertainty, it had decided against taking any chances.

Over 100 suspects involved in Essex's rebellion in 1601 were arrested and detained in London prisons and private houses belonging to loyal councillors. The council acted quickly to examine the accused and judges were told to hear these cases before setting off on their regular circuits. Thus within a few weeks, trials occurred and verdicts were given. Essex and two associates, Merrick and Cuffe, were executed for waging war against the queen, and 36 others were fined. Some rebels paid dearly: Rutland had to pay £30,000, and Bedford and Neville £10,000 each. The Earl of Southampton was also fined and given an extended spell in the Tower of London. Although several hundred rebels had taken part in the uprising, no one else was punished.

Ireland

Martial law was invoked whenever rebellion broke out in Ireland. This allowed English troops to shoot to kill and execute without trial anyone they suspected was involved. Between 1535 and 1537 some 70 English and Irish supporters of Silken Thomas were hanged, the earl and his five uncles were executed in London and over 200 rebels were fined and their lands attainted. During the Munster rebellion, Lord Deputy Sidney executed 800 rebels between 1569 and 1572 and over 20 castles were captured and lands seized. Grey de Wilton, Lord Deputy from 1580 to 1582, massacred the entire garrison of Smerwick and hanged as many rebels as he could find in the course of two years. The head of the Earl of Desmond, who was killed in 1583, was forwarded to Elizabeth and put on display on London Bridge. After each rebellion, lands were seized, fines were imposed and property was destroyed by vengeful troops. The Tudors never showed any sympathy or understanding towards Irish rebels, and as a result treated them quite differently from their counterparts in England.

Summary diagram: How did Tudor governments deal with rebellions?

```
                    (a) Consult advisers    (b) Gather information    (c) Send out instructions

  (a) Buy time
                                               Strategy
                                                                      (a) Military casualties
  (b) Propaganda
                                            Government
                         Tactics            responses               Fate of the rebels
  (c) Pre-emptive
      measures
                                                                    (b) Trials and retribution

  (d) Raise troops
```

2 | The effects of rebellions on government and society

Crown servants

Key question
Why were Crown servants able to survive calls for their dismissal?

All dynastic rebellions against the Tudors failed and most of the rebellions protesting against government policies and ministers fared little better. The Tudors were resolute in their defence of the Crown; having claimed it under questionable circumstances, they were determined to hold on to it. Crown servants who were the targets of attack – Morton, Bray, Wolsey, Cromwell, Audley, Rich, Cranmer, William and Robert Cecil – all survived. True, Wolsey's relationship with Henry VIII worsened as a consequence of the Amicable Grant protests but he remained in office for a further four years. Nor was Henry inclined to bow to pressure to change the council that had served him so well in the 1530s. Men like Cromwell, Cranmer, Rich and Audley had not caused the Pilgrimage of Grace and he ensured they were rewarded for their part in defeating it. Cromwell remained Henry's principal secretary and was granted monastic lands and annuities from confiscated estates. When he fell from office in 1540, it was not on account of the rebellion but the consequence of arranging an unpopular marriage for the king to Anne of Cleves. Cranmer continued to serve Henry as his Archbishop of Canterbury, Rich was rewarded with the office of Chancellor of the **Court of Augmentations** and Audley stayed as Lord Chancellor. The Duke of Somerset was the only minister to fall from office as a result of rebellion and ironically it was not because the rebels demanded it but because he failed to suppress them effectively and was overthrown by his fellow councillors.

Key term

Court of Augmentations
Established in 1536, this administrative and financial court in London handled affairs relating to the dissolved monasteries.

Religious developments

The Tudors were also unwilling to reverse or change their religious policies, which had prompted rebellions between 1536 and 1569. If anything, the Pilgrimage of Grace made Henry even more determined to sever links with the Roman Catholic Church. Participation in the revolt by abbots and monks convinced him that their continued existence presented a security risk and led him to support Cromwell's move to dissolve the larger monasteries in 1537–8. Most abbots and abbesses surrendered their convents voluntarily in anticipation of parliamentary legislation. Ironically the pilgrims, instead of preserving the smaller monasteries, were instrumental in bringing about the closure of the larger ones. Cromwell's Injunctions of 1538 further confirmed the government's reformed stance in respect of saints, pilgrimages and holy days. The U-turn, which Henry made in 1539 when he endorsed the Act of Six Articles, was a result of popular **iconoclasm** and the conduct of overzealous Protestants. If his conservative reaction owed anything at all to the Pilgrimage of Grace, it was his fear of disorder occurring in many parts of the realm that reminded him of the German peasants' revolt of 1525, the more recent Anabaptist disturbances in Münster and the placards incidents in France. Edward VI, like his father, did not recall the English prayer book, which had angered the Catholics in Devon and Cornwall; in fact, Cranmer proceeded to publish an even more Protestant book three years later. Mary went ahead with her marriage to the Catholic prince, Philip of Spain, in spite of Wyatt's rebellion and stepped up her campaign against heretics. And Elizabeth was not intimidated by the reaction of northern Catholics to her religious settlement; in 1571 the council introduced penal laws specifically against Catholic recusants. Not a single religious revolt achieved its prime objective.

Policy changes

In a few cases, however, governments did respond by making policy changes. As a result of the Yorkshire rebellion in 1489, Henry VII agreed not to collect the tax nor did he impose any fine on the rebels. The Cornish were also relieved of having to pay their war tax in 1497. Although the county was heavily fined, the king did not attempt to introduce tax novelties again. The most successful of all protests was against Wolsey's Amicable Grant. No one paid any tax, no **benevolence** was received and a parliamentary subsidy that still had two of its four instalments to be collected was reassessed at more modest rates for fear of reigniting a taxpayers' strike. Of course, failure to impose a non-parliamentary tax did not prevent future governments from trying again, but Wolsey and Henry had learned their lesson. When Henry collected benevolences in the 1540s, he targeted the wealthier groups rather than the poor.

Henry VIII's responses to the Pilgrimage of Grace

The Pilgrimage of Grace also produced two positive changes that would have pleased some of the rebels:

Key question
Did religious rebellions achieve any of their main objectives?

Key terms

Iconoclasm
The smashing and destruction of religious images and icons.

Benevolence
A gift that was occasionally requested to help the government overcome a financial crisis.

Key question
Why did Tudor governments decide to make some concessions to rebels?

- Unlawful enclosures and excessive entry fines had been the cause of rioting in Westmorland and Cumberland in 1535 and accounted for angry outbursts in 1536–7. To try to obviate this, the Earls of Sussex and Derby were instructed by the king to examine the landlord–tenant relations in Kendal, the vale of Eden and Craven, and if they discovered any irregularities, 'to bring such enclosers and extreme takers of fines to such moderation that they and the poor men may live in harmony'. The commissioners appear to have been successful. No further disturbances occurred in this region in the 1540s when much of the country was experiencing severe social and economic difficulties.
- The gentry and lesser nobility had complained about the Statute of Uses of 1536 and called for its repeal. In 1540 this happened when a new Statute of Wills allowed testators the right to distribute two-thirds of their property without incurring the payment of feudal taxes to the Crown.

Edwardian concessions

The rebellions in 1549 produced several responses from the government. The most dramatic event was the arrest and imprisonment of Somerset by privy councillors. They held him responsible for the political crisis partly due to his unwise policies, which were seen as undermining the authority and power of landowners, and partly on account of his failure to deal with the crisis effectively. Confidence was soon restored in the City and among the gentry, and this was further reflected by legislation passed in November 1549 when the new regime tried to prevent further disturbances. An 'Act for the Punishment of Unlawful Assemblies and Rising of the King's subjects' declared it high treason if 12 or more people gathered to alter existing laws or tried to kill or imprison a privy councillor or refused to disperse within one hour. It was also declared a felony if 12 or more people attempted to destroy enclosures, parks, barns or grain stores and refused to disperse, and it became treason if 40 or more people gathered for more than two hours. To improve the quality of civil defence in the counties that had proved ineffective in recent times, lords lieutenant were given control of the shire levies. Privy councillors even suggested that 'idle persons' and rebel leaders should be forced to join the county militia to save on expensive mercenaries but this proposal does not appear to have been implemented. Although further disturbances occurred between 1550 and 1552, there was no repetition of the 'year of commotion'. JPs were more vigilant, privy councillors and lords lieutenant acted decisively and a run of good harvests lowered food prices and so reduced social tension.

Social and economic reforms

Tudor governments also took note of social and economic causes of distress in 1549 and 1596 and sought to remedy them. For example, the Edwardian government in 1549–50 introduced several measures to help the poor. The Subsidy and Vagrancy Acts were repealed and an Enclosure Act was passed that restricted landlords' manorial rights over the commons and wasteland of less than three acres. This was designed to protect rural peasants from future enclosers of woods and marginal land. Further Acts fixed grain prices, prohibited exports and maintained arable land. The Elizabethan council also took steps to stop future anti-social disturbances after the Oxfordshire rising of 1596. All bishops were ordered to give sermons that advertised the good work the government was doing in helping the poor; and wealthier subjects were to be reminded that they had a Christian duty to organise special charity collections. Congregations were expected to 'endure this scarcity with patience' and to reject attempts by 'discontented and idle brains to move them to repine or swerve from the humble duties of good subjects'. Moreover, in 1597 the council prosecuted seven leading Oxfordshire landowners who had enclosed local common and wasteland. Two Acts were also passed to alleviate social distress:

- an 'Act against the decaying of towns and houses of husbandry'
- an 'Act for the maintenance of husbandry and tillage'.

MPs were also ordered by the Lord Keeper to return to their counties at the end of parliament to ensure the recent statutes were implemented. The government's carrot and stick strategy appears to have worked, and there were no further popular risings in Elizabeth's reign.

Measures taken to strengthen royal authority

A major consequence of rebellion was measures taken by the Crown to strengthen its position and weaken that of potential rebels in troublesome areas. Henry VII achieved this in a number of ways. In 1487 following Simnel's rebellion, the Star Chamber Act established additional legal powers to deal with nobles who disturbed the king's peace, and an Act of Livery and Maintenance attempted to restrict the number of servants retained by lords and used as private armies. In the aftermath of the Yorkshire revolt in 1489, Surrey was rewarded by being appointed Lieutenant of the Council of the North, a royal council begun by Edward IV but which had lapsed in 1485, and lands that had belonged to the Earl of Northumberland were transferred to the Crown. Over 30 families now held their land by **knight service** to the king and at a stroke Henry had considerably strengthened his grip on the north of England. Unlike his successors, Henry preferred to travel throughout his realm and stayed for long periods of time in some of the more disaffected areas, such as Somerset, Worcester and York. Gradually Henry built up close ties with county families, which played a key part in the restoration of order. After the Cornish rising and Warbeck's rebellion of 1497, there were no more armed uprisings though Henry still needed to be vigilant. Edmund, Earl of Suffolk appears to have been conspiring against the king between 1501 and 1506, until Henry imprisoned him in the Tower, and 51 attainders were issued to suppress Suffolk's supporters and strengthen the Crown politically and financially.

Key term

Knight service
Men who held land from the king were obliged to do knight service. This entailed fighting for the king and providing troops whenever he went to war or (as was customarily the case) providing sufficient money to hire mercenaries instead.

> ### Essay focus
>
> Essay 2, paragraph 5 on page 100, usefully cites Henry's acts of attainder, bonds and recognizances to show how he strengthened royal control at the expense of the nobility and gentry.

Henry VIII and the northern counties

Henry VIII similarly took the opportunity afforded by the Pilgrimage of Grace to build up royal support in the northern counties. Too many gentry and sons of nobles had involved themselves in the disturbances, either willingly or out of compulsion. Although the older heads of noble families had not participated, Henry and Cromwell decided to reform the Council of the North and the administration of the marches. The death of the Earl of Northumberland in June 1537 was particularly fortunate: he had held the east and middle marches. The wardenship of the west march was taken from the Earl of Cumberland but because he had not supported the rebellion, he was made a **Knight of the Garter**. Another major reform was the appointment of local lesser gentry as deputy wardens while the king assumed overall responsibility for the marches. Changes also occurred in the commissions of the peace between 1536 and 1539. Henry purged the bench of magistrates who had shown sympathy towards the rebels or in whom he no longer had total confidence. No disciplinary action, however, was taken against nobles like Lord Scrope of Bolton, John Lord Lumley and John Lord Latimer, who had co-operated with the rebels. It was not Henry's intention to destabilise the north any further and he needed noble families to enforce his rule. Loyalty, however, was vital and he reminded these men, 'We will not be bound of a necessity to be served with Lords'.

Henry VIII had promised that a parliament would meet in the north, but it never did. Instead reforms to the Council of the North strengthened his political hold. Its judicial and administrative functions were expanded and all JPs and sheriffs north of the Trent (except in Lancashire) were to take orders directly from it. This enhanced its power to act quickly and suppress future disturbances. The council's membership was also reformed. Tunstall, Bishop of Durham, was made president, senior nobles such as Westmorland, Cumberland, Dacre and Shrewsbury were encouraged to attend, but most significant was the inclusion of Ellerker, Bowes and Tempest. Each had taken leading roles in the rebellion but Henry was prepared to give them a prominent part in the political life of the north, and none acted disloyally again.

Elizabethan reforms to the Council of the North

An important legacy of the Northern Earls' rebellion was the reforms to the county militia, commissions of the peace and Council of the North (see Chapter 4, page 112). From 1569 all parishes were ordered to keep a list of men aged between 16 and 60 who were eligible for military service and parishes were

Key term

Knight of the Garter
An honour in the gift of the Crown that Henry VIII generously dispensed. The recipient was entitled to wear blue or crimson robes and took precedence over other knights.

instructed to improve the quality and size of the county muster. The rebellion had revealed the inadequacies of the militia, and better training was introduced in 1573. Reforms to the Council of the North occurred in 1572. The Earl of Huntingdon, Elizabeth's cousin and a puritan with no local connections, became the new president. He was authorised to ensure JPs enforced the penal laws against Catholics, removed illegal enclosures, punished unlawful retaining and assisted the poor. From 1570 most northern counties had their magistrates purged. JPs who had shown leniency towards the uprising were replaced by more reliable men. Though this purge could not be applied in every case, as there were insufficient alternatives, a constant turnover of JPs in the 1570s gradually built up a more dependable bench. It was hoped that these measures would minimise the likelihood of future disturbances and remove the influence of Catholic families from the political social scene in the northern counties. In this way the Crown turned one of the prime objectives behind the earls' rebellion to its own advantage and the absence of any further religious or political revolts in the north suggests that it succeeded.

Ireland

Silken Thomas's rebellion of 1534 was a watershed in Anglo-Irish relations. Henry VIII decided to end the dominance of the Geraldines and, thereafter, English officials replaced Irish office holders in Dublin. A small permanent garrison was established and border fortresses were restrengthened and, though periodically cuts were made, a military presence came to symbolise English rule in Ireland for the next 400 years. The seizure of Kildare's lands and those of his supporters opened the way for granting lands to English loyalists, and the refusal of the Irish parliament to meet the cost of the rebellion led to Henry seizing Irish monastic and episcopal lands instead. There was no immediate reaction to the reprisals, which were fairly lenient, and most Anglo-Irish endorsed Henry's religious changes, but opposition by Gaelic lords and Palesmen to religious reforms did lead to a revolt in 1539 against the Archbishop of Dublin. Though it failed to gather much support and within a year had fizzled out, it was an early indication of nationalist and papist opposition that would characterise Elizabethan Irish rebellions.

From time to time rebellions in Ireland could be a security risk but they never presented a serious challenge to English rule and domestic troubles and foreign wars were always given priority. Nevertheless in comparison with the costs involved in suppressing disturbances in England, Irish rebellions were far more expensive. Henry VIII spent £40,000 dealing with Silken Thomas's rebellion whereas 15 years later, in the 'year of commotions', the Edwardian government spent £27,000 suppressing a multitude of English revolts. The costs spiralled out of control in Elizabeth's reign: the Geraldine rebellion cost the government £254,000 and Tyrone's national uprising an estimated £2 million. Moreover, the Tudors increasingly struggled to suppress disturbances in Ireland; after

Key question
Why did the Tudors not take Irish rebellions more seriously?

fighting the Earl of Tyrone for more than eight years, victory was qualified. The earl renounced his title of 'the O'Neill' and agreed to support English sheriffs and garrisons in Ulster but he was granted a pardon and recovered all that he had held at the start of the rebellion.

Key question
In what ways did rebellions affect Tudor foreign affairs?

Foreign affairs

Rebellions also had an impact on Tudor foreign affairs. The Yorkshire uprising distracted Henry VII at a time when he was preparing to go to war with France over Brittany. Raising money was proving hard and, although Yorkshire's contribution to his war preparations would have been relatively small, Henry felt obliged to visit York to try to prevent future disturbances when his time would have been better spent in London. Support for Warbeck from foreign powers in the 1490s also affected Henry's relations with Burgundy, France, the Holy Roman Empire and Scotland. Henry signed the treaties of Etaples and Ayton to secure his throne from the claims of the pretender, and put a three-year trade embargo on Burgundy. His preparations to attack Scotland in 1497 were also badly affected by the Cornish rebellion. Troops had to be recalled and Daubeny, who was to have marched north to lead the campaign, found himself defending the south of England instead. Eventually a truce was declared between James IV and England but the revolt had proved particularly embarrassing for the government, and encouraged Warbeck to choose Cornwall as the starting point for his own campaign.

Failure to secure the Amicable Grant also had an impact on Henry VIII's plans to invade France in 1525. Without the additional money, which the grant was intended to produce, he could not hope to raise enough troops and equip them for a summer campaign. Within a year, relations with Charles V had deteriorated and those with France improved, and Henry's hopes of leading an army on the continent were dashed. It would be another 17 years before Henry and Charles were again comrades in arms. The rebellions in 1549 also had a serious impact on Somerset's foreign designs and in particular the war against Scotland. The government already had serious financial difficulties and was struggling to meet the costs of what was turning out to be a lengthy and expensive war. Foreign mercenaries were hastily redeployed to deal with the domestic troubles, and the orderly withdrawal of English troops from the Scottish lowlands was thrown into disarray. In addition, news of these rebellions encouraged France to declare war on England, which compounded Somerset's problems.

Relations with Spain were also affected by rebellion. Wyatt may have failed in his attempt to stop Mary from marrying Philip but his revolt brought to the fore xenophobic feelings among many Englishmen and did little to appease the Spanish prince's own concerns about living in England. The legacy of this ill-feeling, which was enhanced by the Marian persecution of Protestants, continued into Elizabeth's reign. Spain also recognised the strategic opportunities that Ireland presented whenever rebellions broke out, and in 1580 and 1601 sent money, troops and priests to assist Irish rebels against the English. Although neither expedition proved successful, they further damaged Anglo-Spanish relations.

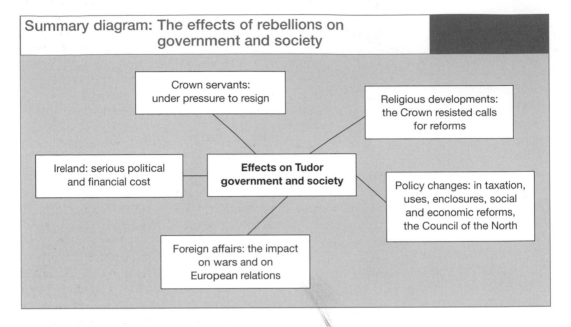

Summary diagram: The effects of rebellions on government and society

Crown servants: under pressure to resign

Religious developments: the Crown resisted calls for reforms

Ireland: serious political and financial cost

Effects on Tudor government and society

Policy changes: in taxation, uses, enclosures, social and economic reforms, the Council of the North

Foreign affairs: the impact on wars and on European relations

3 | Conclusion: were Tudor governments ever seriously threatened by rebellion?

We have seen in Chapter 2 that the strength of a rebellion depended on several factors and if these worked in unison, they were capable of challenging, even threatening, the stability of Tudor governments. The size and support a rebellion received could prove to be too large for a government to confront directly and, if it had the backing of English nobles or foreign princes, then the threat was very serious. The Cornish, Amicable Grant, Pilgrimage of Grace, Western, Kett and Northern Earls all raised a host greater than the royal forces, and could not be easily dispersed. Simnel and Warbeck, though they gathered fewer troops, acquired the support of foreign rulers and, in the case of Simnel, several English and Irish nobles. This rebellion was probably the most threatening in so far as the king had to fight a battle in person to defend his newly acquired throne.

A rebellion's objective largely determined its potential threat. Politically motivated disturbances, such as Simnel, Warbeck, Wyatt, Northern Earls and Essex, were dangerous precisely because they planned to overthrow the monarch. Should a rebellion approach London – as occurred in the Cornish, Wyatt and Essex revolts – then the safety of the government was similarly imperilled. Fortunately for the Tudors, London proved consistently loyal and, as long as the government held its nerve, the citizens were likely to support it. Thus, neither Wyatt nor Essex was able to rally the people against two potentially vulnerable female rulers, and Mary Tudor secured the throne because Londoners backed her legitimate claim against Northumberland's protégée, Lady Jane Grey.

In practice, most rebellions were localised affairs and intent on registering a protest against government policies and ministers rather than seeking to overthrow the monarch. The length of a rebellion could be an irritant, however, which might raise doubts about the government's competence to maintain order and thus weaken its credibility. The reputation of both Wolsey and Cromwell suffered as a result of the Amicable Grant and Pilgrimage of Grace, and the Duke of Somerset fell from office as a direct consequence of the 1549 disturbances. Most disturbances lasted for less than a month, and the Pilgrimage, Western and Kett's rebellions that lasted for more than two months were exceptional. Yet even these rebellions, which wished to reverse government policies and remove unpopular royal councillors, failed to present a serious threat to the government in London.

Governments then were never seriously challenged provided they stayed calm under pressure. Strategies of deploying a mixture of propaganda, persuasion and threats usually kept the nobility and clergy on side, and rebels either lost interest in their protest or went home confident that changes for the better would follow. All governments played for time until they were in a position of strength. Once they felt strong enough to exact reprisals, they isolated rebel groups and picked off the leaders at will. If they made a bargain or offered concessions, it was because they felt temporarily vulnerable and had little intention of keeping to promises made under duress.

Only in Ireland did the Tudors have some difficulty suppressing disturbances. The absence of large permanent garrisons, the harsh terrain which made fighting very tough, and the growing unpopularity of government policies, contributed to an increase in ill-feeling between the native Irish and the English administration and settlers. Yet although the Tudors struggled to keep Ireland at peace, rarely did Irish rebellions present a threat to the government or the monarch. Certainly Irish nobles and clergy could destabilise political affairs in Ireland. They invaded England in Henry VII's reign in the name of the pretender Simnel, and some Irish received support from Catholic Spain in Elizabeth's reign. Only in the 1590s did the Tudors view the Irish as a serious threat, partly on account of the size and widespread support in Ireland for O'Neill's rebellion but mainly because its potential to receive assistance from Spain endangered national security. For most of the Tudor period, the Irish Channel protected England and Wales from disturbances across the water and ensured that what was 'out of sight' stayed largely 'out of mind'.

Summary diagram: Were the Tudors ever seriously threatened by rebellions?

Factors that increased a rebellion's seriousness

- Size, support, and backing of English nobles and foreign powers
- A rebellion's objective, e.g. to overthrow the monarch
- Its proximity to London

Factors that weakened a rebellion's seriousness

- Governments held their nerve or made deals they had no intention of honouring
- Most rebellions were localised protests
- Most of the English nobility and clergy supported the Crown

Further questions for debate

1 How effectively did Tudor governments deal with rebellions in England and Ireland?

2 How far did government methods used to combat rebellions change in the course of the period?

3 To what extent did government reforms made in the aftermath of rebellions help to prevent further disturbances?

4 Assess the role of the nobility in suppressing rebellions in England.

5 Assess why Tudor governments were never seriously threatened by rebellions.

Choose two of the above questions and write plans in the form of notes and/or diagrams. Your plans should outline your main arguments, any relevant supporting evidence and how key ideas are linked synoptically.

Advice on answering essay questions on explanation

Explanation questions are likely to begin 'Assess the reasons why ...', 'How do you account for ...' or 'Why did ...?' In the essays that follow, the question requires students to explain the reasons for the government's effective handling of rebellions. You need to assess several reasons and show that you have understood the links and connections between various developments over the whole period, thereby demonstrating the concept of continuity and change over time. To score high marks, a synthesis of argued explanations not a list of reasons is therefore required.

Read each of the following essays carefully. Each essay was written in one hour and without the use of notes. Note any strengths and limitations and compare your views with those of the assessor. Marks should be awarded for each of the two assessment objectives described in the tables at the end of the book (see pages 142–3).

Essay 1: Assess the reasons why Tudor governments were able to deal so effectively with rebellions

1 The reasons why Tudor governments were able to deal with popular disorder is not clear cut there are a number of reasons why as for example the people accepted laws passed through parliament, the local authority of JPs, lord lieutenants and the nobility. They adhered in the majority to the religion of their king which was certainly a central mechanism which could help a government deal effectively with rebellion and more importantly the Tudor people were loyal to their government and king and in the long term looked towards it in crisis and for authority.

2 By the end of Elizabeth's reign, the government had become more orderly and effective. The positions of Justice of Peace and Lord Lieutenant were well established and generally worked as a means of controlling rebellion. For example, in 1569 when the Northern Earls rebelled and the Earl of Suffolk, Radcliffe, and local JPs and lord lieutenants put down the rebellion as opposed to the rebellions of 1549 where JPs and nobles simply could not cope with the scale of rebellion. Arguably even in 1486 under Henry VII, JPs existed but on a much lower scale. Henry VII set up ways to make the government more effective in terms of dealing with rebellion as he set up the courts of Star Chamber in 1487, which is renowned for dealing with traitors to the regime throughout the Tudor century. What is more Henry successfully put down the Simnel and Warbeck rebellions through using parliament and the government by entrusting nobles to put down the rebellions and through executing Warbeck and Warwick in 1499 and allowing the 12 year old Simnel to spend his life working in the kitchens. Arguably the fact that Henry had established himself in parliament and had an overall trustworthy government suggests how the government was used effectively as Henry was extremely vulnerable to rebellion throughout his reign.

3 The government constantly worked in coherence with the king and the Tudor people, which certainly helped with its effectiveness. For example, in 1525 when the king sent Howard to deal with the Amicable Grant with an army of 1800, they purely refused to fight as they sympathised with the rebels and instead took back the grievances to the king who then subsequently dropped the tax. This conveys how the government and the king and the people worked together. Continuity can be seen in the Pilgrimage of Grace where the rebels complained at the evil councillors Cromwell and Rich as they did in the Amicable Grant where they complained about Wolsey. The Duke of Norfolk was sent with a delegation rather than an army and dealt with the rebellion successfully with less than one per cent of the rebels executed. Therefore it is arguable that the government was able to deal with rebellion by sending the right nobles to suppress it.

4 Another reason the government was able to deal with rebellion continuously and effectively was because of the element of religion for the English people were religious and this acted as de-motivation for

---

1 General introduction that outlines some valid reasons.

2 Sussex not Suffolk dealt with this rebellion. It is unclear what is meant by 'Henry had established himself in parliament'.

3 Suggests the candidate only has a limited understanding of the concept of government. The paragraph ends with a *non sequitur*.

rebellion as even in the Pilgrimage of Grace there were other factors mentioned in the Pontefract Articles such as sheep and cattle tax and debasing of the coinage. Also it is argued that this rebellion was political in terms of the fact that they asked for 'the Lady Mary to be made legitimate' in Article number 3. The government could use religion to make the people abide by laws as a Tudor monarch would not have separated politics and religion. As for example in Henry's reign when the Pope made him defender of the faith and Elizabeth and Mary's reign where heresy truly was not an option especially in Mary's reign where 900 Protestants were burnt at the stake. It was easier for the people to work with the government.

> 4 The argument that religion 'acted as de-motivation for rebellion' is unclear; Mary did not burn 900 heretics; the Pontefract articles did not refer to a sheep and cattle tax or debasement.

5 When the government is not able to work effectively in dealing with popular disorder this is when the nobility or gentry move out of their hierarchical position and pomposity can be seen or when the rebels become out of control and even go as far as murdering members of the government. This can be seen in the Yorkshire tax riots in 1489 where Northumberland was murdered and in the Western rebellion where the government agent William Body was brutally murdered and in Kett's where the lawyer Flowerdew was attacked and his enclosures torn down. It is even more serious when the nobility move away from the government. This can be seen in 1554 in Wyatt's rebellion where the lord lieutenant who had previously dealt with rebellion in 1549 rebelled supposedly about the marriage of Mary and Philip joined by a xenophobic number of 2500. He managed to get as far as Ludgate. The Northern Earls' rebellion was not dissimilar.

> 5 Body was murdered a year before the rebellion began, Flowerdew was not a member of the government, and Wyatt was not the lord lieutenant of Kent in 1554. Weak and unclear reference to the northern earls.

6 To conclude, when all parts of the government work in coherence, then rebellions are dealt with effectively. The fact that every single rebellion was dealt with in one way or another is evident of this and shows continuity and change can be seen and that as the Tudors became stronger then their means of putting down rebellion became more effective. The Tudor governments were seen as moving away from the medieval governing regime and into a revolutionary modern era, developing into the civil war, which did not happen under the Tudors.

> 6 A confusing and asserted conclusion: 'shows continuity and change can be seen' is a vacuous statement; and the final sentence is illogical.

Assessment for essay 1

Some relevant knowledge but of variable accuracy; some unclear and disorganised sections; mostly communicated satisfactorily. [Level IV: 11 marks out of 20]

Satisfactory understanding of key concepts and tries to answer the question set; makes some synoptic comments but synthesis is limited and at times developed inadequately. [Level IV: 23 marks out of 40]

Overall the mark of 34 is a middle D Grade. To achieve a higher mark, the candidate needed to improve his or her powers of expression to develop an argument that used accurate factual evidence synoptically. Irish rebellions have also been overlooked, which weakens the argument since Tudor governments always had difficulty suppressing them.

Essay 2: Assess the reasons why Tudor governments were able to deal so effectively with rebellions

1 Offers several interesting ideas and suggests that the Tudors did not always deal effectively with rebellion. A promising start.

2 Makes a valid reference to Derby's role in the Pilgrimage of Grace, and usefully refers to Irish issues.

3 Good synthesis and use of evidence in support of the role of deference.

1 The ability of the Tudor governments to control rebellion is inextricably linked to the population's willingness to rebel. There were many forces such as the church and societal constraints, symbolism, treason laws and overwhelming force at their disposal. Counter to this however was the fact that they had no standing army. If they had, it would have been seen as a threat to personal freedoms. The country was still much divided, with the north, west and Welsh marches proving to be constantly unstable and violence was a far more popular means of voicing demands, with parliament only becoming a platform for complaint in Elizabeth's reign. Moreover, Ireland was a continuous problem, which arguably the Tudors rarely dealt with effectively.

2 In this unstable situation the connection of the monarch to their nobles was crucial. The nobility represented the main means of control in the localities with them acting as lords lieutenants and sheriffs. A break with the nobility, such as Henry VII faced with his assaults on retaining, Stanley and the Earl of Kildare, whose nature drove him to support Simnel in 1487, compromised these forces of control. To effectively deal with rebellion then the government had to build a good relationship with the nobility in their position as keepers of the peace. This can be illustrated by the Pilgrimage of Grace where the loyalty of Lord Derby to Henry VIII not only protected the spread of the discontent south of the river Don but he in fact also persuaded the counties of Rutland and Leicester to remain loyal. So although the renegade actions of Darcy made the situation worse, the controlling influence of the loyal nobles prevented the spread of sedition towards London and the south east. In Ireland the Tudors relied totally on playing off noble clans against each other, relying on the Kildares to suppress rebellion until 1534 and, thereafter, Irish nobles to support the Dublin administration and counter any dissident groups.

3 The reverse of this was the state of Tudor society where Fortescue's 'chain of being' doctrine allowed the monarch to evoke deference to their power. The Pilgrimage of Grace in 1536 again shows this where the commons were unwilling to fight the smaller royal forces and instead listened to Henry's conciliatory words and disbanded. This idea of deference and loyalty provides one of the best forms of Tudor control, and probably one reason why they could so effectively deal with rebellion. The usurpation of Lady Jane Grey of the throne in 1553 allowed Mary to call upon loyalty to the Tudor name to allow the suppression by her large and passionate force gathered at Framlingham. Again in 1554 the way in which Londoners kept Ludgate shut against Wyatt shows how support for the legitimate monarch was a powerful tool in suppressing rebellion. The defiance of the Lord Mayor of London to succumb to Essex's attack in 1601 similarly stemmed largely from support for the rightful queen and an abhorrence of insurrection. In Ireland discontented nobles such as Shane O'Neill, Desmond and Tyrone, frequently led rebellions but they

still felt the need to respect the English queen and, having made their protest, sought reconciliation.

4 Another means of Tudor control was simply the fact normal people did not generally want to fight and die, particularly if it entailed fighting against the monarch. For example, few people rose to support Simnel in his march from Lancashire, partly due to the fact that they disliked the unstable, brutal Irish forces and German mercenaries. People's unwillingness to fight and die could also be supported by the Northern Earls' rising of 1569 where feudal relationships and compulsion were often the only means of raising a force. Although a passive fact of life, this revulsion of violence was key in the Tudors' armoury for successfully dealing with disorder as it often meant that few forces were sent against them. This is particularly clear when localised tensions like between Devon and Cornwall in 1497 limited rebel forces to 10,000. In addition this localisation meant that rebellion rarely got further than its origins for lack of support, again linking with and emphasising the importance of passive localisation as a method of dealing with disorder. The dukes of Norfolk and Suffolk were therefore able to dissuade the Amicable Grant protesters that they should disarm and disperse rather than march on London in 1525. Although it seems to only present a means of preventing disorder, it was a crucial reason why Tudor governments succeeded. In the case of the Duke of Somerset in 1549, his lenient treatment of Kett's and the Western rebellion present the factor that he did not need to deal with them before he was ready, as he felt confident they would not spread. Wyatt similarly was unable to rouse areas outside Kent in his protest at Mary's proposed marriage to Philip of Spain. The grievances that he and his county gentry felt so strongly were not shared elsewhere. Thus even though the Marian government had very limited resources, it was able to effectively combat Wyatt's challenge.

> 4 A good point, well illustrated.

5 As well as the fact that Tudor people did not want to fight, and especially not for a non-local cause, with only 65,000 of a total 15 million rising at all, most being in the Pilgrimage of Grace, which was largely peaceful, it is important to consider restraining forces. Henry VII passed acts of attainder and imposed extensive bonds and recognizances on his nobility, which discouraged them from rebellion; Henry VIII passed new treason laws to defend his break with Rome, and reforms to the county militia under Elizabeth allowed a force of some 10,000 to be sent against the northern earls. Thus the use of legislation was an important factor of control.

> 5 The use of legislation could have been further developed in respect of details and how it helped prevent/defeat rebellions.

6 Linked to this is the role of state force. The execution of over 400 people after the Northern Earls' rebellion and 800 hanged after the Geraldine rebellion shows a method of deterrent for other rebels. The harsh treatment of the 4 rebels in the 1596 Oxfordshire rising showed the population that the state was not prepared to tolerate violence which, when it did occur such as at Carlisle in 1537, would be crushed with massive force. Royal armies sometimes exceeded rebel

> 6 Good, well synthesised use of evidence.

forces by as many as 10,000 as in the case of the Cornish rebels in 1497, and could result in the deaths of thousands of rebels as occurred in the Western rebellion at Clyst St Mary and in Kett's rebellion at Dussindale.

7 Conclusion should not include a new point about royal councillors; 'public propaganda' has not been discussed in the essay.

7 As well as force and threats to the people and as a reaction against rebellion, with the support of the nobility, the Tudors had a good situation with their rebellions. They could often deal with them because the force was not aimed at deposing them but aiming at grievances against evil councillors, such as Morton and Bray in 1497 in the Cornish rising, or Cromwell and Rich in the Pilgrimage of Grace. With forces not directed at the monarch, problems could be reduced. So a combination of stark violence and threats with public propaganda allowed governments to deal effectively with rebellions.

Assessment for essay 2

Makes use of relevant and accurate evidence and a range of appropriate terminology; essay is clearly structured, coherently and accurately communicated. **[Level IB: 17 marks out of 20]**

Good level of understanding of key concepts of continuity and change over the whole period; synthesises explanations and provides a range of supported judgements that are focused on the question. **[Level IB: 34 marks out of 40]**

The overall mark of 51 is a clear Grade A. To achieve an A*, the essay needed to develop some of the explanations more fully (e.g. symbolism referred to in 1 and public propaganda that is cited in 7), highlight the differences between dealing with rebellions in Ireland and England, and improve the conclusion.

4 The Maintenance of Political Stability

OVERVIEW

This chapter is concerned with the maintenance of stability and seeks to explain how the Tudors ruled their kingdom.

- Institutional developments: the role of central and local authorities, especially the monarchy, church, parliament, royal councils, judiciary and the law, royal commissions and JPs, sheriffs and lords lieutenant
- Tudor policies: continuity and change – the nobility, religious changes, economic developments, social reforms, Ireland
- Conclusion
- An assessment of two A2 essays: Grades A* and C

Revolts and rebellions were exceptions to the general rule of order, which was achieved by rulers developing particular institutions and addressing the key problem areas that commonly gave rise to rebellion. Continuity was more evident than change in respect of Tudor institutions. When changes did occur, they were often short-lived and met specific needs rather than formed part of a coherent programme of reform. The 1530s, however, did see major constitutional, religious and administrative changes, which historian Geoffrey Elton once described as 'revolutionary', but this was an exceptional decade. Generally, Tudor institutions underwent more subtle, evolutionary changes. The main objective of governments was to maintain political stability and this could best be achieved through continuity.

Note making

Use each of the headings and sub-headings as starting points for your notes. Read through each section before writing anything down and then note the main thematic developments. Select the appropriate factual evidence in support of your arguments.

1 | Institutional developments

The monarchy

Key question
How did the monarchy affect popular perceptions of authority?

The institution of the monarchy was the most important element in the maintenance of stability. The monarch was the source of unity and authority in the kingdom, and was directly responsible for the protection of his or her subjects and ensuring that the laws of the land were upheld. The monarch held power from God and, as Henry VIII proclaimed, owed allegiance to no one else. It was commonly believed, and the Tudors never tired of reminding their subjects, that an act against the monarch was not just treason, it was a sin against God. Thus William Baldwin could write in the *Mirror for Magistrates* in 1559:

> Full little know we wretches what we do
> When we presume our princes to resist.
> We war with God against His glory too,
> That placeth in His office whom he list.

Respect for the monarchy

The power of the monarchy, both real and imaginary, did not depend simply upon the awe and mystique that surrounded it. Governments stressed the relationship between subject and master, the need to keep one's place in society and respect the authority of one's superior. Those in authority constantly underlined this idea through the concept of the Great Chain of Being. Each link in the chain, they claimed, connected humans upwards towards God and downwards to the animal kingdom, plants and minerals. Everyone and everything had a place in society and any attempt to usurp one's position was likely to result in chaos. In 1509 Edmund Dudley had stated in *The Tree of Commonwealth*:

> Let not them [the commons] presume above their own degree nor any of them pretend or counterfeit the state of his better.

Not all subjects understood or accepted this philosophy, as uprisings and revolts clearly demonstrated, but respect for authority was increasingly publicised by the Tudors, particularly in the second half of the sixteenth century. As Richard Hooker explained in his *Laws of Ecclesiastical Polity* written in 1593:

> Every degree of people, in their vocation, calling and office, has appointed to them their duty and order. Some are in high degree, some in low, some kings and princes, some inferiors and subjects, priests and laymen, masters and servants, fathers and children, husbands and wives, rich and poor, and every one has need of [the] other.

All Tudor monarchs recognised that if they were to be effective rulers then they had to work at enhancing the respect and aura surrounding the monarchy. From 1534 both spiritual and lay officeholders swore oaths of allegiance and supremacy, and under Edward, oaths of uniformity were added, reversed under Mary and reinstituted by Elizabeth. Like medieval oaths of fealty that bound subjects to the Crown, the oaths of succession and supremacy were taken throughout the country by individuals and by corporate institutions such as universities and cathedral chapters. The Tudors also made increasing use of **proclamations**; nearly 900 were issued during this period. These could be turned into parliamentary statutes but most were issued in the absence of parliament when speed was of the essence and the Crown wished to impart information immediately. Thus Henry VII issued a proclamation in 1509 to end speculation surrounding the claims of a pretender and in 1553 the Duke of Northumberland authorised one to deny Mary's right to the throne. Copies were sent to every county where the message was read out in parish churches and market places. In this way, the Crown kept informed as many of its subjects as was practicable.

Propaganda

Propaganda was an important weapon in the Tudor armoury (see pages 73–5). Henry VII claimed descent from King Arthur, developed the Tudor rose as a symbol of political unity and decked his servants in his coat of arms and royal badges. His Burgundian-style court with its lavish displays and entertainment impressed foreign visitors and English nobles alike and added to the majesty of the king. Henry VIII preferred more visual imagery to highlight his physicality, wealth and imperial bearing. Coins that portrayed a 'closed' Crown were minted to show Henry's '**imperatur**' status, and larger coins contained finer details of his physiognomy. Illustrations accompanied official documents, portraits by Holbein suggested his grandeur, and stately buildings, such as Hampton Court, Nonsuch and Greenwich palaces, were monuments to his magnificence. Neither Edward nor Mary glamorised the monarchy to the same degree: a sickly boy and an introverted woman were not suitable subjects. Nevertheless Edward was portrayed in paintings in the image of his father and Mary's image on her Great Seals reflected a regal bearing. Elizabeth, on the other hand, realised the potential of elevating the image of the monarchy while still maintaining close links with her subjects. Unlike her father, brother and sister, most summers she visited royal castles and manor houses, stayed with county gentry, hunted with her nobility and travelled to provincial towns. Wherever she went, she developed bonds of affection with her people who lined the route of her advertised progresses. Although she never visited Ireland, Wales, the north and south-west of England, she built up a strong rapport with southern, central and eastern England, which was where most people lived. The queen encouraged pageantry that idealised herself as a symbol of eternal stability. Painters focused on her wisdom, beauty, justice and good governance, poets represented her as **Belphoebe and Astraea**, and her court developed an endless round of rituals and ceremonies designed to celebrate her majesty.

Through its use of patronage the Crown had at its disposal the means to win over and keep the political nation subservient. Its

Key terms

Proclamations
Notices that were publicly issued by the Crown and proclaimed in London and the localities.

Imperatur
A 'closed' as opposed to an 'open' Crown symbolised imperial authority, which implied that the ruler was subject to God alone.

Belphoebe and Astraea
Mythical women celebrated for their beauty and sense of justice, respectively.

'Armada portrait' of Elizabeth I painted about 1588. Why do you think the queen would have wanted to be portrayed as a young woman?

capacity to award honours such as peerages and knighthoods, to grant monopolies, land, annuities and pensions, and to make appointments to the Church, court, judiciary, administration and armed forces, gave the Crown an enormous potential to reward loyal and competent subjects. They, in turn, were expected to reward the monarch with unbending service and obedience. The main beneficiaries were the nobles, courtiers and gentry, who may have numbered some 2500 in Elizabethan England. In theory offices were not sold but money certainly changed hands in the form of fees, gifts and unrecorded payments as royal servants benefited from their privileged position and built up a network of clients in central and local government. In this way the interplay between dispensers and receivers of royal patronage bound the counties to the central administration and was a key reason for long periods of stability under the Tudors. Men and women were drawn to the power, wealth and influence of the court, and, as long as the channels of patronage remained fluid and were not monopolised by one individual (which occurred under Wolsey in the 1520s and Robert Cecil in the 1590s), the politically active classes stayed loyal to the Crown.

The Church

Throughout the Tudor period the Church consistently supported the Crown and was an important institution in the maintenance of stability. At Henry VII's accession he was anointed with holy oil, crowned by the Archbishop of Canterbury and imbued with divine authority. For his part, the king looked to his bishops for advice and assistance in administering the realm and appointed the archbishop as his Lord Chancellor. Henry was a devoted son of the Church and expected the pope to support him against rebels and impostors. Innocent VIII duly obliged. Anyone who fought against Henry at Stoke and Blackheath was threatened with excommunication. The use of sanctuary, which Henry believed Lovel and the Staffords had abused, was denied to traitors and rebels by Henry's judges, and the pope made no objection to this ruling.

Until 1529 Henry VIII continued to use clerics as his administrators, advisers and diplomats. Bishops Warham, Fox and Tunstall were key royal servants but they paled into insignificance alongside Wolsey. When he was Lord Chancellor between 1515 and 1529, the Church enjoyed a high profile in central administration. Wolsey made active use of the courts of Chancery, Star Chamber and Requests (see page 113) and his clients, many of whom were in holy orders, sat on royal commissions and helped to maintain order in the country. Henry VIII's divorce and subsequent break from Rome, despite actions by some Roman Catholics, did not weaken Church–State relations. If anything, the relationship was strengthened as bishops continued to be appointed by the Crown and after 1533 they owed their office and loyalty solely to the Crown. Henry in turn continued to use them as administrators and advisers – Tunstall, Bishop of Durham, for instance, became the new President of the Council of the North and Lee, Bishop of Coventry and Lichfield, presided over the Council of Wales – but laymen trained in civil law displaced bishops as his Secretary of State, Lord Chancellor and Lord Privy Seal. Apart from a brief period under Mary when Cardinal Pole was Lord Chancellor, all political offices in Edward's and Elizabeth's reigns were held by non-clergymen. The clergy's role as law enforcers, which had been of vital importance before the fall of Wolsey, was over – at least until the 1630s.

The Church and the doctrine of obedience

The alliance between Church and State, however, remained strong. The Church's support for the monarchy is well illustrated by its public avowal of the doctrine of obedience and non-resistance, which was first fully developed in the sixteenth century. In the 1530s priests received detailed injunctions as to the content of their sermons and were instructed to preach at least four times a year on the subject of obedience. Stephen Gardiner, an orthodox Roman Catholic, had serious misgivings about the royal divorce and the efficacy of the English Church separating from Rome, but he acknowledged that the king-in-parliament had no superior as far as the law was concerned. He argued in *De Vera Obedientia Oratio*.

Key question
How far did people's attitude towards the Church change as a result of the Reformation?

God, according to his exceeding great and unspeakable goodness toward mankind ... substituted men, who, being put in authority as his vicegerents, should require obedience which we must do unto them with no less fruit for God's sake than we should do it (what honour soever it were) immediately unto God himself.

The accession of a minor to the throne in 1547 raised doubts about the Privy Council's legitimacy to rule on his behalf and prompted Cranmer to write a series of **homilies** by which the clergy would educate their congregations. The *Homily on Obedience* reminded people that in obeying the king, they were actually obeying God. It declared:

Let us all therefore fear the most detestable vice of rebellion ever knowing and remembering that he that resists common authority resists God and his ordinance.

Bishop Latimer in his *Sermons* summed up the Church's doctrine of obedience in 1548:

When laws are made against God and his word, then I ought more to obey God than man. Then I may refuse to obey with a good conscience: yet for all that, I may not rise up against the magistrates, nor make any uproar; for if I do so, I sin damnably.

Although timely in their publication, neither Cranmer's *Homilies* nor Latimer's *Sermons* could prevent the outbreak of widespread revolts. Cranmer's reaction was to circulate copies of his sermons to be read out in parish churches throughout the kingdom. Their purpose, he explained, was 'to preserve the people in their obedience and to set out the evil and mischief of the present disturbances'. In citing the Old and New Testaments, he reminded people that they had a duty to be 'patient in adversity' and to be 'long-suffering'. Bishops relayed a similar message in the 1590s at the height of an economic and social crisis. Their sermons spoke of the efforts that the government was making to combat the problems, they reminded wealthy subjects of their Christian duty to help the poor, and they instructed everyone to endure the famine 'with patience'. The Church therefore played an important role in reiterating the need to obey the law. Sermons helped to shape public opinion and ensure the townspeople and peasantry were kept informed of government policies.

The oppressive rule of Mary led to a minority of English writers developing theories of disobedience towards the monarch on the grounds that rulers had an obligation to be just and true to the Christian Church. If they acted like a tyrant or sinned against God, then it was argued rebellion could be justified but only if led by a magistrate, such as a noble, JP or mayor. These ideas however became irrelevant to most Englishmen once Elizabeth came to the throne. Although some Calvinist and Catholic writers on the continent went on to develop more advanced theories of resistance, the Church of England held firm to the doctrine of non-resistance. Archbishop Parker, who was probably responsible for the *Homily against Disobedience and Wilful Rebellion* published in the aftermath of the Northern Earls' revolt, spoke for the majority when he declared:

> The first author of rebellion (the root of all vices and mother of all mischiefs) was Lucifer … Thus rebellion, as you see, both the first and greatest and the very root of all other sins, and the principal cause both of all worldly and bodily miseries … and, which is infinitely worse than all these … the very cause of death and damnation also.

Role of the local clergy

At a parish level, the Church played a vital role in local politics. Increasingly the parish came to be the focal point for administering poor relief and tackling social problems (see pages 129–30). Clerics were encouraged to inform their bishops of any signs of trouble and relevant matters were forwarded to the Privy Council, and the parish clergy were expected to instruct the people on their moral and legal obligations. Not everyone attended church, but those who listened to feast day and Sunday sermons will have received enough reminders from their parish priest of their duty to be obedient and a good neighbour. Moreover, children in learning the catechism were instructed 'to honour and obey the king, and all that are put in authority under him'. Although respect for the Church was undermined by a decline in its political status in the course of the period, the clergy no longer had a majority in the House of Lords after 1540, and Elizabeth expected her bishops to reside in their dioceses and not engage in high politics, she nevertheless gave them her support and they supported her in keeping the country stable and peaceful.

Essay focus

Look at Essay 2, paragraph 6 on page 140, which discusses the role of bishops and the parish clergy in maintaining stability. This is a good example of how to use information synoptically. The section illustrates changes in the way the clergy upheld social stability and the importance of the Reformation as a turning point in Church–State relations.

Parliament

Parliament was not an integral part of Tudor administration. It met infrequently and only when the monarch commanded: for instance, just seven sessions were held during Henry VII's 24-year reign and 13 occurred in Elizabeth's reign of 45 years. Its main purpose was to vote the Crown financial grants and discuss bills that royal councillors and MPs had proposed, yet each of the Tudors recognised that parliament could be a useful tool in preventing disorder and in dealing with rebels and conspirators who threatened the stability of the country.

Parliament, or more precisely, the House of Lords, acted as a court of law. Nobles had the right to be tried by their peers and Hussey and Darcy (1537), Suffolk (1554), Dacre (1570),

Key question
How did parliament contribute towards the maintenance of political stability in England?

Northumberland (1572) and Essex (1601) were all tried and convicted for making war against the Crown. Parliament was also used to bring bills of attainder against rebels. Henry VII's parliaments passed 138 Acts and his successors each authorised statutes in the wake of rebellions. Once lands had been attainted, only an Act of Parliament could restore them. Henry VIII and Mary were quite generous unlike Henry VII and Elizabeth, but it did not serve the Crown to be overly oppressive. For example, much of the resentment felt by nobles and gentry towards Henry VII may have been due to the way he treated them in his later years. Contrary to traditional practice, he only reversed one-third of attainders.

From time to time Acts of Parliament were passed to maintain order and deter would-be malcontents. Early in his reign Henry VII made clear his intention to clamp down on illegal retaining, which was the root cause of so much violence and disorder. The Star Chamber Act, Act of Livery and Maintenance and subsequent Statute of Liveries confirm the king's support from parliament in pursuit of this objective. His De Facto Act of 1495, on the other hand, was intended to draw a line under past indiscretions and acts of disobedience committed by Yorkists against the Crown, and may have helped restore stability in the wake of Stanley's treason.

In the 1530s Henry VIII and Cromwell implemented religious and political reforms through parliament, which ensured minimal resistance and considerable support. It is hard to gauge how far the Commons and Lords agreed with the doctrinal changes. Most Catholic clergy naturally felt uneasy about the break from Rome and some but not all abbots objected to the closure of their monasteries. Parliament as a whole approved of the dissolution and the subsequent disposal of monastic land went a long way towards retaining the support of MPs and peers, many of whom were beneficiaries. In fact the Reformation Parliament of 1529–36 probably marked a watershed in the history of English parliaments. Thereafter, changes to existing religious laws had first to be approved by parliament. Since religion could be such an emotive subject, as was evident in the 1536 and 1549 rebellions, Edward, Mary and Elizabeth understood the political value of having MPs endorse proposed changes. These were the men who in the past might have led protests against undesirable reforms; after 1536, MPs and the gentry they represented stood squarely behind the government and suppressed any extra-parliamentary disturbances. Potential poachers had become keen gamekeepers. In the 1550s the House of Commons provided a forum where the grievances and concerns of the gentry and nobility could be expressed. Whether or not MPs and peers were able to affect policy-making, their voices were heard at the highest level.

The growing support from MPs for the Crown was evident in Elizabeth's reign. Every parliament called on to vote subsidies did so even when they were multiples of two, three and four times the normal request. From 1571 MPs legislated to protect the queen and country from Catholic plots, and in 1581 from Jesuits who, it was alleged, had entered England 'to stir sedition'. The Act to retain the Queen's Majesty's subjects in their due obedience

(1581) and the Act for the Queen's Safety (1584) reflected the increasing patriotic fervour among many MPs. In fact a sea change had occurred in the Commons. At the start of the Tudor period few men aspired to be an MP: there was no salary, it entailed travelling to and finding accommodation in London, and much of the parliamentary business held little interest. By Elizabeth's reign, many gentry wanted to become an MP and wished their sons to follow them. Pressure to create more parliamentary seats steadily grew, and the Crown responded by establishing 80 new seats between 1509 and 1558 and a further 62 between 1558 and 1603. Few MPs were interested in high politics and the affairs of state, but they were concerned about economic and social issues that affected their boroughs and they saw parliament as a way of tackling these problems. The 1563 Statute of Artificers is a good case in point. Privy Councillors proposed the bill to establish seven-year apprenticeships but it was MPs who extended the bill to include the urban economy as well as agriculture. Similarly the Elizabethan poor laws owed much to the initiative of MPs. Parliament did not always agree with royal policies or support Crown-sponsored bills but in the realm of law and order, it proved a valuable ally and sounding board for the political nation.

Royal councils

The Tudors governed their kingdom through councils, initially the king's council (*curia regis*), which became the Privy Council in the 1530s, and, in the course of the period, through the addition of regional councils in the north of England, Welsh borders and Ireland (see page 131). For a brief spell between 1539–40, there was a Council in the West headed by Sir John Russell that administered the south-west counties of England. The prime function of all these councils was to transmit the monarch's wishes into actions and ensure that the country was effectively governed.

Key question
How important were royal councils in the administration of Tudor England and Ireland?

The Privy Council

The royal council changed in its size, character and work in the course of the sixteenth century. Some 227 men attended Henry VII's council during his reign although fewer than 20 councillors were in regular attendance. His principal advisers were bishops, nobles and courtiers, of whom the most important were the Archbishop of Canterbury, who was also Lord Chancellor, the Lord Privy Seal, who acted as the Chancellor's secretary, the Lord Chamberlain, who oversaw the court, and trusted household servants who held key administrative and financial offices. Henry VIII added more nobles to the council though clerics continued to hold important posts especially during Wolsey's ascendancy in the 1520s. By 1540 a small, select group of councillors had emerged into a Privy Council. Its genesis was due to the rebellions that beset Henry in 1536 and its membership came to reflect noble factions according to the king's changing matrimonial circumstances. Thus senior members of the Boleyn, Howard, Seymour and Parr families assumed prominent roles. The size of the council increased from 30 to 40 members under Edward and Mary and continued to contain a mixture of nobles, bishops, law officers and household servants of principally Protestant and Catholic persuasions according to the monarch's faith.

Under Elizabeth numbers in regular attendance fell back from around 20 to fewer than 12, with five or six men doing most of the work. Gradually the frequency of meetings and composition also changed. At first the council met three times a week, contained six nobles and no bishop; by 1603 it was meeting every day, was heavily influenced by the Secretary and Treasurer, and was dominated by members of the household and sons of government officials who had risen through state service and professional training. Cromwell in the 1530s had given the office of Secretary of State a key role in the central administration and, though its relative importance had declined after his fall, Elizabeth's dependence on Cecil and Walsingham, who held the post from 1558 to 1572 and 1573 to 1590, respectively, ensured it survived as a vital administrative office. Walsingham, in particular, assumed responsibility for maintaining stability in the kingdom.

The Council of Wales

The Council in the Marches of Wales and the Council of the North took their orders from the Privy Council in London but also developed in the sixteenth century into administrative and judicial councils in their own right with a president, secretary, chief justice and clerks. Until 1536 there were no changes in the administrative organisation of the Welsh marches and lordships. The Crown held most of the land in Wales and there were few independent lordships though some lords such as the Duke of Buckingham (until 1521) and Henry Somerset were powerful figures. Henry VII restored a council at Ludlow in 1487, placed his uncle Jasper in charge, and invited the leading Welsh and English nobles to attend. After Jasper's death in 1495, its presidents were often bishops, men like William Smith, John Veysey and Rowland Lee, but effective power rested with local landowners until the 1530s when Lee restored royal authority by rebuilding castles and enforcing justice more effectively. He was assisted by the Statutes of 1536 and 1543 which created 12 new counties in Wales and extended the council's authority to cover five English border counties. Wales now had an English administrative and judicial system and elected 24 MPs to Westminster.

The Welsh lords accepted the political and religious reforms under Henry VIII and caused no problems for his successors. No doubt their Welsh descent helped the Tudors but bribes of church land and offices were probably more crucial. The gentry were keen to become JPs and serve the Crown as well as enhance their own position locally. Although order and justice appear to have been of variable standards, there were no revolts or rebellions against the Crown in Tudor Wales. In the 1590s George Owen proudly wrote in his *The Dialogue of the Government of Wales*:

> No country [*sic.*] in England so flourished in one hundred years as Wales has done, since the government of Henry VII to this time ... so

altered is the country and countrymen, the people changed in heart within and the land altered in health without, from evil to good, and from bad to better.

The Council of the North

Henry VII revived the Council of the North after a four-year lapse. The Yorkists had created it in 1473 and at Henry's accession it was dominated by the Clifford, Neville, Percy and Dacre families. The appointment of the Earl of Surrey as his lieutenant in 1489 heralded the king's intention to develop greater control over the northern counties but the council's influence remained limited until the 1530s. Twice it was remodelled – in 1525 and 1530 – and received judicial functions in 1537 acting as a regional Star Chamber under the presidency of Cuthbert Tunstall, Bishop of Durham. Henry VIII invited leading nobles to attend and kept a watchful eye on proceedings by assuming himself the wardenship of the marches, which bordered Scotland, and appointing gentlemen rather than nobles as his deputies of the east, middle and west marches. Nevertheless, the Duke of Norfolk was probably correct when he declared that the 'wild people' of the marches could only be controlled by men of 'good estimation', which may explain the ennoblement of two deputy wardens in 1544.

Although Edward and Mary restored the Dacres and Percys as wardens, Elizabeth from 1563 started to appoint more southern nobles and northern gentry to the wardenship, which greatly assisted the council in attempting to maintain stability in the north. The council, however, underwent further reforms in the light of its failure to deal effectively with the revolt of 1569. The Earl of Huntingdon was appointed president (from 1572 to 1595) and the council's authority was increased to cover all northern counties except Lancashire. Even though there was local sympathy for Mary Queen of Scots and Catholicism continued to be a potential source of conflict, the council played a major part in upholding order and dispensing justice in the north of England. After 1570 there were no more revolts or disturbances in Elizabeth's reign.

The judiciary and the law

One of the most important requirements of any government is to ensure that the law is respected and upheld. Without this there can be no stability. From the outset the Tudors understood that the success of their dynasty largely depended on the restoration of the law. The Yorkist kings had gone some way towards achieving this in the years following the Wars of the Roses, and Henry VII largely built on their foundations. He had at his disposal a range of common law and prerogative courts:

Key question
In what ways did changes in English law and the use of law courts bring about greater stability in Tudor England?

- The common law courts comprised the Court of King's Bench, which heard serious criminal cases, civil cases that involved personal injury, suits in which the Crown had an interest and cases of appeal from other courts.
- The Court of Common Pleas heard civil cases concerning debt, fraud and property.

- The Court of Exchequer handled disputes concerning the Crown's revenue and in the course of the century also dealt with private suits.
- Parliament occasionally met to hear cases of treason.

These courts were well established but in the fifteenth century, when the Crown commanded less respect, juries had been threatened and judges bribed by powerful litigants.

An Act of Maintenance in 1487 was designed to end the pressure nobles could bring on the judicial system but the Crown put more store in supplementing the common law courts by using **prerogative** courts. Courts such as Star Chamber, Requests and Chancery had no jury, gave rulings according to the evidence presented to the king's councillors and flourished during the Tudor period. Wolsey as Lord Chancellor established regular sittings and a recognised procedure in Star Chamber and Requests, which led to an increase in litigation in both courts as the period progressed. For instance, the number of cases brought before Star Chamber in the first half of the sixteenth century rose from an annual average of 12 to nearly 150. The number of Chancery petitions also increased as the court, unlike the common law courts, could hear cases of appeal from inferior jurisdictions, notably the borough courts.

The Tudors also established law courts to meet particular needs. Some courts had a long history; others were short lived. The Councils of the North, Welsh Marches and Dublin each acquired its own judicial status and heard both criminal and civil cases; the Court of High Commission was established in the 1580s to deal with ecclesiastical issues. Some courts only functioned for a few years. Henry VII created the General Surveyors court to oversee his royal estate and the Council Learned in the Law, which investigated cases of suspected malpractice among his tenants-in-chief, many of whom were nobles. Both courts ceased in 1509 though the General Surveyors was revived later in Henry VIII's reign. Financial courts that Cromwell established in the 1530s, such as Augmentations and First Fruits and Tenths, were amalgamated into the Exchequer in 1554, but the Court of Wards retained its separate status and organisation to become one of the Tudors' most important judicial and financial courts. Each of these prerogative courts in time came to be resented by the common lawyers who viewed them as a threat to their livelihood but the Tudors saw the advantage of encouraging both systems. If they wanted to be certain of winning a case, they brought it before a prerogative court and, although such courts lacked the authority to give a death sentence, once a verdict had been reached it was possible to transfer the case to a common law court for sentencing.

In practice, however, the Tudors were not despots. They understood the value of presiding over a judiciary and legal system that was respected and, as far as possible, independent and free from corruption. When, for instance, Henry VII attempted to get his King's Bench judges to give a ruling on sanctuary in advance of the trial of Humphrey Stafford, he was rebuked for interfering in

Key term

Prerogative
Powers held by the Crown. Prerogative courts were presided over by royal councillors who dispensed justice in the interests of the Crown.

the judicial process. This did not, however, prevent the king from intervening in cases of retaining where, in advance of the indictment, he intimated the fines and recognizances awaiting the accused. Thus, the Tudors took full advantage of the law to strengthen their authority and maintain order in the country.

Martial law, sedition and treason

Henry VII and Henry VIII used parliament to pass bills of attainder against rebels and traitors, whereby trials were held and sentences given on absentee offenders. Martial law was also introduced at particular times of crisis, for instance during the rebellions in 1536–7, 1549 and 1569. Mary also used it in 1558 to arrest and prosecute anyone carrying **seditious** or heretical books, and in 1589 Elizabeth granted her provost marshals the power to stop and detain any vagrants. Unlike acts of attainder and treason laws, martial law did not allow the property of the accused to be seized, so it was used sparingly against the landed classes. However, it did have several advantages: it dispensed with the niceties of witnesses and evidence which could be hard to obtain in times of rebellion; it dispensed with trial by juries that could be very unreliable; and it delivered justice quickly and in the Crown's interest.

The law of sedition and the treason law in particular were extended by the Tudors to increase compliance and reduce the likelihood of disorder. The spreading of rumours was a common occurrence in revolts and rebellions and the authorities treated severely those found guilty of causing sedition. For example, whipping, imprisonment and public declamation awaited anyone who spread rumours of Henry VII's death or claimed to know of the existence of impostors. Cromwell in the 1530s insisted that rumours, prophesies or false stories should be thoroughly investigated and the perpetrators punished. For instance, in 1538 the vicar of Muston in Yorkshire was executed for predicting that the pope would soon 'come jingling with his keys' to England, the king would 'flee into the sea', and the Percys would 'shine kindly again and take the light of the sun'. In 1542 rumour mongering became a **felony**. Seven years later in the wake of widespread rebellions, the Privy Council declared rumour mongers would be chained to the galleys, which was virtually a sentence of death. Mary introduced the decapitation of the right hand and Elizabeth went further in 1581 by making sedition a capital offence.

The treason law was also broadened and became more intrusive. Since 1352 treason constituted compassing or imagining the king's death and levying war against the king in his country:

- In the 1530s two Acts extended treason to denying the Act of Succession, refusing to take the Oath of Supremacy and criticising Henry's marriage to Anne Boleyn. Most significant was the 1534 Act that stated treason could be 'by words' as well as 'by deeds'. Treason by words was not an innovation but its application was extended to cover recent developments. By 1540 nearly 400 people had been charged with treasonous words and at least 52 had been executed.

Key terms

Seditious
Liable to cause an affray or act of disorder.

Felony
An offence that carried the death penalty.

- Although this law was repealed in 1547, Northumberland restored it to apply to anyone who declared 'by writing, printing, painting, carving or graving' that the king was a 'heretic, schismatic, tyrant, infidel or usurper of the Crown'.
- In 1554 Mary widened the Act to cover any allegations made against her marriage to Philip or the welfare of the two sovereigns.
- Elizabeth extended the Treason Act even further. In 1571 anyone who possessed papal objects, obtained, published or received papal documents, or claimed the queen was a heretic in writing or by words could be indicted for treason.
- In 1585 a group of people – the Jesuits – were declared to be traitors even before treason was committed in word or deed. And such severe measures were not confined to Roman Catholics.
- In 1597 parliament declared that any group assembled to destroy enclosures was guilty of treason. In the same year, judges ruled that conspiring with arms was high treason on the grounds that 'rebellion is all the war which a subject can make against the King'.

Key terms

Quarter Sessions
General courts held in a county every three months.

Oyer et terminer
A commission directed to justices that empowered them to 'hear and determine' indictments for specific crimes committed in a particular area.

The vast majority of people never came before Assize judges, who twice a year attended county sessions. Indeed few will have appeared at **Quarter Sessions** where JPs presided. In most cases, disputes were dealt with in local courts such as the sheriff's court, manorial, borough and hundred courts or, in the case of matrimonial disputes, sexual impropriety and disputed wills, in the diocesan courts. Whenever possible, arguments were settled out of court, subjects were 'bound over' to keep the peace and the community acted to see that social harmony was maintained. At the beginning of the Tudor period, some people believed it was acceptable to act disorderly in order to achieve justice; by the end of the period, fear of popular disorder was very real. The overall feeling was that the proper way to proceed was to use the judicial system and act lawfully. It was quite a transformation.

Key question
In what ways were JPs the 'workhorses' of Tudor administration?

Royal Commissions and JPs

One of the most important methods of administration used by the Tudors and one frequently underrated by historians was the instigation of commissions to perform particular tasks within the counties. Under the early Tudors, members of the royal household and departmental officials often headed the commissions but in the second half of the period lords lieutenant regularly supervised their work. The range of their activities illustrates the importance that the Tudors attached to them as organs of royal administration. For instance, Henry VII used commissions of *oyer et terminer* when he wanted to investigate and take action against suspected rebels in 1497, and commissions of array were used to authorise nobles to draw up troops to deal with Simnel's rebellion. Henry VIII appointed commissions to assess subsidy payments, survey monasteries and chantries, and sell Crown lands. Enclosure commissioners were sent around the country by

Wolsey, Somerset and Cecil, and after 1570 most counties had commissions to investigate the extent of **recusancy**. Elizabeth made extensive use of special commissions as an effective way of being kept informed of developments at county level. Teams of officials conducted their enquiries quickly, made recommendations directly to the Privy Council and thus made a significant contribution to the maintenance of stability in the country.

The commissions of the peace (or justices of the peace) were by far the most important commissions to develop under the Tudors. JPs had existed since the fourteenth century but the nature of their work and the number operating in each county increased dramatically under the Tudors such that it is hard to see how law and order would have been upheld without them. In 1485 most counties had fewer than 10 JPs and commissioners often served two adjacent counties, such as Devon and Cornwall. By the end of the sixteenth century, most counties had over 50 – Norfolk had 61, Yorkshire 57 and Wiltshire 52 – and JPs were no longer itinerant. The increase in numbers in part reflected an increase in their workload but it was also due to the pressure from the gentry. Many became JPs and enjoyed the authority and prestige that went with the office and the financial and political opportunities it afforded them. Although unpaid and subject to annual appraisal, most JPs held office for life but periodically commissions were remodelled. Wolsey, for example, deliberately appointed non-northerners to several northern counties between 1513 and 1525 to effect greater stability in the region, and between 1536 and 1539, nearly one-third of all JPs in areas affected by the Pilgrimage of Grace were replaced. Edward, Mary and Elizabeth changed JPs in particular counties for religious reasons, and there were wholesale changes in 1569 and 1601 in areas where JPs had supported rebellions.

JPs performed two main functions: judicial and administrative:

- Their judicial role was extensive. For instance, they could order sheriffs and bailiffs to search for robbers; examine felons; commit those who disturbed the peace to gaol; review the empanelling of juries; collect recognizances for upholding the peace; fine recusants and arrest papists; detain and punish vagrants and rioters; hear cases concerning burglary, petty larceny and assault; and resolve disputes between masters, apprentices and servants. Much of their time was spent in travelling the county 'out of session', dealing with cases presented by constables and hundred courts, but four times a year they presided over the Quarter Sessions in the county courts. At these formal gatherings, a cross-section of the county society attended to witness Tudor law in operation. In a typical session these would comprise: the sheriff or his deputy, the county gaoler, constables, bailiffs, coroners, jurors, witnesses and accused. While cases involving the Crown and serious charges of rape, murder and treason were forwarded to the Assizes, JPs fulfilled a vital role in dispensing justice at a local level. Not all JPs were honest and hard working, but most worked for the good of their community and were loyal subjects of the Crown.

Recusant
A Catholic who denied the royal supremacy or refused to attend the services of the Anglican Church.

Key term

- Their administrative role was arguably more important than their work as law enforcers. According to the 1602 edition of William Lambarde's *Eirenarcha*, a handbook for JPs, they were expected to administer over 300 statutes, although clearly some were more important than others. These ranged from ensuring that roads, highways, bridges and sea defences were properly maintained to clearing blocked sewers and drainage ditches; from monitoring weights and measures on market days to fixing the price of grain in times of famine; from assessing subsidy tax returns to overseeing the welfare of the poor; from licensing alehouses to assisting officials at the county muster. In fact there was very little that a JP was not expected to do.

Essay focus

Any essay question that concerns maintaining order and stability will benefit from a discussion of the work of JPs. Their contribution is concisely assessed in Essay 2, paragraph 6 on page 140.

Key question
Why did the lord lieutenant become the Crown's principal representative in English counties?

Sheriffs and lords lieutenant

The decline of the sheriffs

Since the fifteenth century, sheriffs, who were originally responsible for maintaining order in the counties, had been in decline. In 1485 they still played a key role in supervising parliamentary elections, serving royal writs, mustering of troops, organising Quarter Sessions and Assizes, transporting prisoners, empanelling juries, presiding over monthly meetings of the county court and enforcing sentences passed down by JPs and assize judges, and these duties continued throughout the sixteenth century. However, the Tudors never fully trusted their sheriffs to exercise political and military power. Henry VII had viewed with alarm their capacity to undermine royal authority in the shires and sought to weaken their influence. In 1495 he gave JPs the power to monitor their activities and encouraged them to report any malpractices to the royal council. Gradually the sheriff's authority became more honorific and the maintenance of stability in the counties fell to the increasingly over-worked JPs. The outbreak of rebellions in the 1530s and 1540s, moreover, demonstrated that the sheriff's ability to muster soldiers and suppress serious disturbances left much to be desired – some had even joined the rebels – and reform was required.

The rise of the lords lieutenant

In 1549 in the wake of serious disturbances in central and southern England, lords lieutenant were appointed to oversee counties where there had been rebellions or where subjects might become troublesome. Intended as a temporary measure, the Duke of Northumberland in 1551 saw the political advantage of their existence to buttress his position as President of the Privy Council. Lieutenants like Russell in the south-western counties and

Northampton in East Anglia performed military as well as police duties, and the absence of any rebellions between 1550 and 1553 suggests that the 12 men appointed by Northumberland fulfilled their role competently although their unwillingness to support his coup against Mary is a telling comment on the illegitimacy of his claim to rule the country. The office lapsed at Mary's accession but was revived with the advent of war in 1557 when she divided the country into 10 lieutenancies. Elizabeth similarly saw no need to appoint lieutenants on a permanent basis and only appointed them in times of crisis, notably in 1569 during the Northern Earls' revolt and in 1585 at the outbreak of war with Spain. However, the continuance of war and the threat of invasion in 1588 resulted in most counties having a resident lord lieutenant, and since most officers were privy councillors, as many as two to six deputies per county were appointed to carry out their duties in their absence. By the end of the period, lords lieutenant had become a regular feature of county administration. Sometimes they were used to supervise recusants, distribute grain in times of shortage and collect loans on behalf of the Crown, but their main function was to muster and train the county militia.

In the course of the sixteenth century and largely as a result of the rebellions between 1536 and 1570, the Tudors came to realise the inadequacy of the county militia. The law required every free man aged from 16 to 60 years to carry a weapon to defend himself and his country in the event of an invasion. Although this was clearly inadequate, and in most cases never implemented, the Crown without a standing army and police force necessarily relied on the nobility and gentry to supply retainers and, where possible, weaponry and armour. The number of retainers had greatly diminished since the advent of the Tudors and many were reluctant to fight for commanders other than their own lord or to act against their neighbours (see page 72). Moreover the logistics of the Crown raising, equipping and organising troops proved very haphazard when put to the test. In theory, every summer the sheriff mustered all able-bodied men in the county, recorded and checked their weapons, and gave them basic training in warfare. In practice, the Crown had little idea how many men could be put on a war footing ready to suppress rebellions or repel invaders. Wolsey conducted a survey in 1522, which revealed that the most common weapon was the **billhook**, and a survey in the 1540s suggested that few men possessed complete sets of armour and harnesses.

Reform of the county militia

Mary tried to improve the condition of the militia by passing two Acts in 1558. These firstly required everyone to contribute according to their means towards the provision of men, equipment and horses, and secondly attempts were made to achieve a more regular attendance at the muster. If any improvements occurred, they were clearly inadequate to deal with the 1569 revolt and so it fell to the lords lieutenant to overhaul the whole system of raising and training troops.

Billhook
A curved blade attached to a wooden handle that could be used to slash and cut an adversary.

Key term

In 1572 a Militia Act was passed to address the problem. Men aged from 16 to 60 years were required to be trained in the use of arms: they were paid 8*d* (3p) a day for about 10 days' training a year and their equipment was to be provided by the county. However, as this would cost the Crown at least £400 a year per county, only 10 per cent of men were selected for training. The lords lieutenant and their deputies appointed muster masters and provost marshals for raising, equipping and training the troops, and by the late 1580s England had some 26,000 trained bands ready for active service. Their prime task was to fight any Spanish invasion but they could be used to suppress riots and disturbances though Elizabeth was reluctant to send them overseas or even to use them against Tyrone's rebellion in Ireland. Nevertheless by 1603 the Crown had at its disposal a civil defence force that was independent of the servants and retainers that the aristocracy had supplied for centuries. It is difficult to assess the competency of the trained bands as a whole but when they were first put to the test in the Midland counties in 1607, the gentry found 'great backwardness' and relied far more on their own retainers.

Lords lieutenant and their deputies worked closely with the JPs and gentry and were a pivotal link in the chain of command between the Crown and county administration responsible for ensuring the country remained stable and peaceful. The absence of any major rebellion after 1570 in Elizabethan England does not prove that they were an effective deterrent against popular disorder, but a permanent Crown appointee in each county enabled the government to be better informed of local issues and undoubtedly better placed to resolve difficulties before they became too serious.

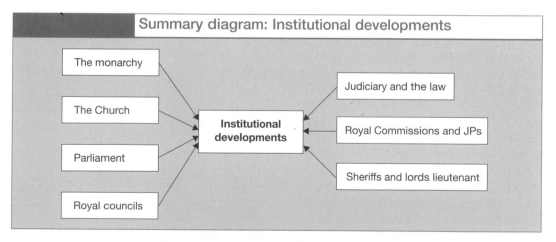

Summary diagram: Institutional developments

2 | Tudor policies: continuity and change

We have seen how the stability and order of the kingdom depended to a great extent on Tudor institutions and administrators, but it was also the case that the policies undertaken by Tudor governments played a vital part in keeping the people under control. Political, religious, economic and social issues needed to be addressed if recurrent disturbances and rebellions were to be avoided.

The nobility

The political role of the nobility underwent a dramatic change during the Tudor period. In the second half of the fifteenth century, families such as the Howards, Percys, Staffords and Nevilles owned vast tracts of land, often consolidated in one area of the kingdom where they ruled their tenants like petty kings. The Percys in the north, for instance, controlled the lives of some 10,000 tenants. Many lords had private armies, waged war against their neighbours from fortified castles and had little respect for the king's laws. While the Wars of the Roses had certainly depleted the resources of many nobles and in a few cases wiped out families altogether, there still remained a small number of nobles who were unwilling to accept Henry Tudor as the rightful king. Moreover many had become accustomed to governing the country with or without the king and, as leaders of the political community, Henry knew they were indispensable if he was to survive. As long as they were competent and loyal, the king would leave them alone; but if they acted independently or against his best interests, he would rein them in.

Henry VII and Henry VIII sought to reduce the incidence of disorder perpetrated by the nobility by dismantling castles in non-strategic sites, confiscating supplies of gunpowder and decommissioning cannons. Most nobles complied, though they were encouraged to keep their suits of armour and harnesses in good condition ready for royal service. Henry VII spent most of his reign trying to eliminate the threat of pretenders and rival claimants and in so doing trammelled the English and Irish nobility into a state of subservience. Statutes of 1487 and 1504 attempted to confine retainers to licensed holders and harsh fines were imposed on nobles who ignored the law. Lord Burgavenny, for example, was fined £71,000 and Sir James Stanley £245,000 in 1506. It was not Henry's intention to eliminate retaining – he needed troops to suppress disturbances and fight foreign wars – but to punish the worst cases of abuse. Other Tudor rulers took the same view. Henry VIII relied on 700 of Norfolk's retainers and Lord Ferrers provided 1000 men to counter the pilgrims in 1536. Mary issued over 2000 licences for retaining and Elizabeth needed nobles' retainers to deal with the 1569 uprising. Private feuding still existed especially in the Welsh marches, Scottish borders and outside the Irish Pale although there is evidence that the number of cases involving **livery and maintenance** declined significantly in the course of the sixteenth century. By the end of the period, the Crown, in Lawrence Stone's words, may have gained 'a royal monopoly of violence' from the aristocracy, but some nobles were still capable of raising and equipping troops independently if they so wished.

The Crown preferred to seize nobles' lands if an act of treason had been committed. Henry VII passed 138 Acts of attainder and, contrary to customary practice, only reversed a minority of them. Henry VIII, Edward and Mary were more generous in restoring lands but few nobles after 1536 were involved in treasonous

Key question
How and why did the role of the English nobility change during the Tudor period?

Key term

Livery and maintenance
Wearing a lords' tunic bearing his coat of arms, and the practice in which some lords attended a law court in order to influence the judge and jury.

activities. Bonds and recognizances were also imposed on the nobility by all of the Tudors. These required Crown servants on taking office, many of whom were nobles, and any subjects who had infringed the law, to stand surety for hundreds and sometimes thousands of pounds. It has been estimated that two-thirds of the English nobility and gentry were at the king's mercy by 1509 and, although Henry VIII cancelled all bonds in a gesture of unprecedented generosity, bonds were the preferred method of controlling unreliable nobles and were again introduced after the rebellions of 1537, 1549, 1554, 1570 and 1601.

All of the Tudors tried to prevent major families from building up large tracts of land and exercising political dominance in their counties. Henry VII discouraged English heiresses from marrying powerful and potentially threatening nobles, made the Welsh lords sign indentures of good behaviour and kept a close watch on Burgavenny, the most powerful baron. When the fourth Earl of Northumberland was murdered in 1489, the king took possession of the young heir as a royal ward to gain control of the Percy estates in Yorkshire and Northumberland. Henry VIII similarly tried to strengthen royal control of sensitive areas. In the 1530s he endowed Russell and Suffolk with lands in the south-west and East Anglia, respectively, and transferred the wardenship of the northern marches from traditional noble families to lesser gentry. The appointment of local gentry who owed their office to the Crown made steady inroads towards reducing the lawlessness in the north. The perceived view was that the northern magnates promoted disorder by either ignoring disturbances or actually encouraging them. However, the demise of the great northern families – the Nevilles, Percys and Dacres – came as a result of the Northern Earls' revolt in 1569 when many of their lands were seized and regranted to gentry from the south of England.

Henry VII did not favour ennobling his subjects. He only raised four men to the peerage, two of whom were relatives, and in the course of his reign the overall number of peers fell from 20 to 10. In contrast Henry VIII, Edward and Mary behaved more generously. Henry rewarded his nobility with lands and titles and was responsible for creating over half the peerage by 1547, but he skilfully balanced new creations with the promotion of existing nobles, and confined his generosity to a small group of courtiers. During Edward's reign, his regents rewarded themselves and many of their associates with peerages. In 1547 alone Thomas Wriothesley became the Earl of Southampton, John Dudley the Earl of Warwick, William Parr the Marquis of Northampton, and Thomas Seymour, Richard Rich, William Willoughby and Edmund Sheffield all became barons. Elizabeth like her grandfather was ungenerous in her creation of peers. Only 10 new peerages were created and as a result the total number fell from 57 in 1558 to 55 in 1603.

In the course of the Tudor period, the nobility also appears to have undergone a metamorphosis that had a significant bearing on their relationship with their tenants, the Crown and society in general. Instead of military honour, war and violence, which had influenced their social mores in the fifteenth century, many by 1603 espoused good lordship, peace and civility. Part of this transition can be explained by the steady decline in feudal relations with their tenants; land tenure came to be based on **copyhold and customary rights** rather than on the 'honour' and 'will' of the lord, and lords retained far fewer servants. And the demise of large households in the second half of the sixteenth century for economic reasons further weakened the bonds of personal ties. The change can also be attributed to an increasing interest in **humanism**, learning and European culture, and a desire to study at one of the universities and Inns of Court. Thus most nobles ceased to be politically ambitious or aggressive towards their neighbours and instead focused their efforts upon managing their estates and working with the Crown to attain political and social stability in the counties.

> ### Essay focus
>
> Compare the two essays on pages 136–41 to see how information on the nobility has been effectively and ineffectively used. Essay 1, paragraphs 2 and 3, asserts rather than explains; Essay 2, paragraphs 2–5, integrates and assesses the role of the nobility with considerable skill. Higher marks are always given to essays that evaluate and explain developments.

The Tudors relied heavily on the nobility as councillors, administrators and military leaders. Henry VII convened five Great Councils of the nobles, and Henry VIII and Elizabeth held assemblies of nobles in the 1530s and 1580s to discuss matters of state. Parliament of course was an occasion when the peers were invited to advise the monarch and all Tudor councils contained nobles. In 1526, for instance, seven out of 20 royal councillors were peers, in 1540 eight were in attendance, and 14 in Edward's enlarged council in 1553. Only in Elizabeth's reign did the number of peers decline from six in her first council to one in 1601. But if Elizabeth was less dependent on her peers in the Privy Council, they served her in other ways.

Every peer and leading gentleman was expected periodically to attend the royal court to pay their respects to the queen. Some nobles resided permanently as servants of the household and chamber; others served as ambassadors and fulfilled diplomatic duties. Some became JPs, some served on special commissions and many more became lords lieutenant. Stanley in Lancashire, Hatton in Northamptonshire and Talbot in Derbyshire for instance were the queen's principal source of authority in these counties. Nobles also presided over the regional councils in Wales, the north and Dublin, and used their influence to impose order in the region. Above all the Tudors relied on nobles to put down rebellions. Surrey, Oxford and Pembroke assisted Henry VII; Norfolk, Suffolk and Shrewsbury suppressed rebellions in Henry VIII's reign; Russell, Warwick and Grey led armies against the Western, Kett and Oxford rebels, and Pembroke, Clinton and Norfolk were sent

Key terms

Copyhold and customary rights
Tenants who held a copy of their tenancy but in practice only had limited rights. Customary rights were more secure and reflected traditional local practices and customs.

Humanism
The study of architecture, art, language, rhetoric and literature that enabled the individual to become more civilised and better prepared to play an active role in the political life of the state.

to deal with Wyatt and his rebels. Elizabeth similarly depended on Sussex, Clinton and Hunsdon to combat the northern earls, she sent lords Grey, Essex and Mountjoy to suppress the Irish rebellions, and the Earl of Nottingham was called upon to arrest Essex himself in 1601.

Religious changes

Key question
Why were there no wars of religion in Tudor England and Ireland?

Henrician reforms

Ecclesiastical and doctrinal reforms could be a potent source of conflict, as both Henry VIII and Edward VI discovered. All governments feared rapid change and much effort was made to explain and justify religious reforms and minimise popular instability. Although uniformity of belief was the preferred goal, a more realistic objective was to implement changes with as little disruption as possible and only to target extremists who could not be accommodated in the English Church. As a result, Henry persecuted a minority of Roman Catholics, who would not be reconciled to the new headship and Protestant reforms, and those sects that threatened the unity of the Church of England such as Anabaptists and **sacramentarians**. After the Pilgrimage of Grace he faced no more religious uprisings, partly due to his decision in 1539 to halt further Protestant reforms in the face of growing iconoclasm and partly because few English and Irish were prepared to rally to the papal cause. The government nonetheless remained on its guard against popular insurrections. In 1543, for example, an Act for the Advancement of True Religion declared 'no woman (except noble women in private) nor artificers, prentices, journeymen, serving men of the degrees of yeoman and under, husbandmen or labourers' was to read the Bible because these 'lower sort' might acquire 'naughty and erroneous opinions, and by occasion thereof fall into great division and dissention among themselves'.

Key term

Sacramentarians Protestants who denied the real presence of Christ in the Eucharist.

Edwardian reforms

Apart from the Western rebellion and disturbances in counties such as Hampshire and Oxfordshire in 1549, there was little negative reaction to the Edwardian religious reforms. Although the government played down the radical nature of religious change, the Dukes of Somerset and Northumberland introduced reforms slowly and cautiously. They were for instance concerned that itinerant preachers and unlicensed printing might be provocative, and from September 1548 banned all preaching. A year later censorship was introduced to prevent the printing of radical tracts, sermons and ballads. In fact reforms were greeted more by apathy and indifference than by active opposition. Of course it may be that by 1552, when the country experienced the most radical doctrinal reforms to date, people who might have opposed the changes were biding their time in anticipation of a Catholic restoration under Mary. It is equally possible that the introduction of legislation, which made the gathering of 12 or more people a felony, deterred potential protesters.

Catholic restoration

Mary Tudor, in spite of her harsh treatment of Protestants, faced no religious revolts. Wisely she and her council encouraged recalcitrant Protestants to emigrate rather than spread opposition internally. Of course, the government's decision to burn nearly 300 heretics must have deterred some would-be rebels, although it was concerned that public burnings might generate popular protests and a proclamation in 1556 attempted to bar servants, apprentices and young people from attending these ceremonies. Also the knowledge that Mary was childless and would be succeeded by her Protestant sister perhaps convinced many people that it was better to suffer in silence. In reality outside London and certain dioceses such as Canterbury, York and Winchester, where Catholic bishops were keen to enforce a Counter-Reformation, the religious reforms in the 1550s had little impact on the spiritual condition of the people. Both Catholic and Protestant gentry are known to have acquired monastic and chantry property, there was no real appetite by clerics or laymen to see a restoration of the papacy, and as many as 2000 priests resigned or retired from their benefices after 1554 rather than give up their recently acquired marital status.

The Elizabethan Church Settlement

Elizabeth famously announced that she would 'open windows into no man's soul'. Her principal desire to achieve outward conformity and to establish a religious settlement that was acceptable to the vast majority of the nation largely explains the absence of popular resistance and revolts in her reign. Only a small number of Catholic priests were unwilling to subscribe to the oaths of supremacy and uniformity. A minority of English counties, notably Lancashire, Sussex, Hampshire and Cornwall, and most of Ireland had a Catholic core but none was prepared to revolt against the Elizabethan Church. Significantly none of these areas joined the northern earls in their pseudo-religious revolt of 1569.

The arrival in England of Mary Queen of Scots in 1568 and the excommunication of 1570 increased the potential for Catholic conspiracies and disturbances, which the government effectively countered. Counties known to favour Catholic beliefs had their JPs systematically remodelled, Assize judges were ordered to readminister the oath of supremacy to all JPs in 1579 and Walsingham's agents alerted the Privy Council to plots linked to Mary. In practice few Catholics sympathised with her plight or showed much interest in the activities of Jesuits and missionaries who were roaming the country in the 1580s.

Anti-Catholic penal laws from 1571 made it clear that Catholics had to choose between obeying the queen and the pope, and the majority of the noble and gentry families stayed loyal to the queen. In return she periodically protected them from attempts by zealous Protestants in parliament to increase the severity of the penal laws. In 1571 for instance the Commons and the Lords passed a bill to force Catholics to take Anglican communion once a year or pay a £66 fine. The queen vetoed the proposal. Similarly no concerted attempt was made to force the Church Settlement on Ireland. As a result religion was never a serious issue with Irish clans in spite of its potential to cause instability.

Protestant challenges

Wherever religious grievances underpinned rebellions against Tudor governments, the protagonists were Catholics. English Protestants, in contrast, were consistently loyal to the monarchy: a minority in 1549 wanted further reforms, none rebelled against Mary and even puritans acknowledged Elizabeth's entitlement to be the Supreme Governor of the Church of England. In fact Elizabethan Protestantism was not that popular: it was too academic and unattractive to most rural people, who disliked long sermons and had little time for Bible reading. Attendance at church was generally low and some parishes had difficulty keeping order during services. In practice playing football, hunting and going to the pub were preferred Sunday activities in many parishes. Although by law everyone should have attended Sunday service, the authorities were reluctant to proceed against absentees. The emergence of Protestant non-conformists in the 1580s, however, led to the government taking action to stamp out possible dissension. Sects like the Brownists and Barrowists were forced into exile, leading members who returned from the continent were arrested and the Court of High Commission was used to censor literature and issue licences to preachers. At a time of growing national crisis, the government again took no chances. An Act of 1593 restricted all recusants to a five-mile radius from their homes and imprisoned indefinitely known trouble-makers, both puritan and Catholic. None of the radicals posed a threat to civil or religious stability though this Act may have been a factor in ensuring dissidents were kept under control.

Economic developments

Key question
What initiatives were taken by the central government and towns to combat economic problems?

The Tudors did not have a coherent economic policy; they simply reacted to events as they unfolded. Governments were, however, influenced by the need to raise revenue to administer the country and by a desire to prevent disorder and look after their subjects' welfare. Grievances over taxation, enclosures, high food prices and unemployment were the root cause of several rebellions and generated riotous behaviour in most English counties at some stage under the Tudors. No government set out to provoke disquiet and in most cases Tudor governments only intervened in economic affairs to rectify a problem. Even then the main objective was a short-term fix, not complete reform. As a result over 300 statutes were passed, mainly to improve trade and industry, and to control labour relations and social welfare, which JPs were expected to enforce. In practice few cases seem to have been presented to JPs at a local level and even fewer prosecutions were brought by the Crown, which suggests that once legislation had been introduced the Crown was more interested in its own fiscal welfare. It is also likely that JPs were reluctant to prosecute for fear of exacerbating unemployment and fomenting trouble.

Government finance

Raising taxes was always unpopular: then as now people resented handing over their money. The government's response was to try to justify the need and to avoid making excessive or innovative demands. The Amicable Grant amply demonstrated the danger of trying to collect a non-parliamentary tax and farmers expressed similar concern in 1536 and 1549 when rumours circulated that the government was planning to increase indirect taxation. Medieval rulers had been expected to 'live of their own', to utilise their own lands, profits of justice and customs duties to meet the costs of running the country and maintaining the royal household – but by the end of the Tudor period this was no longer the case. To meet the rising costs of administration, which more than doubled in the sixteenth century, governments employed a variety of expedients:

- Henry VII and his successors used parliamentary grants to pay for wars and the practice of receiving peacetime subsidies began in the 1530s.
- Henry VIII and Edward debased the coinage, sold off Crown lands and negotiated loans from continental bankers.
- Mary and Elizabeth cut back on expenditure, made their administrations more efficient and avoided wars for as long as possible.

Above all, Elizabeth made no attempt to reform the system of self-assessment whereby land, property and goods were rated for tax and confirmed by JPs at levels well below their acknowledged value. Since 1547 MPs and peers had begun to revise their parliamentary assessments downwards. By 1558 the assessed landed income of nobles had on average fallen by 25 per cent, and continued to fall such that, in the 1570s those rated at £100 or more were taxed at around 10 per cent. William Cecil, for example, had estates and goods rated at £133 a year that were valued at over £4000, and he was the Lord Treasurer! This collusion between landowners, merchants, nobles and gentry ensured that, while the wealthy classes did pay taxes from time to time, as long as the government kept its demands within reasonable limits, there was never going to be any serious resistance or opposition. Even during the last decade of her reign, when Elizabeth requested very large subsidies, MPs approved. War needs and national security outweighed any thoughts of complaining. Indeed by judicious financial management and by avoiding excessive demands, neither Mary nor Elizabeth experienced tax revolts.

Enclosures

The enclosing of land was not a major issue except when it occurred illegally or in times of economic hardship, and then only in areas where fertile land was in short supply. Every Tudor government legislated against unlawful enclosures. Thus Acts were passed in 1489, 1533, 1549–50, 1555, 1563 and 1597 to prevent the conversion of arable to pasture, the engrossment of farms and the destruction of common rights. Commissions of enquiry were periodically held in 1488, 1517, 1548, 1549 and 1565–6 to ensure illegal enclosures had not occurred, and there is evidence to suggest that plaintiffs increasingly turned to litigation rather than violence to right a wrong. Wolsey charged 264 landlords and corporations with unlawful enclosure and the Privy Council took action against illegal enclosures in the wake of the Pilgrimage of Grace. Northumberland, in contrast, sided with the landlords in 1550 and took action to deter protesters, although the collapse of the wool trade and a series of good harvests may explain the absence of complaints in the 1550s. Generally enclosures became less of an issue in Elizabeth's reign such that by 1593 the government was confident enough to repeal all existing anti-enclosure legislation. Unfortunately the repeal coincided with the start of five poor harvests, grain shortages, rising inflation and urban unemployment. Yet even allowing for this downturn in the economy and the disturbances in Oxfordshire in 1596, there was no strong call to reverse the law. In fact an Act was passed that made protests against enclosures treasonous, which no doubt contributed to a spate of enclosure activity in the last years of Elizabeth's reign.

Food supplies

Economic historians have estimated that one in every four harvests failed in Tudor England and that at least one-third of the population lived at or below starvation level. If this is so, it is perhaps surprising that the period did not see more grain riots and rebellions due to rising prices and the scarcity of food. Part of the explanation lies in the lack of interest shown by nobles and gentry in leading rebellions or participating in local riots; but principally the answer is to be found in government legislation, the enforcement of statutes and proclamations by JPs, and the initiatives taken by municipal authorities in tackling the problems locally. Acts were passed in 1534, 1555, 1559, 1563, 1571 and 1593 to limit the export of grain and encourage imports, and measures were taken in 1527, 1544, 1545, 1550, 1556 and 1562 to prevent the hoarding of grain. In many cases towns such as Norwich, London and Ipswich bought up cheap corn, stockpiled it and sold it to the poor at below market rates in times of dearth. JPs were also ordered to search houses for grain and farmers were forced to sell corn at a fair price. Books of Orders were issued by the royal council in 1527, 1550, 1556 and 1586, that gave detailed advice on how to deal with food shortages, and Orders in the 1590s required towns to transport surplus corn to the most affected areas. Perhaps on account of the sensitive nature of food prices and the fluctuating availability of grain, the government was more willing to intervene when there were food shortages than in other fields of economic activity. Its success rate, however, is hard to judge. It remains true that in spite of continuing poor harvests and food shortages in the last 20 years of Elizabeth's reign, there was little sign of disorder. JPs did their best to enforce regulations but towns often looked no further than helping their own citizens and some merchants were primarily interested in profiteering.

Essay focus

The role of local authorities in tackling economic problems is dealt with very successfully in Essay 2, paragraph 7 on page 140. The relationship between the localities and central government is often overlooked but here the essay gives examples of problems, solutions and town officers, to illustrate their contribution to the maintenance of stability.

Unemployment

The steady rise in population and fluctuating trade markets meant that levels of unemployment rose during periods of depression, which increased the likelihood of unrest. The 1520s, 1550s and 1590s saw short-lived but significant slumps in the woollen cloth trade and resulted in corresponding bursts of government interventionism. Admittedly the Crown had a personal interest in maintaining high levels of cloth production since its customs revenue was directly affected by exports of wool and cloth. The problem of large numbers of unemployed fullers, carders, weavers and dyers only became serious in the 1550s. Northumberland's council issued rules in 1552 to control the quality of manufacturing different types of cloth in an attempt to raise export sales, and Mary's government passed laws in 1555 designed to force weavers to join guilds and maintain a good standard of work.

By far the most important legislation came in 1563. The Statute of Artificers introduced a range of measures intended to restrict the movement of labour as the unemployed travelled from town to town in search of work, and to ensure relations between employers and workers were put on a fair basis. Thus the Act declared:

- no one could practise a craft without first completing a seven-year apprenticeship
- workers and servants could not be hired for less than a year
- masters were not allowed to dismiss a servant nor servants leave their employment without good reason
- JPs were told to set maximum wage rates for every occupation
- all unemployed aged between 12 and 60 were to be found work in their parish: the men in agriculture and women in domestic service.

The Statute represented a real attempt to control the economy, to find work for the unemployed and to preserve order across the country. It is, however, difficult to say how effective it was in practice. There were no revolts or rebellions involving unemployed workers and farmers in the second half of the sixteenth century but JPs appear to have been reluctant to impose regulations strictly and only in years of severe economic depression, notably in the 1590s, were laws enforced. In reality, JPs usually sided with the masters, employers and craft guilds, and only fully applied the laws when it was in their interest to do so.

Social reforms

Key question
In what ways and to what extent did the poor threaten the stability of Tudor England?

How best to deal with the rising number of beggars, vagrants and poor people was a concern for all Tudor administrations. Although the poor were unlikely to cause a rebellion, they could swell the ranks of protesters and exacerbate social and economic problems for the authorities, particularly in towns and cities. The measures that were taken by central and local governments reflect the need to tackle a problem before it got out of hand. Not all remedies were successful and in retrospect some seem quite inadequate, yet Tudor society for the first time in 300 years introduced reforms that remained on the statute books until 1834. Moreover, in spite of the population doubling in the course of the period, severe trade depressions that increased the numbers of unemployed and the closure of the monasteries that had been a source of relief for many destitute beggars, urban and rural authorities succeeded in keeping the poor under control.

The first Tudor administration to address the growing number of beggars was that of Cromwell in the 1530s. Until then, itinerant beggars were put in the stocks for three days and then returned to their place of birth or previous known residence. Impotent beggars were allowed to stay but none was permitted to roam the countryside. The depression of the 1520s led to large numbers of unemployed taking to the roads, which galvanised the government and some towns into action. In 1531 an Act made a distinction between the impotent and idle poor; the former were licensed by JPs to beg, the latter were to be whipped. London took a more benevolent approach and introduced voluntary alms' collections in 1533, a measure that was extended nationally by an Act of 1536, which also required parish authorities to find work for the able-bodied but lazy poor. In practice, however, few collections were made, village constables were given neither money nor raw materials to set the poor to work and, like so much Tudor social legislation, the reforms proved ineffectual.

The Edwardian government also made little headway in helping the poor. Vagabonds continued to be punished, most notably between 1547 and 1549 when a proclamation sentenced them to two years' slavery for a first offence of begging and life imprisonment thereafter. The genuine poor, on the other hand, were to receive dole money from church donations but as these remained discretionary and the threat of being admonished by the parish priest or bishop awaited non-contributors, this attempt in 1552 at stopping begging was a failure. Already cities such as Norwich and York had instituted a compulsory poor rate levied by the parish and it is clear that measures adopted by town authorities were much more effective than government legislation. By 1553 several hospitals in London had been founded and endowed with ex-monastic and chantry property, and important distinctions were made between different types of poor. Bridewell, for instance, housed vagabonds, Christ's looked after 400 orphans, and St Thomas's and St Bartholomew's took in the sick, aged and impotent. Later in Elizabeth's reign, cities like Norwich, Ipswich and Exeter came to accept their responsibility for funding and managing the welfare of their citizens.

The most important legislation occurred in Elizabeth's reign:

- The 1572 Act recognised that the deserving poor – the aged, sick and impotent – were to be helped, and vagabonds severely punished (they were whipped and had their ears bored), but it required JPs to assess how much was needed to keep them and for the first time overseers were appointed to collect compulsory parish taxes. Since the onus fell on the parish to provide for the poor, parishioners developed a collective responsibility for maintaining order and were naturally keen to discourage begging and vagrancy. A fundamental flaw in the Act – it made no provision for men and women who wanted to work but were unable to find any – was rectified four years later.

- The 1576 Act required parishes to provide wool, flax, iron and hemp so that all able-bodied people had to work. A run of five bad harvests between 1594 and 1598, large numbers of young people who were 'out of service' (i.e. neither apprenticed to a master nor employed in a household) and many disbanded soldiers and sailors, combined to alarm the government to pass a comprehensive poor law in 1598.

- The 1598 laws modified and codified previous legislation, and introduced two new reforms. First, the 'Act for the Relief of the Poor' replaced overworked JPs with churchwardens to oversee the welfare of the genuine poor and unemployed. Second, the 'Act for the Punishment of Rogues and Sturdy Beggars' separated vagabonds into two groups: dangerous vagabonds were to be rounded up by provost marshals and sent to the galleys or banished; other beggars were to be returned to their parishes of birth (if known) or placed in houses of correction and made to work.

Much had been achieved in the course of the Tudor period to reduce the likelihood of the poor disturbing the peace and, coincidentally, to alleviate their distress. By 1603 the deserving poor had been distinguished from the wilful vagrants, and the wandering poor from the settled poor. Local overseers administered relief that was compulsorily levied on parishioners and went towards food, clothing, providing work and treating the sick, elderly and infirm. Vagabonds were discouraged from begging or becoming nomadic, and punished if they refused to work. Once again, it fell to the JPs to ensure this system of social welfare actually worked. The genuine poor were therefore assisted by a combination of state, municipal and private charitable relief and, although the range of statutes and proclamations may not have been consistently enforced, enough was done to ensure the poor did not pose a threat to the stability of the country.

Key question
How far can Tudor rule of Ireland be described as 'successful'?

Ireland

The maintenance of permanent order in Ireland was all but impossible. The only effective areas of law enforcement were the lowlands of Munster and Leinster centred around Dublin and the Pale where the Anglo-Irish mainly lived. Feuding between rival clans such as the Geraldines and Butlers, or O'Neills and O'Donnells was endemic, whether in or out of office. Tudor monarchs were not recognised as sovereign rulers by Gaelic lords, who controlled most of the island, and instead English kings depended on the most prominent Anglo-Irish family – the Geraldines – to govern on their behalf. Relying on the Geraldines was a high-risk, low-cost strategy. The eighth Earl of Kildare, Gerald, acknowledged Simnel and Warbeck as kings of England and his brother, Thomas, died fighting Henry VII at Stoke. Moreover, the family used its political status to extend its power at the expense of rival clans and, though revolts were commonplace, a semblance of order was maintained. Disturbances in Ireland were after all not in the Kildares' best interest because they could not govern without a royal commission, and this could be revoked as in 1492, 1522 and 1528. However, attempts to rule through Kildares' rivals, the Butlers, proved equally unsatisfactory as they were unable to command much respect from the other lordships. In practice, English laws were only occasionally enforced and Gaelic customs and language were encouraged by the Irish administration. In return the Crown's landed interests were protected and the cost of governing Ireland was met by the feudal dues paid to Kildare.

Both Henry VII and his son sent troops to Ireland when trouble flared up: Edgecombe went there in 1487, Poynings in 1494 and Surrey in 1520, but the conquest of Ireland was never seriously considered by the early Tudors. Poynings only took 400 men and Surrey had 500 troops and the king's Yeomen of the Guard. Nevertheless in 1519 Henry VIII took a more proactive interest in Irish affairs, establishing a council in Dublin and sending Surrey to see 'how Ireland may be reduced and restored to good order and obedience'. The earl made a shrewd assessment of the situation when he reported that the Irish 'will not be brought to no good order, unless it be by compulsion, which will not be done without a great puissance of men, and great cost of money, and long continuance of time'. As Henry had neither men nor money to spare, he returned to a policy of relying on the Irish magnates.

Changes

The year 1534 marked a turning point in Anglo-Irish relations. Until then the main colonial grievance had been royal neglect: no Tudor ever visited Ireland, the administration was expected to be self-funded, and rulers seriously underestimated the difficulties that faced the lord deputies and deputy lieutenants in maintaining peace. After 1534 the main colonial grievance was royal interference. English-born officials held all the principal offices, which naturally caused resentment among old English families, who had hitherto monopolised royal patronage, as well as among Gaelic lords, who resented the increasing interference in their way of life. Moreover, Henry VIII's Reformation brought religion into the political arena. The new Lord Deputy, Leonard Grey, made clear his intentions in 1536: he called a parliament, attainted Kildare, imposed Henry's Reformation Acts, ordered the collection of First Fruits and Tenths and sold off half of all monastic lands. Although the garrison in Dublin was reduced from 700 to 340 troops, the cost was borne by the locals and army captains were granted lands on the borders of the Pale.

The appointment of Anthony St Leger as Deputy in 1537 heralded further changes. He increased the garrison to 2000 men (although it was again reduced to 500 in 1543) and tried to get the Gaelic chiefs to recognise Henry as the King of Ireland rather than 'Lord'. In 1541 his diplomacy eventually worked. The chiefs agreed to surrender their lands to the king and he regranted them according to English laws and customs. They swore an oath of allegiance and rejected the authority of the pope. For his part, Henry gave up claims to land under Gaelic occupation and surrendered many feudal rights, which gave the Irish greater security of tenure as their lands were now hereditary. Progress was also made at getting the Gaelic chiefs to attend Irish parliaments, to adopt English customs and refrain from tribal conflict. The idea of a united and non-partitioned kingdom of Ireland was slowly taking shape.

Under Edward VI the garrison was again enlarged to 2600 troops and more fortresses were built in the marcher borderlands. Both Somerset and Northumberland took an aggressive stance towards Ireland, which won them more enemies than friends. When disturbances broke out between the O'Connors and O'Mores, for example, the lands confiscated from the warring families were granted to new English settlers at low rents and subject to English law. Resentment further grew as more Englishmen in Dublin saw the opportunity to gain lands and wealth at the expense of the Irish. In Mary's reign more garrisons were built in Leix and Offaly, plantations (proto-colonies) were set up in the vicinity and **purveyance** and military service imposed on local tenants and Irish natives. The Anglicisation of Gaelic lordships and the establishment of colonies outside the Pale, accompanied by a growing military presence, increased the likelihood of instability and worsened Anglo-Irish relations.

Elizabeth's policy towards Ireland was characterised by inconsistency. Reluctant to spend money on maintaining her garrisons and regularly changing her deputies, justiciars and lieutenants (between 1580 and 1603 there were six deputies, six justiciars and one lieutenant), the queen condoned numerous experiments to keep effective control of Ireland that were underfunded, poorly organised and guaranteed to antagonise both the Old and New English inhabitants. The Old English favoured a peaceful and gradual expansion westwards; the New English wanted an instant occupation of border lands which could be best achieved by force. Under Lord Deputy Sussex's administration

Purveyance
The right of the Crown to purchase supplies or to obtain transport for the royal household at prices fixed below prevailing market rates.

Key term

(1559–65), the Old English complained that 'their kingdom was kept from them by force and by such as be strangers in blood to them'. Their complaints were reminiscent of those later voiced by the English northern earls. Following the suppression of Shane O'Neill's rebellion in 1567, junior branches of the clan were made to surrender their land in Ulster and have them regranted according to English law, the Scots in Antrim were expelled, three garrisons were set up and two English colonies established in Ards by Thomas Smith and Walter Devereux. Both colonies failed largely because of the attitude adopted by the founders. Smith, for example, planned to expel the 'wicked, barbarous and uncivil people, some Scottish and some wild Irish', force remaining natives to work for the colony at low wages and deny them the chance of owning land themselves.

Some lessons, however, were learned and subsequent colonies that were established in Connaught in 1585 and Munster in 1586 were more successful. Each colony was overseen by a provincial council and president, who were keen to extend English law and customs, and was modelled on the councils in the northern and Welsh marches. All landowners, both new and Gaelic, registered their entitlement to land, abolished customary practices and paid a yearly rent towards the administration and defence of the province. Elsewhere this **composition** scheme was less well received and Elizabeth's policy of land resumption, which entailed claiming rebels' land as well as concealed properties, led to ill-feeling. Moreover, attempts to enforce recusancy laws in the 1580s were rejected by the Old English, most of whom were Roman Catholic. By the early 1590s much of Ireland outside Ulster was subject to English rule within acceptable terms of administration. Revolts and disturbances occasionally occurred in Munster, Connaught and Leinster, but they were suppressed by local garrisons and Gaelic chiefs intent on preserving the *status quo*. Colonies were slowly spreading eastwards and provincial councils gave passing credence of a centralised administration. Many of these developments were even infringing into Ulster itself although the northern province remained an implacably hostile region.

By 1603 Ireland was in a poor condition as a result of the lengthy and exhausting Tyrone rebellion. Much of Ulster was devastated, cattle and crops had been destroyed, the colonies in Connaught and Munster had been swept away, and social divisions between the New and Old English and Gaelic natives had resurfaced. Elizabeth had failed to maintain order and stability mainly because she had not been willing to devote enough resources to administer the provinces nor allowed colonial initiatives enough time to succeed. If lessons were learned, they were not always consistently applied. English governors needed to work with Gaelic chiefs, as had occurred in the effective strategy of surrender and regrant. In contrast, the development of colonies and small, underfunded garrisons only caused resentment. And when military solutions were considered, the queen despatched too small an army that failed to protect the Old English or control the borders and Gaelic lordships from rebellious clans.

Key term

Composition
Taxes paid in lieu of military service, billeting and purveyance.

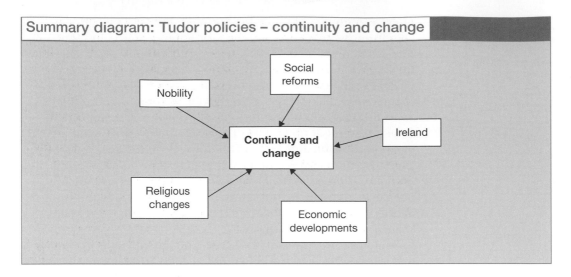

Summary diagram: Tudor policies – continuity and change

3 | Conclusion

The development of central and local administration under the Tudors was instrumental in producing a political and social structure that made government more effective and reduced the likelihood of provincial disturbances. Institutions such as the monarchy, Church, parliament and judiciary strengthened central government and, together with the ubiquitous JPs and newly created lords lieutenant, ensured that there were more direct links between the central and county authorities.

The Tudor period saw many political, religious, economic and social changes. Most people sought stability and never considered challenging the authorities. Those in authority stressed the need for people to know their place and to keep to it, and Elizabethan society in particular was obsessed with maintaining order and degree. In practice, social relations were upheld and stability maintained not because people were brainwashed by concepts of the Great Chain of Being or frightened by sermons recounting tales of 'hell, fire and damnation', but by being good neighbours, by resolving personal problems privately and by behaving responsibly. A 'reformation of manners' appears to have occurred in which people tried to control their behaviour for the good of the community. They sought compromise not confrontation. At a local level, those who ensured that order was upheld were yeomen and husbandmen. They bound over potential trouble-makers and inculcated a moral obligation to obey the law. If all else failed, individuals might consider litigation, and if this proved unsatisfactory, then possibly civil disobedience as a last resort. The imposition of order was achieved by magistrates and manorial courts, but the maintenance of stability also owed much to the ordinary, 'middling' sort of people, who became parish officers, constables and bailiffs.

By the end of the period, the gulf between rich and poor, and between governors and governed, had widened. Prosperous farmers, merchants and gentry had little in common with day labourers, husbandmen and men 'out of service'. They often had their own property, they had an interest in upholding the social mores and, if they had any grievances, they felt confident enough to use the law courts. Under no circumstances would they lead or join popular demonstrations and disturbances. The increase in town charters particularly in Mary's reign and the explosion in local government offices led to towns acquiring greater responsibility for their own welfare. Local people sought to remedy their problems and selected their own citizens to manage the administration, and increasingly these people were yeomen and craftsmen, men whose ancestors might have participated in rebellion. By the end of Elizabeth's reign, they were serving as constables, churchwardens, watchmen, overseers of the poor, and as keepers of the gaols, houses of correction and customs houses, and, like other local officers, assumed a collective responsibility for maintaining order. For the most part they succeeded.

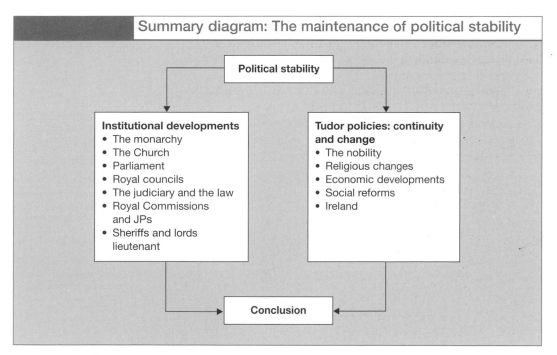

Summary diagram: The maintenance of political stability

Political stability

Institutional developments
- The monarchy
- The Church
- Parliament
- Royal councils
- The judiciary and the law
- Royal Commissions and JPs
- Sheriffs and lords lieutenant

Tudor policies: continuity and change
- The nobility
- Religious changes
- Economic developments
- Social reforms
- Ireland

Conclusion

Further questions for debate

1 How far did the political stability of Tudor England and Ireland depend upon government legislation?

2 Assess the importance of landed groups in maintaining political stability in Tudor England.

3 To what extent did political stability in Tudor England depend upon the Crown maintaining popular support?

4 Why were Tudor authorities so concerned about popular disorder?

5 How far did England become more politically stable during the period from 1485 to 1603?

Choose two of the questions on page 135 and write plans in the form of notes and/or diagrams. Your plans should outline your main arguments, any relevant supporting evidence and how key ideas are linked synoptically.

Advice on answering essay questions on relative importance

In the essays that follow, the focus of the question is on the importance of the nobility in maintaining political stability during the Tudor period. Students need to assess the role of the nobility throughout the period to show change and continuity over time, and to compare their role with that of other groups and factors, such as the clergy, gentry, urban authorities and the monarchy itself. They need to demonstrate that they have understood any links and connections between various developments, thus showing that they can synthesise ideas and concepts.

Read each of the following essays carefully. Each essay was written in one hour and without the use of notes. Note any strengths and limitations and compare your views with those of the assessor. Marks should be awarded for each of the two assessment objectives described in the tables at the end of the book (see pages 142–3).

Essay 1: How important was the nobility in maintaining political stability in Tudor England?

1 The English nobility played an important part in maintaining political stability. Though at times they were responsible for threatening the Crown and even leading armed uprisings, the majority of nobles were loyal and used their social influence to command obedience from people in the counties.

> 1 The start could do with being more focused on the importance of the nobility rather than on what they did.

2 The nobility was often a key cause of rebellions. They had the personal power as landowners and the political duty of upholding stability in their county by enforcing legislation and suppressing rebellion but sometimes they actually were the cause of disturbances. In the Kett's rebellion of 1549, the rebels were infuriated by their noble landlords continuing enclosures and other policies which they felt affected them. Sometimes the nobility led rebellions against the Crown, as happened in 1487 during Simnel's revolt, when Simnel gained the support of nobles like the Earl of Kildare, the Earl of Lincoln and Viscount Lovel. In 1553 another noble, the Duke of Northumberland, tried to oust the legitimate heir Mary Tudor and replace her with Lady Jane Grey, and in the following year Sir Thomas Wyatt, the Duke of Suffolk and others plotted to overthrow Mary. Finally, in Elizabeth's reign, the northern earls, Northumberland and Westmorland, aware that their political influence at court was in decline, rose in revolt just as, and for similar reasons, the Earl of Essex did a generation later. These rebellions indicate that though the nobility was seen as leaders of society, sometimes they led or gave their support to rebellions against the monarchy.

> 2 Much of this section needs to be better focused on the question. The information has been presented as a list of occasions when the nobility caused problems for the Crown. In starting with this line of approach, the argument is seriously imbalanced and in danger of becoming irrelevant.

3 The nobles were used by the Tudors in a number of ways which made them very important. They were sometimes royal advisers and

3 A better paragraph insofar as it focuses on how the nobility helped the Crown to maintain political stability. It contains a good range of examples though devotes too much space to the role of the lords lieutenant.

attended court and the House of Lords. Men like the Duke of Norfolk and the Duke of Suffolk were important members of Henry VIII's council in the 1520s and 1530s, and the Earl of Hertford (later Duke of Somerset) was a key figure in the Privy Council in the 1540s. Some nobles held leading political positions in Tudor administration. The Earl of Surrey, for instance, presided over Henry VII's northern council and the Earl of Pembroke administered the Welsh council. In Elizabeth's reign, the Council of the North was first managed by the Earl of Sussex and then by the Earl of Huntingdon for over 30 years. Another important task the nobles came to fulfil was that of lord lieutenant — the Crown's representative in the counties. This office began under Northumberland when he needed to restore order after a summer of disturbances in central and southern England. His solution was to appoint 12 men, all privy councillors and mostly nobles, to take control of law enforcement. Once order had been restored, the lords lieutenant were disbanded. Mary resurrected them in 1557 and Elizabeth did the same in 1585 but only from 1588, when England was threatened by the Armada, did they become permanent. Their responsibility for training and leading troops in the event of civil disobedience shows how much the Tudors regarded this office. Not all lords lieutenant were nobles, but most were.

4 A good idea to compare the nobility with the gentry. There is some assertion rather than analysis of why the JPs were so important.

4 Other political and social groups also contributed to upholding order and stability in the country. The gentry, for example, held important offices in the county, especially that of JP. Their job was to enforce hundreds of statutes passed by parliament to ensure the country was well run, and to supervise the Quarter Sessions that took place in counties four times a year. As a magistrate they upheld Tudor laws, or at least they tried to; a minority however was corrupt, incompetent or lazy, and it was often easier to do nothing than to attempt to impose a law on unwilling friends and neighbours. The gentry have been described as the 'workhorses' of Tudor administration, and they certainly worked harder than the nobles.

5 Some narrative sections weaken the paragraph, although it makes a perceptive point about the clergy's role as propagandists.

5 The clergy, on the other hand, were not expected to work at all. Their function was to pray for the people and teach them to be law-abiding citizens. The early Tudors used them as advisers and administrators but their real contribution to the maintenance of stability came after the Pilgrimage of Grace. In the rebellion of 1536, many monks, abbots and priests supported the rebels who objected to the dissolution of the monasteries, break with Rome and Protestant reforms. After the uprising was crushed, all the monasteries were closed and the clergy forced to take an oath of allegiance to the king. Those who refused lost their jobs. Those who complied were required to preach obedience to the Crown as the Supreme Head (later Governor) of the Church of England. This role of preacher and teacher was a key element in the propaganda campaign used by the Crown to persuade people they had a duty to God as well as to the king to be obedient. Cranmer even wrote a Homily on Obedience, which ministers were expected to read to their congregations four times a year. Parker, Elizabeth's Archbishop of Canterbury, wrote a similar prayer immediately after

the Northern Earls' revolt entitled: Homily against Disobedience and Wilful Rebellion. In their own way, therefore, the clergy were just as important as the nobility in helping the Crown uphold the law.

6 In conclusion, the nobility's contribution to the maintenance of political stability changed during the period in question but was always key. They were less threatening at the end of the century and were not the only group on whom the Tudors relied to govern the country effectively.

> **6** A fair conclusion to the main arguments in the essay.

Assessment for essay 1

Uses relevant evidence but there are some narrative passages; uses relevant historical terminology. A structured answer, generally well communicated. **[Level III: 13 marks out of 20]**

Satisfactory understanding of continuity and change and, apart from paragraph 2, it focuses on the question set; but explanations are uneven in development – some assertions. Assesses several relevant factors but makes limited synoptic judgements over the whole period. **[Level IV: 24 marks out of 40]**

The overall mark of 37 is worth a low Grade C. To raise the grade, the answer needs to be more focused on evaluating the work of the nobility. Arguments should be fully and synoptically developed.

Essay 2: How important was the nobility in maintaining political stability in Tudor England?

1 The English nobility played an extremely important role in maintaining political stability throughout the Tudor period. Though this role changed in the course of the sixteenth century, at no time could the Tudors ignore the nobility who served the Crown as advisers, administrators and military leaders.

> **1** A focused and promising start.

2 All of the Tudors sought advice from their nobles – Henry VII called five Great Councils and regularly consulted men like Oxford, Derby and Pembroke; Henry VIII always had nobles around him and even during Wolsey's administration, when the cardinal tried to monopolise royal patronage, the king frequently confided in Norfolk, Suffolk and Boleyn. Edward VI and Mary I increased the number of nobles in their Privy Council and relied heavily on their peerage to uphold stability at a time of social unrest. If Elizabeth appointed fewer nobles to her council and only ennobled ten men, she nevertheless regularly sought their advice at court, during parliamentary sessions and on her summer progresses. The English nobility was never far away from the monarch.

> **2** A detailed and comprehensive survey of nobles who served the Crown as councillors.

3 The most direct way in which the nobles helped to maintain stability was in their capacity as major landowners. Noble families like the Percys in Yorkshire and Northumberland or the Howards in Norfolk and Suffolk exercised considerable influence in their counties. They employed hundreds, sometimes thousands, of servants and some, as permanent retainers, provided the Crown with a ready-made army. Thomas Howard, Duke of Norfolk, for instance, supplied 700 men for Henry's army in 1536 and Lord Ferrers contributed some 1000

> **3** Good synthesis of a range of nobles who served as military leaders.

troops to deal with the Pilgrimage of Grace. The Crown had no standing army and needed noble retainers in times of rebellion. Henry VII called upon Surrey, Oxford and Daubeny to help suppress the Cornish rising; Edward VI needed Lords Grey and Russell to put down the Western rebels and Kett's rebellion was defeated by the Earl of Warwick and the Marquis of Northampton. Mary relied on Lords Clinton and Pembroke to lead her troops to counter Wyatt's rebels and Elizabeth appointed Sussex, Hunsdon and Clinton to suppress the Northern Earls' revolt. Without the noble leadership and the backing of their retainers, the Crown would have been doomed.

> **4** An excellent section on the work of nobles as administrators. Aware of change over time.

4 Nobles expected to be consulted by the Crown and to receive commissions to lead armies but they also took a key role as administrators. Regional councils were regularly presided over by a noble. For example, the Council of the North was under the stewardship of the Earls of Surrey, Sussex and Huntingdon, and the wardens of the northern marches until Elizabeth's reign regularly came from the Neville, Percy, Clifford and Dacre families. In the fifteenth century the office of sheriff had often been held by a noble but under the Tudors this county official declined. Responsible for maintaining law and order and for organising parliamentary elections, the Crown saw fit to transfer many of its administrative duties to JPs, most of whom were gentry. Nobles, however, still served on royal commissions and saw themselves as the Crown's leading representative in the county. This notion became more concrete after 1549 when the office of lord lieutenant was created, first as a temporary measure to deal with recurrent disturbances, but from the 1580s on a permanent basis. Elizabeth appointed nobles such as Stanley, Talbot, Parr and Hastings as lords lieutenant in their native counties, a position they held at her majesty's pleasure. These officers were responsible for overseeing the work of JPs and sheriffs, and for the recruitment and training of the county militia, reformed in the 1570s to become the 'trained bands'. These amateur soldiers were Elizabeth's first line of defence in maintaining order if and when trouble broke out. In the 1580s and 1590s they were on hand to deal with food riots and local disturbances but were never put to the test of a major uprising. Nevertheless, the lord lieutenant was another royal officer in the provinces and largely the preserve of the nobility.

> **5** A counter-argument is posited here that makes good use of noble involvement in Tudor rebellions and explains why many nobles had weapons and retainers.

5 It should be recognised, however, that not all nobles stayed loyal to the Crown. Henry VII had to face several rebellions that had support from Yorkist nobles and the Pilgrimage of Grace was led by minor nobles, men like Lords Hussey, Darcy, Latimer and Lumley. Even after a long period of political stability, Elizabeth in 1569 faced a serious revolt from the Earls of Westmorland and Northumberland, and at the end of her reign, from the unpredictable Earl of Essex. The potential of nobles to destabilise the country and threaten the Crown remained throughout the period, partly because they kept large households and retainers could easily be converted into private armies, and partly because many nobles lived in castles and had their own supplies of ammunition. Henry VII had tried to confiscate the latter and control

the former, but the Crown often needed to obtain an army quickly – mercenaries were only employed under Edward VI and proved far too costly to retain – and actually encouraged the nobility to keep supplies of weaponry. Gradually the Crown weakened noble control in politically sensitive areas such as the Welsh borders, the northern marches, East Anglia and the South West. Henry VIII in particular granted lands to the Russell family in Devon and transferred the wardenship of the northern marches to gentry rather than noble families. By Elizabeth's reign, the nobles were less politically ambitious, more sophisticated in their outlook and altogether more respectful of the law than had been the case at the start of the Tudor period.

6 English nobles were very important to the Crown but so too were the gentry and clergy. As the number of county and local offices expanded and Tudor bureaucracy spread its tentacles to all corners of the kingdom, it was the gentry (landowners and merchants below the rank of noble) who dominated county administration. As sheriffs, MPs, commissioners and above all JPs, the gentry played a vital role in maintaining political stability. The clergy also were important but their contribution changed as a result of the Reformation. Until then both Henry VII and Henry VIII had relied on their bishops as leading advisers, administrators and diplomats – reaching a dizzy height in the 1520s. But the administrative reforms of Cromwell led to the emergence of the office of royal secretary who became more prominent than the Lord Chancellor. After Wolsey's fall, no chancellor except Pole in Mary's reign was a clergyman for the rest of the Tudor period. Elizabeth in fact deliberately overlooked her bishops when making political appointments; their duty was to reside in their diocese and ensure religious conformity, which most did very competently. The clergy, however, had a crucial role to play in re-enforcing political order and in particular stressing the importance of obeying a magistrate. Archbishop Cranmer set the standard by producing a Book of Homilies in 1547, and insisting that his Homily on Obedience was read four times a year in parish churches. The clergy reminded congregations of their duty to obey the law, to know their place in society and to suffer any grievances in silence. Not all subjects complied. Not only was there a rebellion in 1549 of 6000 protesters against the new English prayer book, the rebels were actually led in eight parishes by their priest. These, however, were an exception and in the second half of the sixteenth century, the Church and its clergy stayed loyal to the Crown.

> 6 The argument broadens to consider and compare other groups.

7 Finally, in addition to the nobility, gentry and clergy, the Crown depended heavily upon town authorities for maintaining political stability. The population of England and Wales doubled in the course of the Tudor period and urban centres bore the brunt of tackling social and economic problems. Town corporations, led by the mayor and burgesses, were responsible for keeping order and to a great extent they succeeded. Though they were assisted by government legislation in, for instance, dealing with the poor, stabilising food

> 7 The role of urban authorities is often overlooked; here it is compared with the nobility.

prices and finding work for the unemployed – all potentially troublesome issues – it fell to the JPs and local authorities to put government measures into operation. In practice, many towns took the initiative to maintain order and officers, such as constables, bailiffs, churchwardens and overseers of the poor, all helped to serve their community. Though the nobility was still regarded as the natural leaders in society, people became increasingly responsive for combating local problems and rather than rebelling against the government, set out to cure them themselves.

8 The Crown's contribution could have been given more prominence in the essay rather than this aside in the conclusion.

8 Strong leadership from the Crown was essential if the country was to be effectively governed and the laws upheld, but the part played by the nobility – militarily, administratively and as councillors – was always important. Nevertheless, without the contributions of the clergy, gentry and urban authorities, both great and small, the Tudors would not have been able to maintain stability in the country.

Assessment for essay 2

Makes use of relevant and accurate evidence and a range of appropriate terminology; essay is clearly structured, coherently and accurately communicated. [Level IA: 19 marks out of 20]

Good level of understanding of key concepts of continuity and change over the whole period; synthesises assessments and provides a range of supported judgements that are detailed and focused on the question. [Level IA: 39 marks out of 40]

The overall mark of 58 is a good A*. There are few weaknesses and, given its length, to expand on, say, the monarchy's role in maintaining stability, would have been at the expense of another comparative element.

Mark Schemes for Assessing the Essays

How to use the mark schemes

Mark schemes are used by assessors and examiners to determine how best to categorise a candidate's work and ensure that the performance of thousands of candidates is marked to a high degree of accuracy and consistency. Few essays fall neatly into the mark levels. For example, some essays give a good overview but provide few supporting details, and some address the topic in general but not the question in particular. As a result, examiners seek to find the 'best fit' when applying the mark levels. Assessment

	AO1a Mark Scheme for Levels I, II, III and IV
Assessment Objectives	Recall, select and use historical knowledge appropriately, and communicate knowledge and understanding clearly and effectively.
Level IA **18–20 marks**	Uses a wide range of accurate, detailed and relevant evidence. Accurate and confident use of appropriate historical terminology. Answer is clearly structured and coherent; communicates accurately and legibly.
Level IB **16–17 marks**	Uses accurate, detailed and relevant evidence. Accurate use of a range of appropriate historical terminology. Answer is clearly structured and mostly coherent; writes accurately and legibly.
Level II **14–15 marks**	Uses mostly accurate, detailed and relevant evidence, which demonstrates a competent command of the topic. Generally accurate use of historical terminology. Answer is structured and mostly coherent; writing is legible and communication is generally clear.
Level III **12–13 marks**	Uses accurate and relevant evidence, which demonstrates some command of the topic but there may be some inaccuracy. Answer includes relevant historical terminology but this may not be extensive or always accurately used. Most of the answer is organised and structured; the answer is mostly legible and clearly communicated.
Level IV **10–11 marks**	There is deployment of relevant knowledge but level/accuracy of detail will vary; there may be some evidence that is tangential or irrelevant. Some unclear and/or under-developed and/or disorganised sections; mostly satisfactory level of communication.

Objective Ia assesses candidates' ability to use information relevantly, accurately and consistently to answer the question set. Assessment Objective Ib assesses their level of understanding and their ability to explain, analyse and synthesise key developments across the whole period. Synthesis is the most important skill in a synoptic exam and as a result carries most marks. When you read an essay, think about the two assessment objectives that are being tested. Decide which level best suits the overall quality of the essay and be positive, rewarding candidates for what they have done rather than penalising them for what they have failed to do. When you have decided upon the most appropriate level, start at the top of the mark band and work down until you reach the mark that best reflects the essay. The two marks will give you a final mark out of 60. Note that only the top four levels (out of seven) have been used to assess the essays in this book.

	AO1b Mark Scheme for Levels I, II, III and IV
Assessment Objectives	Demonstrates an understanding of the past through explanation and analysis, arriving at substantiated judgements of key concepts and of the relationships between key features of the period studied.
Level IA **36–40 marks**	Excellent understanding of key concepts relevant to the question set. Excellent synthesis and synoptic assessment of the whole period. Answer is consistently analytical with developed and substantiated explanations, some of which may be unexpected.
Level IB **32–35 marks**	Clear and accurate understanding of most key concepts relevant to analysis and to the question set. Answer is mostly consistently and relevantly analytical with mostly developed and substantiated explanations. Clear understanding of the significance of issues and synthesis of the whole period.
Level II **28–31 marks**	Mostly clear and accurate understanding of many key concepts relevant to analysis and to the topic. Clear understanding of the significance of most relevant issues in their historical context. Much of the answer is relevantly analytical and substantiated with detailed evidence but there may be some uneven judgements.
Level III **24–27 marks**	Sound understanding of key concepts relevant to analysis and mostly focused on the question set. Answers may be a mixture of analysis and explanation but also simple description of relevant material and narrative of relevant events, or answers may provide more consistent analysis but the quality will be uneven and its support often general or thin. There may only be a limited synthesis of the whole period.
Level IV **20–23 marks**	Understanding of key concepts relevant to analysis and the topic is variable but in general is satisfactory. Answers may be largely descriptive/narratives of events and links between this and analytical comments will typically be weak or unexplained or answers will mix passages of descriptive material with occasional explained analysis. Limited synoptic judgements of part of the period.

Select Reading List

I. Arthurson, *The Perkin Warbeck Conspiracy 1491–99*, Sutton 1994.

I. Arthurson, 'The Rising of 1497' in J. Rosenthal and C. Richmond (eds), *People, Politics and Community in the Later Middle Ages*, Sutton 1987.

B.L. Beer, *Rebellion and Riot: Popular Disorder in England During the Reign of Edward VI*, Kent State UP 1982.

M.J. Bennett, *Lambert Simnel and the Battle of Stoke*, Sutton 1987.

G.W. Bernard, *War, Taxation and Rebellion in Early Tudor England*, Harvester 1986.

M.L. Bush, *The Pilgrimage of Grace: A Study of Rebel Armies*, Manchester UP 1996.

P. Caraman, *The Western Rebellion*, Tiverton 1994.

J. Cornwall, *The Revolt of the Peasantry*, RKP 1977.

S. Cunningham, 'Henry VII and rebellion in North-Eastern England 1485–1492', *Northern History*, 32, 1996.

C.S.L. Davies, 'The Pilgrimage of Grace Reconsidered', *Past and Present*, 41, 1968.

C.S.L. Davies, 'Popular religion and the Pilgrimage of Grace' in A. Fletcher and J. Stevenson (eds), *Order and Disorder in Early Modern England*, CUP 1985.

S.G. Ellis, *Tudor Ireland: Crown, Community and the Conflict of Cultures 1470–1603*, Harlow 1985.

G.R. Elton, *Policy and Police*, CUP 1972.

N. Fellows, *Disorder and Rebellion in Tudor England*, Hodder & Stoughton 2001.

A. Fletcher and D. MacCulloch, *Tudor Rebellions*, 5th edition, Pearson Longman 2004.

P. Griffiths, A. Fox and S. Hindle (eds), *The Experience of Authority in Early Modern England*, Basingstoke 1996.

S.J. Gunn, *Early Tudor Government 1485–1558*, Macmillan 1995.

C. Haigh, *Reformation and Resistance in Tudor Lancashire*, CUP 1976.

R.W. Hoyle, *The Pilgrimage of Grace*, OUP 2001.

M.E. James, *Society, Politics and Culture*, CUP 1986.

M.E. James, 'Obedience and dissent in Henrician England: the Lincolnshire Rebellion', *Past and Present*, 48, 1970.

S.K. Land, *Kett's Rebellion: The Norfolk Rising of 1549*, Boydell 1977.

D.M. Loades, *Two Tudor Conspiracies*, CUP 1965.

D.M. Loades, *Power in Tudor England*, Macmillan 1997.

H. Miller, *Henry VIII and the English Nobility*, OUP 1986.

G. Moorhouse, *The Pilgrimage of Grace*, Weidenfeld & Nicolson 2002.

D.M. Palliser, *The Age of Elizabeth 1547–1603*, Longman 1983.

E. Shagan, 'Protector Somerset and the 1549 rebellions', *English Historical Review*, 114, 1999.

H. Speight, 'Local government and the South-West Rebellion', *Southern History*, 18, 1996.

P. Thomas, *Authority and Disorder in Tudor Times*, CUP 1999.

A. Wall, *Power and Protest in England 1525–1640*, Arnold 2000.

J. Walter, '"A rising of the people". The Oxfordshire rising of 1596', *Past and Present*, 107, 1985.

P. Williams, *The Tudor Regime*, OUP 1979.

J. Youings, 'The South Western Rebellion of 1549', *Southern History*, 1, 1979.

Glossary

Act of Six Articles   This Act upheld the orthodox Catholic faith and remained in force until 1547.

Act of Ten Articles   This Act stressed the importance of baptism, the Eucharist and penance, and put less significance on confirmation, marriage, holy orders and the last rites.

Act of Uniformity   An Act that enforced the Protestant prayer book, which was first introduced in 1549, and modified in 1552 and 1559. It imposed punishments on those who did not conform.

Anglicise   To make English.

Attainted lands   Acts of attainder were passed by parliament on traitors and their entire property and that of their family were attainted and forfeited to the Crown.

Belphoebe and Astraea   Mythical women celebrated for their beauty and sense of justice, respectively.

Benefit of clergy   The privilege of exemption from trial by a secular court that was allowed in cases of felony to the clergy or to anyone who could read a passage from the Scriptures.

Benevolence   A gift that was occasionally requested to help the government overcome a financial crisis.

Billhook   A curved blade attached to a wooden handle that could be used to slash and cut an adversary.

Bonds and recognizances   Bonds were written obligations binding one person to another (often the Crown) to perform a specified action or to pay a sum of money; a recognizance acknowledged that someone was bound to fulfil a commitment.

Bonds of allegiance   Financial and legal penalties were imposed on rebels and on anyone of doubtful allegiance.

Break from Rome   The name given to Henry VIII's separation of England from the Roman Catholic Church by a series of parliamentary Acts culminating in the Act of Supremacy of 1534.

Cade's rebellion   Jack Cade led a revolt in Kent that briefly occupied London before being defeated in battle. The rebels were protesting at high taxes and governmental incompetence.

Castleward   Tenants had once been required to defend Norwich Castle but this military service was later commuted to paying a rent.

Catechism and prymer   A catechism was a book of basic religious instruction in the form of questions and answers; a prymer was an elementary book of religious instruction.

Commissions of array   Authority given by the Crown to nobles to raise troops.

Commonwealth   The 'wealth' or welfare of the common people.

Composition   Taxes paid in lieu of military service, billeting and purveyance.

Convocation   The general assembly of the clergy that usually met when parliament was called.

Copyhold and customary rights   Tenants who held a copy of their tenancy but in practice only had limited rights. Customary rights were more secure and reflected traditional local practices and customs.

Court of Augmentations   Established in 1536, this administrative and financial court in London handled affairs relating to the dissolved monasteries.

De facto   By deed, as opposed to *de jure*, 'by law'. Henry VII descended from an illegitimate line and based his claim to the English throne on the fact that he had killed the alleged usurper, Richard III, in battle.

Despotism   The government of an absolute ruler who rules without regard for the law.

Devise   The means by which Edward disinherited his half-sisters, Mary and Elizabeth, in favour of Lady Jane Grey.

Embargoes   Trade restrictions such as those imposed on Burgundy in 1493.

Entry fine   A fee paid by tenants when renewing their lease that allowed them to re-enter their property.

Escheators   County officials responsible for overseeing Crown lands and collecting feudal payments such as wardships and escheats.

Factions   A small number of like-minded people who rivalled an established and larger group for political, religious or social power.

Felony   An offence that carried the death penalty. ·

Feodary   An officer of the court of wards.

Feoffees   Property trustees and administrators.

Firebrands   People who cause unrest.

First fruits and tenths   Taxes on the first year's income of a new bishop and one-tenth of the value of ecclesiastical benefices received by the Crown after the Reformation.

Folding   Allowing cattle and sheep to graze and manure the land.

Gaelic clans   Some native and older Irish families spoke Gaelic and were distinguished from the families of Norman descent and more recent immigrants who spoke English.

Harness, arquebuses and morions, with matchlight   Body armour, long-barrelled handguns, metal helmets, and fuses to ignite the arquebuses.

Heir presumptive   An heir who it was presumed would inherit unless an alternative claimant was subsequently born.

Homilies   Lessons that could be read directly or improvised into a sermon.

Humanism   The study of architecture, art, language, rhetoric and literature that enabled the individual to become more civilised and better prepared to play an active role in the political life of the state.

Hundreds   Norfolk, like most counties, was divided administratively into hundreds.

Husbandmen   Small farmers or landowners of a lower social standing than yeomen.

Iconoclasm   The smashing and destruction of religious images and icons.

Imperatur   A 'closed' as opposed to an 'open' Crown symbolised imperial authority, which implied that the ruler was subject to God alone.

Inflation   A rise in prices and an accompanying fall in the purchasing power of money.

Inquisition fines   Fees paid for an enquiry and valuation of a deceased person's estate that was believed to hold freehold land in chief of the Crown.

Knight of the Garter   An honour in the gift of the Crown that Henry VIII generously dispensed. The recipient was entitled to wear blue or crimson robes and took precedence over other knights.

Knight service   Men who held land from the king were obliged to do knight service. This entailed fighting for the king and providing troops whenever he went to war or (as was customarily the case) providing sufficient money to hire mercenaries instead.

Liturgy   An order of church service.

Livery and maintenance   Wearing a lords' tunic bearing his coat of arms, and the practice in which some lords attended a law court in order to influence the judge and jury.

Martial law   Military law that replaced civil law during a political crisis.

Masterless   Adolescents who were not apprenticed to a master or an employer and so were more likely to be itinerant and ill-disciplined.

Melanchthon and Oecolampadius   Philip Melanchthon was a moderate Protestant who succeeded Luther as the leader of the German Reformation. Johannes Oecolampadius was a leading Swiss Protestant who implemented reforms in Basel in the 1520s.

Middle march The marches were the lands between England and Scotland that were divided into three and administered by wardens.

Midland Revolt A serious peasant uprising in Leicestershire against landlords who enclosed common fields and converted them from arable to pasture.

Muster To summon soldiers for an inspection.

Oak of Reformation An old oak tree on Mousehold Heath outside Norwich.

Oyer et terminer A commission directed to justices that empowered them to 'hear and determine' indictments for specific crimes committed in a particular area.

Pale A region near Dublin that was one of the few well-governed areas of Ireland.

Peasants' Revolt In 1381, peasants in Kent and Essex led by Wat Tyler and John Ball marched on London, in protest against a poll tax and calling for the abolition of serfdom.

Plantations Lands that were confiscated from rebels and granted to English and local landlords at reduced prices.

Prerogative Powers held by the Crown. Prerogative courts were presided over by royal councillors who dispensed justice in the interests of the Crown.

Prince of the blood A prince who was a blood relation of the monarch.

Proclamations Notices that were publicly issued by the Crown and proclaimed in London and the localities.

Purveyance The right of the Crown to purchase supplies or to obtain transport for the royal household at prices fixed below prevailing market rates.

Quarter Sessions General courts held in a county every three months.

Recusant A Catholic who denied the royal supremacy or refused to attend the services of the Anglican Church.

Retainers Nobles retained servants in their households who might be used as private armies.

Richard II In 1399 Henry Bolingbroke had seized the Crown from Richard II. The re-enactment of Shakespeare's play (written in 1595) reminded Londoners that the deposition of Elizabeth I would not be unprecedented.

Sacramentarians Protestants who denied the real presence of Christ in the Eucharist.

Sanctuary A place that provided a haven for outlaws. Every parish church, cathedral and monastery had the privilege to offer sanctuary, although in practice certain crimes such as treason were rendered ineligible.

Scutage Rather than fight in person for the king in times of war, tenants-in-chief could commute their feudal obligations into a tax known as a scutage or 'escuage'.

Seditious Liable to cause an affray or act of disorder.

Strategy and tactics Strategy is an overall plan and management of troops designed to achieve an objective; tactics are the means by which the plan is carried out.

Tenants at will Tenants who could be ejected from their land at the will of their landlord when their lease expired.

Tithes Payments made by the laity to the parish church of one-tenth of their agricultural profits or personal income.

Villein A tenant who was obliged to perform any services that his lord commanded.

Wardship The Crown acted as the guardian of the son or daughter of a deceased tenant-in-chief until he or she came of age at 21.

Index